# MARKING TIME

# Marking Time

a prison memoir

## Michael Bettsworth

with a foreword by Ludovic Kennedy

MACMILLAN
LONDON

First published 1989 by
MACMILLAN LONDON LIMITED
4 Little Essex Street London WC2R 3LF
and Basingstoke

Associated companies in Auckland, Delhi, Dublin, Gaborone,
Hamburg, Harare, Hong Kong, Johannesburg, Kuala Lumpur,
Lagos, Manzini, Melbourne, Mexico City, Nairobi, New York,
Singapore and Tokyo

British Library Cataloguing in Publication Data

Bettsworth, Michael
    Marking time: a prison memoir.
    1. Great Britain. Prisoners – Biographies
    I. Title
    365'.6'0924

ISBN 0-333-47489-9

Photoset by Rowland Phototypesetting Limited
Bury St Edmunds, Suffolk
Printed and bound in Great Britain
by Richard Clay Limited, Bungay, Suffolk

# CONTENTS

# ACKNOWLEDGEMENTS

I would like to express my thanks and appreciation to my agent, Jeffrey Simmons, without whose honest advice and tenacity this book would never have been published. I am also grateful to my editor, Brenda Thomson, for her encouragement and help with the manuscript, and to Peter James for his careful copy-editing.

*Michael Bettsworth*
*May 1988*

# FOREWORD

Anyone who reads this book may conclude that its author, Michael Bettsworth, was punished beyond what society demanded of him. He was convicted of having sexual relations with a fifteen-year-old girl at the school where she was a pupil and he headmaster. In mitigation it was said that the girl was physically mature, by no means a virgin and, from all accounts, agreeable to what was said to have occurred. From a strictly legal point of view his sentence of eighteen months' imprisonment, of which he served just over six, was probably about right.

It was Mr Bettsworth's misfortune, however, that because of his social position, the case received wide publicity; with the result that when he had completed his sentence, the slate could not be wiped clean. The profession of teaching to which he had devoted twenty years of his life to good effect was thereafter barred to him; while the stigma of having once been in prison will, he says, never leave him. His immediate family suffered as much if not more than he. One of his sons was so psychologically damaged by the experience that he requires psychiatric treatment to this day.

Yet Mr Bettsworth's misfortune has been our gain. The majority of prisoners have not been blessed with the skills to describe the prison experience; a smaller majority, having been there before, have long ceased to notice anything unusual about it. But for him the experience was horrific; from the cosy security of the headmaster's study and a loving home he was pitchforked, within hours of the verdict and manacled to his guards, to a prison cell whose facilities, or lack of them, he was obliged to share with two other men, and where they were all incarcerated for some twenty-three hours a day. 'I had been curious all my life to know what the inside of a prison was like,' he writes, 'and I resolved to record all I saw or heard.'

In the first few days shock followed shock. A man who was used to bathing daily found that he was allowed only one bath a week, so that there were times when crotch and foot odour permeated the cell. 'I found living in my own stench for days on end quite foul.' Family visits were restricted to one a month. Letters were severely rationed. Time hung heavy. Gradually he came to realise that the old adage about going to prison as punishment, not for punishment, was not true: the real punishment in the shape of a life without meaning and with petty restrictions of all kinds only began when you got there.

But the worst of Michael Bettsworth's early experiences resulted from his being placed on Rule 43. Rule 43 prisoners are those who, for their own safety, are segregated from other prisoners. Mostly they are child sex offenders for whom murderers, rapists, muggers and thieves nurture a peculiar loathing; and whenever and wherever he went on brief forays from his cell, he was greeted with shouts of 'Fucking nonce', 'Hang the bugger', and so on, and, while on exercise, was the target of spittle and small objects raining down from upper-floor cells. That the girl involved in his case was not a child but a physically mature female was not a distinction his fellow inmates cared to make. 'Nonces fulfil a useful function for the rest of the population,' he writes, 'in that sex offenders give the other convicts a feeling of superiority: they feel that if there is a group down upon which they can look, then perhaps their own offences are not so venal.'

On transfer from Exeter jail to Leyhill open prison he was taken off Rule 43, with the results that taunts and ostracism for being a nonce continued and there were times – for it has been known for nonces to have the contents of a scalding tea urn tipped over them – that he felt in physical danger; and it wasn't until he had been there a full three months that he came to be accepted. In other ways too, and although the regime at Leyhill is supposed to be progressive, he preferred life at Exeter where staff and inmates had been more friendly. Expecting some easing of the petty restrictions, he found them to be as bad if not worse; and one of the worst was the absurd situation that entitles prisoners to buy so much of tobacco, toiletries and letters each week, but only pays enough for a fraction of them. 'I cannot for the life of me understand', he writes, 'why visitors cannot bring stamps, tobacco and other necessities to the prisoner or why he cannot buy them out of private cash.' The result, inevitably, has been the flowering of the tobacco barons.

# Foreword

The importance of tobacco in prison is that it helps to relieve stress; and the stress of prison life on the individual is something that Mr Bettsworth brings vividly home to us. Its basic cause is the artificiality of the existence. A prisoner becomes an automaton with no rights or independence of action, little freedom of choice, less a person than a thing; and whose guards at Leyhill, he found, treated the inmates with a lack of respect which he would never have shown to his pupils. Small things become exaggerated out of all proportion. Most evenings a free man can relieve his stress by taking a drink, visiting the cinema or friends, making love to wife or girlfriend. In prison all these are denied him – except for tobacco which, if government health warnings are true, can endanger his health. No wonder that some prisoners, unable to contain their stress, run amok. 'Riots will continue', says Mr Bettsworth, 'until society rethinks its custodial practices.'

At Leyhill he discovered for himself the truth that prisons are breeding-grounds of crime. Not only do young prisoners become introduced to drugs and learn from older lags new ways of robbing and thieving, but the system begets criminal activities within the prison. He had intended to be of good behaviour throughout his sentence, but incensed by the punishment meted out to him by some trivial breach of prison rules, he took on the system by smuggling in tobacco and nicking goodies from the kitchen where he worked. It afforded some satisfaction. 'A constant battle against the regulations gave prisoners a *raison d'être*. It was part of the survival kit prisoners need to alleviate boredom and maintain an identity.' When a fellow inmate said to him, 'Prison is turning you into a thief, Mike,' he had to agree.

But the most deeply felt grievances of many prisoners concerns disparity of sentences and the question of parole. If the punishment is to fit the criminal, as I believe it should, rather than the crime, then disparity in sentencing is to some degree inevitable. But parole is another matter. A prisoner's date of release, says the author, is what occupies his mind more than anything else; but the vagaries of the parole system means that he can never be certain when that date will be. 'It is', he says, 'a source of indescribable anguish by its unpredictability and unfairness.' There are many who feel that a prisoner who knows that his sentence is for a fixed term which can be neither shortened nor lengthened will serve his time more equably than in a situation where his hopes are raised and dashed; and who think that offences that occur in prison should be punished by loss of privileges rather than by loss of remission.

As Michael Bettsworth says, once a prisoner has been convicted and taken to prison, society is no longer interested in what happens to him. But if it is still government policy that felons are sent to prison *as* punishment and not *for* punishment, there is room for many small improvements which would raise the morale of prisoners and staff alike. Why cannot a prisoner have more than one bath a week? Why cannot he have the tobacco ration to which he is entitled? Why, to prevent marriages crumbling, cannot families visit more than once a month? Why only one telephone for three hundred inmates? Why such a restriction on outgoing letters? Any small improvement in the living conditions inevitably brings complaints of 'feather-bedding' from the popular press, but they should be firmly resisted: for as Mr Bettsworth says, only those who have experienced deprivation of loss of liberty can know what living in prison is like.

More important though is the whole question of the usefulness or otherwise of prisons generally. 'Too many people are in prison too long,' says the author, and after reading his book, one can only agree. Clearly those who remain a menace to society – murderers, rapists, gangsters and so on – must be kept locked up until such time as they are deemed safe to be released; clearly, too, a sentence must not ignore society's abhorrence of the offence. But it is high time that the government's belief in the efficacy of prison – a belief that has resulted in Britain having more prisoners *per capita* of the population than any other country in Europe – was challenged. Other countries are more progressive than ours in the use of non-custodial punishments, whereby an offender can repay his debt to society in useful employment instead of being taken out of circulation. Countries which have given priorities to these schemes have found that the great majority of those taking part have not offended again; while here the reconviction rate is around 70 per cent.

Michael Bettsworth says that no one who has been a prisoner is ever consulted about the experience when it comes to discussing changes or reforms. He has done the next best thing in writing a book which should be required reading for all those, in government and without, whose business it is to study prison reform. His time in prison was the debt we required of him for his offence; but it may be that he has given back to us more than he owed by his revealing and disturbing account of it.

*Ludovic Kennedy*
*July 1988*

# PREFACE

On 29 September 1982, I became headmaster of a new school which I had co-founded with thirteen of my colleagues after the closure of the 437-year-old Truro Cathedral School of which I was deputy headmaster and head of the department of English. I had been appointed to that post, after teaching at Winchester for more than a decade, less than three years before.

On Friday 13 December 1985 after a week's trial, I was convicted, on a majority verdict, of having had an affair with a fifteen-year-old girl pupil and sentenced to eighteen months' imprisonment.

I waited seven months for my trial, during which time I led a nomadic existence; my only home, my school, was out of bounds to me and I could see my wife, who remained working at the school until shortly before my release, only when she had an occasional free hour and by previous appointment.

However, this book is concerned solely with my experiences of prison; how I reacted to it and how my many friends and colleagues were affected is recounted here. I have a twofold purpose.

First, *Marking Time* is an historical record. It is based upon my prison diaries and, though I cannot vouch for the veracity of every opinion I record, I can promise that what I record was what I saw and heard. Some of the facts will shock; others will appear incredible. Everything in this book 'happened' to me.

Second, I have sought to define the essential nature of the prison experience – particularly as it applied to the first-time, almost petty, offender – and to suggest that there are ways of treating convicted persons which may make the experience more bearable for them and for their guards.

I hope the story told here will open closed minds and cause more of us to become more intellectually involved with this major social problem. Daily publicity in the national media has brought about heightened awareness of 'the prison problem' but this awareness is, at best, superficial and ill-informed. I know, for example, that the majority of people in this country, perhaps in every civilised country, would not feel easy about the subversive effect prison had on me.

Sadly, the general public's consciousness is limited to scenes of recurring prison riots – scenes I predicted when I was in prison three years ago and scenes which now I predict will continue to be enacted unless changes are made in the system. Such eruptions harden the views of those who think criminals must be 'kept down' and cause the views of 'reformers' like Lord Longford to be distorted.

I hope, then, to enable public awareness to be better informed so that as our penal policies become more widely debated in the coming months, awareness rises above a superficial level. We must consign to oblivion the Pavlovian response of, 'Yes, prisoners do have a degrading time. They live in jails built by French prisoners-of-war in overcrowded and insanitary conditions. But what can we do about it? Crime is on the increase; we must protect ourselves.' Never once does the conscience demand that thought should be profounder; never does the charitable face of society wonder at the strain caused when the sins of the father are visited upon the children. This book may stimulate that conscience.

*Michael Bettsworth*
*July 1988*

# 1

# THE VERDICT

*Stone walls do not a prison make*
*Nor iron bars a cage*

Richard Lovelace, 'To Lucasta, Going Beyond the Seas'

Imprisonment does not begin with the judge's sentence. It does not even begin with the defendant's appearance in the dock, though in the British system the sight of a man or woman sitting in the segregated area of the courtroom flanked by prison officers can only give to the jury the impression that he or she is 'in custody' and therefore guilty. No. Imprisonment of a far more painful kind begins when the person is charged – or even before then.

Once one knows that the end of the whole mysterious and terrifying process can be imprisonment one is a prisoner to one's thoughts and feelings. In the seven months leading to my trial I was a hostage to fortune, and my family had been taken prisoner too. No person awaiting trial is free. Wherever one goes the thought of the trial is paramount. One envies the people walking the streets with, compared to the accused person, no care in the world. Nothing appears to be real. Sleep becomes difficult. Social intercourse is strained and meaningless. Sexual behaviour disappears into irrelevancy.

I remember on the family holiday we took in France while I was awaiting trial my youngest son Tim, with tears streaming down his face, asked me if there had been a trial and if 'you have been found guilty and got a long sentence'. For the first time I had to speak directly to him about all that was happening and tell him that I *could* go to prison. He had been told so many things about the case – filthy and mendacious things – that I thought my heart would break when I considered his suffering. I waited for him to cry himself to sleep, went to my wife and told her that at that moment I could have committed murder. Even now I dare not fully contemplate my children's sufferings.

I

My wife, Jen, too, was in this infernal prison with me. She and I had discussed six months before the trial the fact that I might be imprisoned and had outwardly accepted the fact as one logical outcome of the experience. Indeed, I had practised sleeping in the tiny back bedroom of our cottage as if it were a prison cell; I am slightly claustrophobic and wanted to condition myself to the possible incarceration. The experiment did not really work for I knew I could leave the room at any time. Mentally, too, we were incarcerated – prisoners of horrible imaginings, of a nightmare that would end we did not know when. We waited seven months for the trial. Each one of those months was worse than being in prison. My sentence – I ought to write 'our' sentence – was in its eighth month before I had spent one night in a prison cell. Unlike prisoners remanded in custody, none of my 'remand time' could be subtracted from the eventual sentence I received.

It was impossible, hard as I tried, to become mentally adjusted to the possibility of going to prison – and of going there for many years. It was not so much a feeling of 'this is not happening to me' – although the air of unreality was there; it was more a feeling of being a permanent and total outsider. I remember envying everyone in the local town, because I saw them as 'free'. I felt jealous of every driver on the motorway as I endured my nomadic, pre-trial existence. That I had to ring up Jen to make an appointment to meet her for tea or for a snatched lunch intensified this feeling of loneliness, of not belonging.

There were no practical steps I could take to prepare for the outcome of my trial, for that outcome was uncertain. If I assumed I would be in prison I would have had to realise the few assets I had and clear as many decks as possible for my wife; if I did that and was acquitted, I would have destroyed the basis of our 'normal' existence. Mentally I was in a limbo as dark as anything in Dante.

At one moment I would feel elated and certain of an acquittal; at the next, insomnia, doubt and helplessness tormented me. On the rare occasions that I saw my wife we would often have fierce arguments – never about the case but always stemming from our mutual stress. Tim sometimes witnessed these rows and on one occasion I remember going into his bedroom to find him sobbing, oh so quietly but oh so tragically, into his pillow. My self-contempt surged up as I realised that I was the cause of his suffering and that, instead of supporting and encouraging him now, I was adding to his awesome burden. That feeling is still with me and I suspect it will never go.

The second stage of prison begins as the charges are read out when one stands in the dock and the trial pursues its ineluctable course. One is centre stage with spear carriers who wear 'HMP' on their shoulders. What does the jury think? Is it not reasonable for them to assume that the man is being held in custody and is therefore regarded as dangerous, or at least that he is more likely to be guilty than not guilty? One could argue that acquittal rates in Crown Courts would mitigate against this but it would be hard for a jury to disregard the daily vision of the 'man in the dock' when subtle points of truth are being debated. How often after my conviction did I long for a judicial system like the French – inquisitorial rather than our less sound, accusatorial one.

'Guilty.' The jury foreman pronounced the verdict in a clear but strained voice. Eleven people believed me to be guilty. Only one felt able to save my wife and sons from the unspeakable horror and humiliation of a conviction. This Christmas would be unlike any other. The future would forever be bleak. Happiness was now a forgotten feature of our past lives.

Though I was prepared intellectually for this verdict the result stunned me. I remember my heart surging. I remember saying to myself, 'Stand up straight and look the judge squarely in the face. You don't want the *Sun* tomorrow to print that "The accused stood with his head bowed in the dock as the judge passed sentence."'

I remember the speed, or so it seemed to me, with which the judge sentenced me to three concurrent terms of eighteen months' imprisonment. It just was not happening to me. The red robes, the clerk of the court's black gown, the darkness of the evening sky, and the total, total silence in the court room are vivid memories. Then I did not know what to do. I felt the touch of a prison officer's hand on my waist to indicate that I should leave. I think I bowed to the judge – not merely out of courtesy but because I had resolved to make a dignified exit. I was led downstairs and put in a narrow cell.

I remember being interviewed by a prison officer and signing various forms. I do not remember what they were. I think I was searched and my pockets emptied. Just before going into court to hear the verdict I had given my watch, pipe, tobacco, wallet and lighter to my eldest son. I wanted to hear the verdict with nothing in my pockets. I argued that if I were going to prison I would rather go there with nothing and come out with nothing than enter with anything that would remind me of my former life. All I possessed was a metal comb – now taken from me and handed to my wife – and a handkerchief which was taken away when I entered the prison.

I sat alone on a wooden chair with my feet up on a bench, saying over and over again to myself, 'Well, you're going to prison. So, you're going to prison.' My mind did not think of such things as appeals, parole, loss of livelihood, separation from my family. I vaguely thought that I would be out before the next Christmas and consoled myself with the thought that I could have got six years. In a peculiar way my mind seemed to have adjusted to my new state immediately. I did not want to weep, though I was easily moved to tears on other occasions.

After a short time Jen and my eldest son, Jamie, came to the cells.

'Don't worry about me; I'll be all right,' I said to her.

'I know you will,' she said.

Jamie said nothing but was close to tears. He kissed me on the lips and left quickly – a six-foot-two eighteen-year-old who suffers from acute claustrophobia and who had been my 'minder' for the previous six months.

Jen was concerned that I would be assaulted by other prisoners because I was now a convicted sex offender – 'nonce' is the jargon term, a word I came to dread. A kindly prison officer assured her I would be all right. She and I spoke for a few more minutes – I do not know what we said – and she left. When would I see her again? When would I see Tim, whom I had kissed goodbye that morning as he was taken to school. 'See you tonight, Moth.' 'Bye, Dad.' Jason, my middle son, was still away at his boarding school and was travelling home overnight. He would not learn until the next morning that I was in prison. These thoughts unsettled me mightily and I fought back the tears.

My barristers and solicitor then came into the cell. I felt sorry for them. I thought they had conducted a masterly defence and said to them, before they could make whatever professional solicitations are appropriate to the occasion, that I was grateful for their magnificent efforts. My QC thought that an appeal was impossible on technical grounds but that I would be eligible for parole in six months. My junior counsel had recently broken his leg partridge shooting and I remember wishing him a good season.

I was told I would probably be on 'Rule 43', which is a sort of protective custody for sex offenders, informers and any other prisoner who feels himself at risk from the main prison population. So I was to be an outcast even among outcasts. 'In disgrace with fortune and men's eyes, I all alone beweep my outcast state,' I thought.

Without my watch I could not gauge the passage of time. I sat on a wooden bench, this time with my feet on the chair. The cell was narrow and dimly lit. I folded my arms across my chest and let my thoughts wander. After a while a man was brought into my cell by prison staff. He had just been convicted of indecent assault on a young girl and given eighteen months. My immediate reaction was one of disgust until I remembered that I, too, was tarred with the same brush. We were fellow convicts and of a particularly nasty type. He offered me a roll-up cigarette which I smoked with great pleasure. I was already regretting the absence of my beloved pipe and tobacco.

The man told me of his case and said that he was lucky, because a fortnight ago he had found Christ. This was the first of many sudden conversions I was to encounter among sex offenders. He expressed the hope that he and I would share cells at Exeter prison. He told me there would be no need for him to go on 'Rule 43' as his case had attracted no publicity; he would enter the prison as a burglar or some such and no questions would be asked. My case was entirely different because of the national publicity my trial had attracted. I envied him.

An hour or so later the cell door was opened and we were ordered into the corridor to be handcuffed in pairs for our journey to prison. I was surprised by the existence of the handcuffs – I should not have been – and by their weight. They are much heavier than I had believed. We were allowed to go to the lavatory before being driven by coach the fifty or so miles to Her Majesty's Prison, Exeter. Our exit was barred by a press vehicle trying to take photographs of me through the coach window; a considerate officer drew the curtains to hide me from the prying eyes and lenses. At last we were on our way.

There were about seven of us, some just convicted, others still on remand. I remember a chap who had received five years for conspiracy. His cheerfulness put spirit into me. Another man, a drug offender, turned out to know two of my former colleagues at Winchester.

'You're the headmaster, aren't you?' I was asked by a friendly face.

Another man who had been on remand in Exeter for quite some time told me what it was like. I remember his complaints about the food and his advice to take paper tissues with me on exercise; there was never paper in the lavatories in the exercise yard, he explained. What good advice that turned out to be.

The journey continued through the typical Bodmin Moor and Dartmoor mist that I knew so well. I watched the familiar landmarks pass by and wondered when I would ever travel that road again as a free man, even though I knew that in the real sense I would never be free again. We arrived at the prison.

# 2

# FIRST DAYS

*And therefore never send to know for whom the bell tolls*

John Donne, Meditation XVII

I had been curious all my life to know what the inside of a prison was like. When the huge doors closed behind me I resolved to record all I saw and heard.

We were led into a long, narrow, doorless cell. An old lag brought two cups of tea to be shared by the seven of us. It was a human and most welcome gesture. I quickly learned that anonymity was not to be my lot, for the same inmate suddenly said, 'I'm an old lag with thirty convictions. I know the system. Public opinion put you in here.' He went on to misquote John Donne, 'Do not ask for whom the bell tolls . . .' That was my second surprise. The first had been the unexpected mouthfuls of tea, and now I was having the Meditations of a seventeenth-century divine quoted at me by a recidivist. Soon after, a second man was to quote from *Alice's Adventures in Wonderland* – I forget the import of his quotation but I would have been forgiven for wondering if I had come to a literary college rather than a prison.

By now it must have been at least 8.00 p.m. One by one we were processed through Reception by a rather loud-mouthed, bad-tempered officer in a white shirt. My turn came. I was ordered to undress, shower and put on some prison clothes. I was weighed and given more prison clothing and equipment. The last included mug, toothbrush, blankets, pillowcase, denims, shirts, under-clothing, shaving brush and a copy of the Prison Regulations. The Reception Officer yelled a list of instructions at me which I could not take in. I interrupted him to ask for clarification but was immediately told to shut up and reminded in unequivocal terms of my new status. This was an unexpected shock, but I remember thinking it must be part of the induction process. I think I was told that I would not be allowed to hold a firearm for five years; this injunction seemed rather irrelevant in the circumstances but I nodded automatic agreement.

After about half an hour a bearded man in civilian dress escorted me to my cell. He was an assistant governor and treated me with what amounted almost to deference. He explained that 'for your safety' and because of the publicity in my case I was being put on 'Rule 43'. This move would be confirmed by the Governor in the morning.

By now I was very hungry and after the months of waiting for the trial I felt strangely relieved. I asked for food, for I had eaten nothing all day. The AG left me in my cell, saying he would arrange for food to be sent to me.

I took stock of my surroundings and found there was a bunk bed and a single bed in the cell. The lower bunk was occupied. The single bed was made up but empty. The occupant of the lower bunk rose – a thin man in his early thirties – and proceeded to make my bed, explaining that the occupant of the single bed was in the prison hospital. I was struck by the friendliness of this chap – as I had been by that of the old lag in Reception. The camaraderie was unexpected. At the time I did not realise that those of us 'on the rule' were a despised sub-group whose only security was in mutual self-help.

Food was brought – cold, burnt chips and a Cornish pasty. I ate with no relish, undressed and climbed wearily into bed. I think some conversation passed between my cellmate and me but I remember none of it. I expected to endure a sleepless and agonising night like the months of pre-trial insomnia. To my surprise and delight I was asleep in seconds and slept the sleep of the just.

I was awakened, refreshed and (it seemed) totally at one with my surroundings, by the cell light coming on at about 6.30 a.m. My cellmate warned me to be out of bed by the time the officers came round to open the doors. My first drill was 'slopping out'. This is a well-known prison phrase and is subject to much discussion. Parliamentarians call it a 'degrading and sub-human anachronism'. The general public seem to regard it as a glorified nappy-changing session with attendant 'used potty'. I found it to be neither. It is a ritual which occurs in closed prisons after each meal and before breakfast. The occasion is one during which the lavatory is used and, if necessary, one's 'slops' bucket is emptied.

During the night or even during the day, the bucket may be used as a receptacle for urine or even faeces by the less fastidious. Other rubbish is put into it. At slop-out time the bucket is emptied and washed as appropriate. The time is also used for refilling one's water jug and washing bowl. The idea that long queues of men are carting ordure from place to place is entirely erroneous and I have spent many a worse time using public lavatories in rural France.

The more bashful of men find sitting on the lavatory while others watch and wait a little unsettling but as a friend wrote in a letter to me after I had mentioned this process, 'I hadn't thought of that. But one might just as well have a chat as read a book.' So slopping-out is the time of ablutions and a welcome relief from the tedium of twenty-three hours locked in a cell.

Before breakfast shaving water is collected and taken back to the cell. One razor at a time is issued and may be exchanged only in return for another. During the early morning slop-out all 'applications' are made. An officer stands on the landing with a book in which applications are recorded. These include requests for the weekly issue letter, for a probation visit, for a visitors' order, for permission to see the Governor. After all this and before breakfast, we are 'banged up' again. An onomatopoeic phrase of great accuracy. We shave and wait for breakfast.

Because we are 'on the rule' we may not be out of our cells while the other prisoners are around and are never allowed to go anywhere without escort. We listen to the noises of the other prisoners slopping out and collecting their breakfast. Eventually it is our turn and we walk in single file to the serving area to collect our food.

I am quickly spotted by the servers. 'There's the headmaster. He'll give you six of the best.' The comment is not offensive nor does it seem hostile, but some of my fellows on the rule receive threatening glances and some verbal abuse. I wish the ground would swallow me up. It is bad enough being in prison but being with the vilest of the vile is almost unbearable. Food is taken back to the cells where we eat our breakfast. After a decent interval we put out the metal prison trays and have slop-out again.

The first morning is totally confusing. A side of me seems to have adapted instantaneously – it has never been part of my make-up to worry about things over which I have no control –

another side just cannot come to terms with the experience. It is all still a blur. I am the new boy who will hear all, see all, obey all and say nothing. Later in the morning we have exercise. We are escorted through the prison to a small yard bounded by high walls. In pairs we walk round and round in an anti-clockwise direction. The rest of the prison is either banged up or exercising in a larger yard. We number about fifteen. Some of us wear blue; others are in brown denims. I learn that the distinction separates the convicted from the remand prisoners respectively. Surprisingly I am in a cell with two remand prisoners.

Suddenly, after a lap or two, screams of execration come from the adjoining cell block. It has been spotted that the nonces are on exercise. I receive my first experience of the horror of being 'on the rule'. My name is shouted but I have the sense not to look up and identify myself. 'You dirty, fucking bastards.' 'Hang the cunts.' 'We'll fucking get you.' 'Beasts.' 'Animals.' I am struck dumb with horror but I observe that my fellows ignore the insults and threats. 'Don't look up,' I am advised by a pleasant-looking man. Spittle comes floating down to join the other detritus of the yard. A battery is thrown and pieces of bread roll. I have never experienced such naked, feral behaviour. No wonder there is a Rule 43. What would happen if they got their hands on us? A few try to make conversation with me but I walk on unheeding.

One or two peel off to use the lavatory in the yard, having first received the officers' permission. I remember the advice I was given on the coach and plan to synchronise my bowel movements with exercise. It is a well-known fact that one of the hardest things to adjust to in a closed prison is that of synchronising bowel movements with slop-out periods. It takes time to adjust. Well, as I noted in my diary, I have time to adjust.

It was with some relief that we came off exercise – totally unexercised, of course – and went back to our cells. The Wing Officer, the first of many officers at Exeter who treated me with great respect and courtesy, allowed me a special visit to the library where I selected a Flashman novel, a volume of short stories and an Agatha Christie novel. Before this, a fellow con and non-smoker, who had noted that I was without that most important of all commodities, tobacco, had given me five tailor-made cigarettes. This man, an ex-North Sea diver, well spoken and reasonably *cultivé* had followed my case in the press and had great sympathy for me. He was still on remand and so was allowed food and drink from outside. His wife regularly brought him smoked salmon and white wine, which he chilled on his window sill. He was up on indecency charges against young children and later received five years.

How I regretted giving my pipe and tobacco to Jamie. I had forgotten that I could not pop out for tobacco when I ran out of it. I did not miss my watch – it was destined for the wrist of my middle son, so at least a part of me was with him all the while I was away. My other good watch was permanently on Jamie's wrist. As a friend was to say after my release when I told her of this, 'You've all been doing time together!'

Later on that first morning a beefy, cheerful-looking officer escorted me to the photographic 'studio'. I had already been photographed at the police station months before but now it was the prison's turn. I sat in the chair holding my number. I faced the wall for a profile shot. I was now a fully paid-up member of the criminal class. The thought sank reluctantly into my bones. My sons' father is in jail. I could imagine the taunts Tim would receive, and Jen still had to work at my school and be pointed at. My thoughts were interrupted by the officer saying, 'I was in court during your trial and thought it went hard on you.' I felt cheered. I had been there less than fifteen hours and an old lag and now an officer had told me I was wrongly convicted. 'Yes, I'm going to appeal.' I was escorted back to the cell feeling, if not *primus inter pares*, at least *inter pares* with the officer. I had much to learn about my status but at least the foul memory of the abuse during exercise evaporated.

The absent cellmate had returned from the hospital so there were now three of us. The other two were not my sort and I found conversation impossible. The new man was scruffy and looked filthy. Both men were smoking and I longed for tobacco. After about half an hour I asked for a smoke and was given a gossamer-thin mixture of paper, spittle and tobacco rolled so tightly that drawing on it was a physical challenge.

Next came the Governor's interview and a medical. The second lasted less than a minute and I have no recollection of what happened. For the Governor's interview I was told to go into his office, stand on the mat in front of his desk and give my name and number. I explained to the escorting officer that I had no idea what my number was, so I was told to give just my name. Ought I to know my number? No one had told me to memorise it. The Governor asked me to confirm if I wanted to stay on the rule. My reply was that I had no idea, that I had been told to go on it on arrival, that I knew nothing about prison ethics but that my wife feared for my safety. I would do what was advised but my wife's peace of mind was uppermost in my mind. I stayed on the rule.

Just before lunch my equilibrium was unbalanced. An avuncular officer called me from the cell to say that Jen had phoned. The man spoke so softly and feelingly that tears pricked the back of my eyes. 'How is she?' I asked. 'She's all right and sends her love. She's visiting you on Monday.' Tears welled up and I made little attempt to hide them. For a few hours I had forgotten about the outside world. It was as if I was deliberately separating my loved ones from me to spare them the pain of being in prison. I was 'enjoying' the novelty and it had not sunk in that I would see them for only a few short minutes every twenty-eight days. I went back to my cell trying to put on a brave face. I might just as well have been on the moon. I climbed on to my bunk and turned my face towards the brick wall, fighting a losing battle with my tear ducts. I wept silently with a reasonable show of control. My cellmates affected not to notice or, as I came to think later, were too stupid to observe. Over and over again I could hear the officer gently utter, 'She sends her love.' 'She sends her love.' I hear it still and it evokes the same lachrymatory response. It had been her love that had kept me going over the months. Never once had she doubted me. Never had she even hinted criticism. This is the punishment of prison.

The rest of Saturday is a blurred memory. A senior officer told me, 'It'll get better.' I wondered how it could get worse at that moment as I watched Christmas decorations being put up on all landings except ours. Lunch was over by noon and I went back to my reading. Saturday afternoons, I discovered, were the worst time of the week. Tea was over by 4.00 p.m. and the long, long spell until lights-out began. 'She sends her love.' 'She sends her love.' 'She's all right.' How can anything be 'all right' after this? Is Tim 'all right', knowing his Dad's in prison? How did Jason take the news after his long, overnight train journey?

Sleep did not come easily that night and I remember several

times leaning over from my top bunk to shake the snoring man in the single bed. Sometimes I stared out of the tiny cell window and looked at the high wall and the orange-coloured floodlights. Occasionally the sound of jangling keys and the footfall of the night patrol echoed along the corridor. I had already resolved to keep a diary but probably could not get writing materials until Monday. As I languished in self-pity I thought of the line in Pepys' diary which so haunted my current emotions and concerns: of *my* wife, 'poor wretch, who is troubled with her lonely life'. She deserves a better man than me. Eventually I slept but not before seeking God's blessing on my family.

I remember little of the first Sunday. After exercise those of us who wanted to went to chapel. We entered the building after the service had started and left before the end. As we came and went, a chorus of boos and hisses greeted us. We were not allowed to communicate during the service. In the past, convicts of Rule 43 had been attacked while going up to the altar to receive. The chapel was quite full but this reflected more a desire on the part of the men to spend the maximum amount of time out of the cells than a wish to commune with their God.

After the service the Chaplain entered my cell to leave me a copy of Dean Milner-White's *My God, My Glory*. We chatted briefly about York – I had lived there for several years and worshipped daily in the Minster just after Milner-White's death. My comments seemed to fall on deaf ears.

After exercise an officer had told me that the Governor was 'disappointed' that I had elected to stay on the rule. 'With your background in Physical Education and with your intelligence, you should be able to handle this lot. You shouldn't be on the rule; they're the lowest of the low.' I replied that I had been put on the rule and told to stay on it by the Wing Officer. Should I apply to come off it? Was I being cowardly? Was I being set up? I resolved to discuss the matter with Jen at the visit.

On Sunday afternoon we have a video show. Again, we enter the hall separately at the start of the show and leave it thus at the end. As always the accompanying cat-calls and insults are hurled at us. I recognise my cellmate from the court; if the others knew who he was he would be in real trouble. The drug offender sees me but makes no sign. In the evening we have 'association'. This is the three-hour period during which groups of prisoners mingle together for recreation. In our case we are stuck in front of a television from 5.30 p.m. until 8.30 p.m. It is a good time, for we may talk to each other and enjoy the freedom of being out of the cell. Sadly for us, the video and evening association mean that we spend a large part of Sunday not banged up but pass more time in the cells on other days. All our treats come together.

During the afternoon I am taught how to split matches to enable the box to go further. Lighters are not allowed in cells and, as we smoke roll-up cigarettes which seem to go out more often than 'tailor-mades', matches are at a premium. The secret is to be able to split the sulphur head with a ballpoint pen. I find it astonishingly difficult but manage to increase my supply somewhat. The more enterprising inmates have secret razor blades for the purpose. How they acquired them I have no idea. I am still without my own tobacco and generously my cellmate keeps me minimally supplied. I feel a strong urge to smoke but my libido has gone. I wonder if the tea is doctored.

Monday arrives and with it some mail. This is brought to the cell at lunchtime. My first ever prison letter is a wonderful one from my ex-secretary. She says that Jen is well and that everyone is coping. I look forward to the visit in the afternoon. I have arranged for tobacco to be sent in to two remand prisoners and passed on to me. I have written their names and numbers on a minute piece of paper which I hope I can give to my son during the visit.

I am called for the visit. Under escort I walk with other prisoners to the visitors' room. Outside it we are searched and all possessions are put into a pigeon-hole and locked away until after the visit. My piece of paper is nearly found but I manage to get it through. I am told to go to a particular table, whose number I forget, and sit and wait. After a few minutes Jen and Tim enter with Jason. I stand up but do not go towards them. As I shake Jay's hand I tell him there is a piece of paper in mine which I want him to secrete. He does so. 'Where's Jamie?' I ask and am told that he could not face coming to a prison. Well, he *is* claustrophobic, but I am disappointed.

I remember little of the visit except that Tim, very amused to see me in denims, burst into laughter. My own rules at school about casual clothing had been strict and denims had been outlawed. My plan to smuggle tobacco lifted their spirits, too, I think. It was a silly symbol that whatever else I was feeling my spirit was unbroken. The worst moment was when Jen asked me if I was all right. At that moment tears trickled uncontrollably down my cheeks. I wanted to stop them but I could not. She put her hand on my wrist and said, 'It's all right.' 'Don't ask me if I'm all right. I am all right but not if you ask me,' I said to her. The boys wonderfully affected not to notice. I learned, too, that the school's disco had gone ahead as planned and that every record was dedicated to me. Jamie had had Elvis Presley's 'Jailhouse Rock' played as I had asked him to but there had, apparently, been more tears than laughter at the function. A parent wrote later to say that 'The school disco was a weeping tribute to you.' A second, private disco had been held the following day when, again, I was the sole dedicatee. The news heartened and saddened me but it was good to know that the huge support was still there. It had not yet dawned upon me that I had lost my school and the pupils I loved so much. The sense of loss is still there and will never go.

Jen seemed, unsurprisingly to me, to be coping well. We were together for over two hours. The official ration is a half-hour meeting every twenty-eight days, so my lengthy visit was a generous concession on the part of the Exeter authorities. One of the remand prisoners on Rule 43 had his visit ended after thirty minutes. Once back in my cell I climbed on to my bunk and wept silently. I could not conceive that I would not see my family for another month. Even when I had had trips across the Atlantic in the old days I had never been away from them for more than three weeks. How much easier it must be to have no one to love or be loved by. My eleven-year-old son was being punished for something his father had been convicted of – it is a bloody awful system.

Later in the day a female probation officer came to see me. As with all visits we were brought out of the cell to talk on the landing. She talked of the possibility of going to Leyhill, an open prison near Bristol. She was brisk and efficient but there was little warmth in her. Other cons reckoned she was a trouble-maker in that she would intimate that they had been familiar with her. I cared nothing for this or for her. I had had two hours' conversation with my family and I wanted to relive every moment over and over again.

I learned that we were allowed only one bath a week. I discovered that combs were at a premium and that tooth powder was hard to get. It is these little luxuries that make the difference between a bearable and an impossible life in custody.

Bedtime comes and I find myself wondering if, after the initial shame and shock, I am actually 'enjoying' the novelty of the place. I have been well received by all in prison. Fellow inmates have begun to use me as a sounding-board and I find it hard to believe that some have committed the crimes for which they have been convicted or charged. But then, they feel the same about me. My friends – and some of my enemies I am told – feel as strongly as ever about me despite my conviction. Jen still has her job at the school; the boys' education will continue uninterruptedly. Am I being given an enforced rest? I need one, but so does Jen.

Just before going to sleep I hope that I shall be transferred to an open prison but muse that being locked up with two very odd fish is not too unpleasant. I am conscious of foot and crotch odour. I think of Christ again and note that the secular aspects of Christmas seem irrelevant. The morrow will bring me writing materials and who knows what else.

# 3

# ROUTINE AND RITUAL

*Oh wearisome condition of humanity!*
*Born under one law, to another bound.*

Sir Fulke Greville, 'Mustapha'

The experience of prison is largely one of survival. The man or woman in prison has to survive alone. His family and friends on the outside also have their own painful experience of surviving to undergo. But there is one difference. The prisoner has no friends. He has casual acquaintances and strikes up relationships. Willy-nilly he is advised to get on with the people in his cell. Common sense dictates that he should co-operate with authorities upon whom he relies for everything. He is told when to use the lavatory, when to collect his food, when he can apply for a letter to send out, when he can get a new razor blade, when he will go on exercise, when he sleeps, when he is to rise. He is allowed no independence of thought and has no rights.

His loved ones on the outside are deprived of his company and financial support but – and they do not know this – they have freedom. They decide their own destinies in ways which become significant to those who have been deprived of their freedom. It becomes, for example, a matter of great significance to the convict that he cannot decide when he shall use the lavatory – unless he wishes, in front of his cellmates, to defaecate into a bucket. Paradoxically the real freedom of individuals becomes the privilege of privacy. Being deprived of the opportunity to weep or reveal deep human feelings is, perhaps, the harshest aspect of the punishment.

Inevitably, then, different men work out different survival ploys. Some spend a great deal of their time trying to buck the system. For their pains they are put into the 'block' – segregated punishment cells. Others pretend a bonhomie they do not feel; but as soon as an unwelcome letter comes or their parole application is rejected, for example, the true misery of their inner condition is revealed. They weep or fight or swear. Thus it is that there is always an underlying tension in prisons. To ease this, as in hospitals, a routine has to operate. Anything that occurs outside the routine is an added bonus.

In Exeter prison I spent the best part of twenty-three hours locked in a cell every day. I left the cell for meals, exercise, bath, library visit and canteen. Each of these rituals is an eagerly awaited treat.

Meals are served hideously early, and after the 7.00 p.m. cup of tea there is nothing to look forward to until slop-out the following morning. At weekends 'tea' – the evening meal – is served at about 3.45 p.m.

Exercise – a misnomer if ever there was one – is a daily ritual, weather permitting. Remand prisoners do not have to participate in this mindless game. Once the call to exercise comes – and it generally does just as one settles down to write a letter or becomes immersed in a book – we decide whether or not to wear a denim jacket *and* a sweater and line up on the landings. We are marched crocodile-fashion along the landings, down the stairs and out into the small exercise yard. Hand-holding is optional but we might just as well be at infants' school. Once outside, in pairs, we walk anti-clockwise through the débris. 'Keep moving' is the instruction. Two bored officers station themselves at each end of the yard and smoke tailor-made cigarettes. With numb fingers some of us roll thin cigarettes. The first lap is accompanied by the English ritual of discussing the weather. By the end of the third lap we inspect the litter all around. Pages torn from magazines are covered with bird droppings; it seems as if the food thrown from the adjacent cell block is feeding the gull, pigeon and sparrow population of the whole county and beyond. Dead batteries and exhausted ballpoints are kicked as we have a game of makeshift soccer.

Conversation is varied and over the days one learns a great deal about one's fellows. The opportunity is given to use the lavatory in the yard. As I was warned in the coach, there is never any paper, but I am accustomed to bringing my own. The drill is to ask permission of the officer before peeling off into the comparative privacy of the little building. In the early days more often than not time doth not cohere with place and the basic problem of internal discomfort remains.

The steady tramping continues. I am called 'Prof' and 'Teach' by the others, who seem to know all about me. As the days pass I am to learn much about them and their, sometimes quite hideous, crimes.

My early diary frequently refers to the physical discomfort all cons experience. We were warm, regularly fed, washed daily and seemed to be well catered for. But the 'degradation' of slopping-out was as nothing compared with the stench of remaining unbathed for a week.

I had been used to at least one bath daily – and in my days as a teacher of PE was accustomed sometimes to three showers a day as well as my evening bath. I found living in my own stench for days on end quite foul. I had got into the nightly habit of soaking my feet in cold water but I was certainly not going to strip-wash in my cell. My shoes and socks I put out on to the window sill overnight but nothing would remove the stench of crotch odour. My feet were in a bad enough condition because the shoes were ill-fitting, and for the first few days my toes bled and stained my socks. Thus the weekly bath was a monumental treat. I recorded it in my diary on Wednesday 18 December:

> Today is bath day. Luxury . . . BATH. I don't think I've luxuriated so much. Cellmate lent me shampoo. Bath was large, private, unhurried and with limitless hot water. I managed to obtain two pairs of socks and three pairs of pants. Stupidly I gave one pair back – conscious that I must obey the rules – and was told what a fool I was by the prisoner attendant . . . both pairs are US tent variety but I got – unheard of – on request, a pair of Y-fronts with strict instructions not to tell the others. I don't think I'm being fanciful but it seems the whole nick knows who I am and sympathises with my plight . . . Bathtime finished with communal nail-clipping.

After this particular bathtime we were taken straight to the canteen. We regretted this for it meant that two treats were following each other; it was preferable to have a different treat each day if possible. But Christmas was approaching and decks were being cleared for the festive season when skeleton staffs would operate so that the maximum number of officers could spend the largest part of their time with their families. We were convicts. We had no families now.

Canteen is a sort of prison tuck shop. I learned to my surprise that I was to be 'paid'. I had done no work but that was because there was little work at Exeter and, anyway, I was on the rule. I was to receive £1.19 per week; 3p was to go to the 'common fund' which provided recreational facilities. We were allowed to buy one canteen letter a week in addition to the issue one we received weekly. Thus we could write two letters per week. With my money I bought half an ounce of tobacco – 95p; one box of matches – 5p; one packet of prison cigarette papers – 4p; one letter – 13p; and with the common-fund levy, I was spent up. If I had chosen to buy confectionery or fruit, for example, I would have had no tobacco. One irony of the system is that regulations allow a prisoner to have two and a half ounces of tobacco in his possession at any one time. My pay allowed me to buy one-fifth of that ration. Many inmates formulated their own equation. It went something like this: I am allowed five packets of tobacco. I can afford to buy one packet. *Ergo* I must obtain the rest of my entitlement by other means. And the authorities wonder why there are tobacco barons and smuggling. The simple law of supply and demand operates and I am totally convinced that if prisoners were allowed to buy up to the maximum limit per week many problems would cease. Again, though, it may be that one is sent to prison to be punished and not just as a punishment.

A further absurdity was that although private cash, as it was called, could be sent in we were not allowed to spend it on basic necessities. It could not be spent on toiletries, tobacco or letters. It could be spent on a radio – batteries-only and not VHF – and on radio batteries. Additionally one could buy a daily or weekly newspaper with it. It was as if dole money could pay for a television licence but not food. Without doubt the richest people in prison were those who did not smoke – later it was to be the drug pushers.

Gradually I became aware of sickening vicious circles. Prison was a stressful environment. For the majority stress is alleviated by drugs – alcohol or nicotine for most of the population. Increased stress results in the need for increased doses of relief. Prison, itself stressful, reduces a person's opportunity to alleviate the stress by depriving him of drugs. So stress increases, and explosions occur. To this mental pressure is added the physical tension associated with the discreet and natural performance of bodily functions. Nature dictates when one needs to use the lavatory. Practice accustoms one to privacy. In prison we have a man yearning for a smoke who has to get used to the public and often unsuccessful use of a lavatory. Stress increases.

On top of all this he has to live with his own genital stench with people not of his choosing and whom he may hate or be hated by. Where, normally, does one find relief from this sort of pressure? In most cases – even the most hardened – the relief lies in contact with one's family. For the poor man or woman yearning for a smoke or to use the lavatory this luxury does not exist. The monthly visits are short and unnatural. Letters are severely rationed. As I shall describe later, the visits produce stress.

Hardliners in our society will derive pleasure from this picture of severe deprivation. They will comfort themselves with the thought that the pariahs of society are suffering. There would be substance in that thought if the result was that offenders did not reoffend, but the truth is different. Murder and treason did not cease once the first murderer and first traitor were hanged. But our hardliners forget that prisons are not full of Moors Murderers or Yorkshire Rippers. They are full of people who failed to pay fines or who committed relatively minor driving offences. They are full of people with mental disturbances who cannot be treated elsewhere. They are full of other people's Mums and Dads and kids. And they are full of people who have been caught. A recent Home Office report suggests that 13 per cent of our growing prison population (above 50,000 again, despite the Home Secretary's executive release of three thousand prisoners early in 1988) are innocent of the crimes of which they were convicted.

Basic psychiatry has long recognised that, after food and shelter, sex is the next most powerful drive. Prisoners have no sex life. The inexplicable love bonds that instinctively exist in the most under-privileged families are torn apart by custodial sentences, often irretrievably. Heterosexual man is turned into homosexual beast. Almost the same deprivation is levied on one's innocent loved ones outside. A wife has no husband. Children have no father.

It is small wonder that prisoners advise each other to forget entirely the life outside. It is, to me, a matter of the most monumental wonder that politicians and others feel that the answer to the problems of our criminal society is to inflict longer and more frequent custodial sentences. No one who has not been in prison can begin even partially to conceive of the misery that is prison. Only those who have had loved ones 'weighed off' can vaguely perceive the nature of the experience. But the con must plod his weary way homeward – and for most the fact that release will come keeps them going. Some fail to make the journey. I was told that the bricked-up cells in Exeter prison had once contained suicides and that such sad cells were never used again.

So, our hapless, deprived adult looks forward to his third treat of the week. For me this took the form of a visit to the prison library. The initial pleasure of these visits lay in the fact that one was out of the cell. For me, the rows of books were a glorious sight. It was amusing to note how the other cons were intrigued by my choice of reading material. It was of interest to me that one hardened rapist was reading a biography of the poet Alexander Pope and another recommended the Flashman books to me. The con librarian was a quiet, well-spoken man of about sixty who was later to become a firm friend when we were both transferred to Leyhill. He was a jewel thief known as Raffles.

While in the library I had tried to sharpen my pencils. I made a mess of the operation and was taunted by the others. 'Fucking headmaster, can't even sharpen pencils.' The accompanying prison officer had the last word: 'Now you won't be made fucking milk monitor,' he said to the inmate who had teased me. Already on exercise I had been asked if I would be playground monitor! I cite these two comments to show that despite all the deprivation there is humour in prison. As time went on I was to laugh loudly and often – but it took me a long time to realise that I had changed my ideas of what was normal behaviour – or rather I had not changed them. They had subtly changed as part of a sort of 'survival' adaptation. The change was degrading and frightening and was noticed by my wife.

But armed with a new selection of books I could go back to the cell with some hope of being able to pass a little of the time in blissful oblivion.

I was grateful when I reached Leyhill for that prison's library, too. It seems that the authorities recognise the need for many books and they supply them in full measure. The Exeter library was rather limited and had the sort of eclectic range one would expect at a jumble sale. Old copies of Gibbons' *Decline and Fall of the Roman Empire,* along with countless paperbacks. Leyhill's library supplied all quality newspapers, many journals and an excellent range of books.

Interesting to me was a large section of books about the custodial experience as well as an extensive selection of art books. Crime novels and westerns nestled alongside Iris Murdoch and Saul Bellow. The books were modern editions, mainly hardback, and the library building was bright and welcoming. Many a town would have been grateful for such a superb facility and on the one occasion I used the inter-library service I received the book I wanted within three days.

It genuinely gives me pleasure to record this. We were not short of books. In fact so extensively was the library used that regular sweeps of our accommodation were made to collect overdue books.

On Friday 20 December part of my diary describes my cell.

My cell measures 6' 9" by 12' by 8' high. The ceiling is vaulted. Constructed of brick it has institutional green paint on the walls, white paint on the ceiling and dark-brown tiles on the floor. There are three rush mats on the floor, one single bed and a bunk. Two chairs, two tables, two triangular tables of which one is a corner fitment. The door is steel and, of course, contains a spy hole. The barred window is about six feet off the floor. From my (top) bunk I look out on to the small exercise area, other cell blocks and, I think, workshops. In the cell there is also a bucket, bowl and large jug for each inmate. That plus knife, fork, spoon, mug, comb, razor, shaving brush, tooth-brush, tooth powder and soap are one's sole possessions. Books give the cell a homeliness as do my, as yet thirteen, Christmas cards.

Cells have a bellpush on the wall. By pressing it a bell sounds and a metal bar on the wall outside the cell is lowered to indicate to the officers which cell is calling for attention. One may ring the bell after 7.00 p.m. supper if one wants to use the lavatory. After 8.00 p.m. the bell should be used only in dire emergency.

So what does one do all day? Many men sleep but that affects sound sleeping at night. I decided to keep a detailed diary.

Nothing of significance *to me* went unrecorded. The books I read, the letters I received, the sights and sounds and smells I perceived went into the journals. At first I wrote in pencil until I could afford to buy ballpoints. Indeed, one inmate lent me a propelling pencil which I used until I had exhausted all his leads. And I was not the only scribe.

The first cell I was in contained two remand prisoners, one of whom spent the greater part of the day copying out the Old Testament into an exercise book. I do not know what the purpose of this activity was; I do not think he ever read over what he copied. He never tired of his occupation, though. The other man spent most of the time lying on his bunk listening to pop music. Occasionally the two of them quarrelled or indulged in childish boasts. They were both, to use an old-fashioned phrase, 'mentally defective', and, though accused of horrible crimes, required treatment in a hospital. While they bickered like young children I read or wrote.

Later I was moved to a cell with a convicted man, a youngster in his early twenties who chattered constantly. 'My Dad always said I had mental constipation and verbal diarrhoea.' He was a more pleasant man than the others but he did not smoke. He possessed a radio but insisted on using the headphones or listening to the local radio programme so that I found no solace in his machine. I was not to get mine until Christmas Eve.

Routine became ritual. Breakfast, exercise, lunch, tea, bed. In between, if we were lucky, a letter would arrive or we would bath, go to the library or to the canteen. After a while I managed to borrow a chess set and would play innumerable games. I am not a good player but I do not remember losing more than one game out of about sixty.

Once a week the cell would be searched – not so much for contraband as to see if we were tunnelling out! On one occasion the officer remarked that he was 'just checking to see that no one was breaking in for Christmas'.

I read many books, wrote tens of thousands of words, learned how to write letters. The last was an art, for not only was space severely rationed but the knowledge that the censor would read the letters to one's wife and loved ones made the task stressful. No one likes to wear his heart on his sleeve and perhaps be the butt of jokes.

## Routine and Ritual

My extra tobacco arrived eventually and I was never to run short of it again. Life was tolerable once I accepted each day as it came and spent little time thinking about life in the free world. My own experience in the closed prison was brief and untypical.

# 4

# ON THE RULE

*To be worst,*
*The lowest and most dejected thing of fortune*

William Shakespeare, *King Lear*

There is an instinctive feeling of horror at the mention of prison. Few expect to go there, for few offend. The stigma attached to being a convict is ineradicable and this mark of ignominy is placed as much upon one's family as upon oneself. It is, hence, even more loathsome to be part of a despised sub-group within a loathed sub-group. All men of Rule 43 are universally hated.

Anyone who is deemed by himself or by the authorities to be at risk from the other inmates is put on the rule. The majority are sex offenders – a vile phrase which has so many nasty connotations. Informers and those who have got into debt within the system also endure this segregation, as do 'bent' prison officers and policemen. I was placed compulsorily on it and advised not to leave it. Indeed, on more than one occasion the landing cleaner told me that 'the lads' did not think I should be on the rule. They thought my case was 'a load of bollocks'.

Being set apart meant that I could go nowhere unescorted. My small group exercised alone and generally in a tiny yard. Strictly speaking no other convict should have been around when we were let out of our cells. In practice this did not happen and often, as we queued for lunch, we would be screamed at by other prisoners. At the serving place my fellows were given short shrift but my diary records that on several occasions I was given extra helpings by the kitchen cons and was always given a friendly smile. I have already recorded that in the bathhouse I was privileged to be given Y-fronts and my diary records that on one occasion I was given a scruffy change of shirt and the con told his assistant to get me a decent one.

None of this affected my status, though. I was a nonce with the nonces. A further effect of being on Rule 43 was that each day we were visited by a priest. Sometimes it was the Chaplain or his assistant, but the whole spectrum of the Broad Church trooped into the cell at one time or another. Our spiritual life was well catered for; even though we were observers rather than participants in the regular church services there was a weekly event known as 'Chaplain's Hour' which my diary describes as follows:

> Eleven of us in a small office . . . the wino [one of our number] kicked up a fuss and swore at the beginning. By the middle he had volunteered to read and read Psalm 23. By the end this apparent drop-out had partaken of the sacraments. This proves he is literate; I cannot make up my mind whether he is a superlative actor laughing at us all or a man who would really like help . . . Today's was my first Mass, interrupted twice by the telephone and the first at which, after the Blessing, the priest's next words were: 'And now jigsaws.' The occupational games are stored by the Chaplain. The discussion centred on the love of God and the need to rid ourselves of evil. One inmate said he had rid himself of evil. When asked how he replied, 'By divorcing the wife.' The priest was cliché–anecdotal in parts but came out with such *bon mots* as, 'We are God's polo mints; we have God-shaped holes.' All in all the man managed to bring an air of grace and peace into his office. He has a beatific smile – I can see why angry cons are soothed by him.

Later in the same extract I record a postscript:

> Footnote to Chaplain's Hour. Much concern was expressed about the safety of Rule 43 inmates when they go, as it were anonymously, to other prisons on a reallocation scheme known as P2. Should they as Christians lie about their offence? the Chaplain was asked. His answer was that they should grow a stubble and answer the questions of any curious inmate with the word 'Assault', uttered in a gruff voice. One was not lying; one was just failing to use the qualifying adjective 'sexual'. An interesting piece of prevarication!

My memories of the Exeter Chaplain and the elderly Assistant Chaplain are happy ones. The older man was constantly bombarded by my cellmate for favours. The cons seemed to use the priests as magicians. The attitude of a number of officers was different, as my diary entry for Sunday 22 December shows:

> Then off to church. We were asked to wait in the Chaplain's office while the service – to which guests had been invited – started. It was a hotch-potch. Pseudo Nine Lessons and Carols, 'Good News Bible', Evangelical approach and an appalling rendering of 'The Virgin Mary had a baby boy'. Various readers were selected but the inmate reader – a member of the choir – could not be found so a senior officer yelled across to the Chaplain, 'Keep talking and I'll go and find him.' The officer returned, having failed to find the reader, with the words, 'I hope he hasn't gone over the top.' This thoroughly disgraceful remark was received with laughter by the cons. A new con reader was appointed from the choir. The choir mistress read and pointedly emphasised her remarks by looking hard at all the cons. You know the type of woman. The Pentecostal minister read one of last year's entries to the prison poetry prize – a well-written lyric though the scansion defeated the reader in the second stanza! An RC priest, every inch a Rowan Atkinson and with trouble pronouncing his Rs, led the prayers and we, amid hissing, were led out during the final hymn. The best bit for me was the reading of the 'Proper' Bidding Prayer by the Chairman of the Prison Visitors and the 'decent' version of John by the Deputy Chaplain.
>
> I had time to study the chapel. It is modern with two crosses on its walls and an image of Mary. It is dark green and white with modern furnishings. North-east of the altar is a small organ and piano. Officers sit round the walls. The roof is high and impregnated with fire sprinklers. The floor is parquet. One magnificent oak beam lies to the south – the other roof beams are huge reinforced steel joists. It is light and roomy but the smell of farts and feet coupled with the largely indifferent attitude of the cons makes worship a depressing experience. The choir was clapped even after it had slaughtered its carol.

I was once in the chapel alone with the Lord Bishop of Truro, an old friend of mine. Not only had he presented testimony at the trial but he had bothered to trek all the way to see me. Of his visit I wrote:

Bishop just gone. Wonderfully uplifting visit. Present of Paul Jennings' *A Feast of Days*. Chaplain tells him I've impressed the staff by my humility and illustrates the point by saying that a member of a very rich family, who was doing about ten years for manslaughter in Exeter prison, found the slopping-out process so unpalatable and public that he offered £3,000,000 to build new recesses so that he could have a crap in private. My humility should come as a shock to all who know me. How kind of Peter to have come all this way. . . . He further hinted that he had received some flak about his involvement with my case. I'm sure he did – not least of all because he had the guts, the sheer act of faith, to support me. Like everyone else he says Jen is being magnificent. I've asked him to ask her for £15 for a radio. . . . He'll ring her tonight. That's the only bit I find hard – separation from the family – but for the last three years I've not seen much of Jen and the boys, and since May 28th precious little of Jen. . . . I suppose now that I'll only see them once a month I'll adjust to that fact.

Poor Peter was nobbled by the Chaplain for some episcopal chore while we were having a cup of tea – in a china cup! Later an officer was to ask me if 'a bishop' had come to see me; he evinced surprise when I said the Bishop was an old friend. A few days' after Peter's trip another priest breezed into the cell and said patronisingly, 'Hmph. Bishops don't come to see me.'

As far as was possible the spiritual needs of our pathetic group were met. And what a motley crew we were. An ex-headmaster convicted of unlawful sexual intercourse and indecent assault. I was to become their confidant and adviser. Let me describe them.

The man who had made my bed on the first night and who spent hours copying from the Old Testament was on remand. A divorcé, he was accused of a number of indecent offences. I was told by him that he was facing a possible fourteen years' imprisonment. He was an amateur photographer who had taken indecent photographs of young boys. I received the impression that he had sexually assaulted them, but I know no details. He was simple-minded, looked weak and ineffectual but was quite a hard man. He had a ready temper but subsided with equal speed. I have reason to be grateful to him for it was he who kept me supplied with cigarettes in the first few days, and he was my mentor. Of low intelligence, he could not be conversed with at anything except the simplest level and was happiest quarrelling with the third man in our cell.

This man was altogether nastier. Scruffy, mendacious and filthy, he was charged with a brutal assault on a three-year-old girl. He spent a great deal of his time protesting his innocence but my diary notes that after I had asked him one or two simple questions I had come to the conclusion that he was guilty. He was more loathed than anyone. Even in our group he was despised. I learned that the father of the girl he was alleged to have assaulted had plans to kill him when he was in court. The man told me he was safe because he would be on the rule for the rest of his life if he was convicted. His victim's father was a cripple and known to another man on the rule. It seems certain that a reception committee would do away with the prisoner if ever they got their hands on him. I had no sympathy for this simple-minded piece of flawed humanity. If he had not boasted, if he had washed thoroughly, if he had told the truth – anything and I would have tried to find some fellow feeling. I had none.

I have no idea what happened to either man, though after I had been transferred to Leyhill rumour reached me that the second man had been committed to a secure hospital. My new cellmate was very different. He came from a prosperous middle-class background and seemed the odd man out in his family. His sister knew my QC and had been helped in her legal studies by him. He had been in prison before and seemed content with his lot. He was the first to tell me that 'Dorchester's a good little nick'. As far as I could make out he was convicted of indecently assaulting a nurse at a psychiatric hospital he had been attending as a patient, and of indecent exposure. He could not tell me why he had exposed himself. He showed no signs of wanting to reveal his unruly member to me. I think he had been sent to another prison earlier on the P2 scheme but had been 'made' (identified) and threatened with a pair of scissors in one of that prison's work-shops. He chatted incessantly – on one occasion I was treated to a non-stop ninety-minute harangue. The man was more intelligent than the other two, no danger to society and looking forward to working with his father at the end of his, I believe, fifteen-month sentence. Once he had learned that I was not good at small talk we lived together quite happily for the three weeks I shared his cell.

The first two men I have described were sad cases because I do not think they knew what they were doing. Another chap filled that description. I met him twice only on exercise. He was known, ironically, as 'Rambo'. I do not know what his offence was but it was sexual. He had been sent out on the P2 scheme only to return shortly afterwards badly beaten up. He was verging on the educationally sub-normal and would have given himself away at the earliest opportunity. Eventually he was sent to one of the prisons which have separate wings for men on the rule.

Even more unfortunate was what my diary describes as 'a sad little man in a suit'. He was on remand, facing charges of unlawful sexual intercourse. He admitted the offence but said that he had known the girl a long time through a Youth Club connection, had seen her birth certificate and had been egged on by her. His story rang very true. He had a visit at the same time as me and derived comfort from the fact that his wife had noticed that my wife was keeping faithful to me; his wife would do the same for him. Happily he was released on bail before Christmas and I heard nothing of him again. That he was guilty of the offence was true; that he was, in the particular circumstances of his case, on remand in prison and likely to receive a prison sentence because of the actions of a teenage girl, was a painful thought to me. I remember consoling myself with the thought that he may have been one of the 'lucky' ones who was given a suspended sentence or put on probation. There had been several such cases reported in the papers. But I do not want to get into the question of disparity of sentencing here.

To me by far the most interesting man was the former North Sea diver, Dave. He was lame as the result of a diving accident, reasonably well read and well spoken, and he enjoyed the good things of life. He was the remand prisoner whose wife brought smoked salmon and white wine. Remand prisoners could have daily visits and unlimited tobacco. He was waiting to go on trial for charges relating to little children. I believe he, too, had photo-graphed and interfered with boys and girls at his local yacht club. I read later that he was sentenced to five years' imprisonment.

He was an interesting raconteur who on one occasion re-counted with great distress how his wife had given to his daughter his supplies of turbot and wine stocks. Clearly he was going to be convicted and his wife had acted accordingly. On another occasion, when we noticed the page of a magazine blowing across the exercise yard and looked uncomprehendingly at the illustration on it, he remarked, 'I don't know what it is. But I'm here for looking at things I shouldn't have looked at – at least until they got older.' It was an odd remark and showed little remorse for his deeds or concern for his victims – an aspect to which I shall return.

Without doubt the most disgusting of our number was an old dosser whom we nicknamed 'the Bin Rat'. He was forever diving into dustbins or swooping on to the ground for cigarette ends. A chain smoker, he dunned us continually. At first I had great sympathy for him and when my large stocks of tobacco came I kept him supplied. The others hated him. On one occasion they filled a cigarette paper with matches held in position by tobacco. This incendiary device was dropped on the floor outside his cell. Predictably at slop-out he saw the 'cigarette', swooped on it and lit it with rather disastrous effects.

On one occasion the Bin Rat urinated in the middle of the exercise yard and was taken back to the cells. On another he went out of control in the middle of the night and started to throw his furniture about. He was removed to the block from where he emerged a couple of days later. No one would share his cell with him and there was a sudden con-inspired change of accommodation which left one cell conveniently empty for him alone. The officers had the sense to keep him in isolation. He defaecated in his bucket and caused such a stench at slop-out that several times I retched when he was near. I finally lost sympathy with him when he taunted me about my case in revenge for my refusing to give him yet more tobacco. 'I'll see you right in the morning, mate,' was his gambit. When I refused on that occasion he called me a 'fucking cunt'. I went to strike him but an officer's attention was drawn to the scene and that was that. Later I was upbraided by one of the cons for not living up to my previously propounded doctrine of charity and non-violence. This was the first occasion of several when I threatened violence. Prison does change a man.

Two other remand prisoners were tried and sentenced when I was at Exeter. One was an ex-seaman who had lived for a while in America. He was a surprising mixture. Outwardly he exuded an air of toughness yet it was he who enjoyed reading the biography of Alexander Pope. He often gave me tobacco, unsolicited. I am not sure of his offence but I believe it was violence of some sort –

not against children. He was sentenced to three and a half years and came back from the court happily saying he had expected seven. Within three days he changed utterly. Initially his sentence gave him, in his phrase, 'just time for a shit and a shave'; once the enormity of the punishment had sunk in he became moody, and on more than one occasion threw punches on exercise. He was transferred to a semi-open prison and I lost track of him.

His cellmate received three years for indecency against a young boy. He had apparently sucked the boy's penis and fondled his genitals. He knew the boy but had no idea why he had committed the offence. He was a quiet man who once asked me if he could call me by my Christian name. 'I can't keep calling you "Prof" and I know you don't like being called Mr Bettsworth.' He was the only con to be ill while I was at Exeter; he caught a cold and kept to his bed for a couple of days – which caused my cellmate to lend him his radio.

Halfway through my sojourn at Exeter a bruiser whom I nicknamed 'the Mohican' came on to the rule. He was a remand prisoner, but I do not know what he was alleged to have done. He looked a nasty piece of work but turned out to be a sublimely thick, almost cuddly, grizzly bear. I threatened this oaf in the bathhouse once when he asked me for the address of the girl 'you had it with'. I could not do much because I was naked at the time but I left him in no doubt about the error of his way. He often went to the block but was happiest when reading soccer results and it did not matter how old the results were. He was 'two'd up' with 'Doc', who gave sickening accounts of this man's masturbatory habits. Suffice to record that Doc had no objection to masturbation *per se* but to the manner. This was the first reference to sex that I had heard in prison.

Doc was another enigma. He enjoyed the role of 'hard man' of the wing but readily took all my teasing. He modified his language in my presence, once even saying that he was swearing too much. This amused me, for my language had never been free of swear words, though oddly enough I swore virtually not at all in prison. This man was a trained children's nurse who hoped to take up his calling again. His family had deserted him and he felt he had nothing to live for. I think his offence was rape but I am not certain. He was a fitness fanatic who enjoyed his many outings to court. Often he came back from a remand hearing saying his day out had been 'magic'. He recounted a story of filling the lock of his handcuffs with Blu-Tack so that the key would not work. I do not know if the tale was true, although he did show weals on his wrist where he claims the blacksmith cut off the 'cuffs'. I bequeathed him my *Times* copies when I left; I had been unable to cancel my order because of some petty rule, and as Doc had shown an interest in the crossword I left a couple of weeks' supply with him. He was looking forward to telling his current girlfriend what newspaper he was taking. On my last day he stated that he would miss our 'intelligent' conversation on exercise.

His closest friend was also on remand. He was a man who missed his family and his dog with pathetic desperation. A tiny, bearded man who never spoke of his offence, he had some expectation of a light or even suspended sentence. We became a close trio on exercise and he was the first to share intimate photographs of his family with me. He was the cause of my having photographs sent in eventually. At first I had decided that I wanted nothing of the kind with me in prison; I wanted to be a non-person. But as time went on and I feared I would lose my parole for smuggling offences at Leyhill I asked for photographs.

The second man to show me photographs was, perhaps, the most confused and tortured soul of all. He was sentenced to six years for incest; he told me he had had sexual intercourse with his teenage daughters. He did not know why he had done this and went through daily purgatory but with no cathartic effect. His wife and family had stayed faithful to him. Indeed, his daughters, so he told me, renewed contact before their mother. He was visited by them and hoped to rebuild his shattered existence. Once he had been on the P2 scheme, had been discovered and had been beaten up. On the day that I was told I was to go to Leyhill he was told he must try reallocation in Birmingham Prison. He refused, saying he would rather do his six years in the block as long as he had the company of his Bible and his family photographs. He became *persona non grata* with the Assistant Governor, who told him he could not go to the '43 Wing' of another prison until he had tried the P2 scheme twice. I have no idea what happened to him but think of him with great affection and much sorrow.

As time went on I was to encounter a number of incest cases. I remember years ago reading of an incest case between adult brother and sister. At their trial the judge uttered words which I never forgot: 'You have both suffered enough. Go and live your lives in peace.' Why those particular words affected me as an adolescent schoolboy I do not know. I suppose it seemed to me the epitome of deep, human compassion and understanding. For all the horror the word 'incest' invokes, I have never been able satisfactorily to classify the act in my own mind. I suppose it is, like cannibalism, 'against the laws of human nature' – but people do eat people.

Certainly I could not comprehend the actions of many of my colleagues on the rule, but when I got to know them as people I found it hard to reconcile the sentient, normal human beings with the literally perverted offenders that they were designated. The same thought occurred frequently at Leyhill when I became friendly with many murderers. Once again I mused at the connotative power of language, just as I had done during my career as a teacher of literature. I imagine a number of my fellows on the rule had been consigned to prison with the 'tabloidese', 'sex beast caged'.

Certainly my fellow 'sex beasts' laughed and loved, wept and worried like ordinary people, for that is what they essentially were. They yearned, like me, for their wives and children. Their families suffered as acutely the loss of a father as did mine or as did those of any family whose father had died. Before going to prison I would have been shocked to hear myself uttering such appallingly 'liberal' sentiments. Before I was interned I just did not *know*. Now I do and powerfully wish that the hardliners who advocate stiffer penalties for certain crimes would spend some time in prison so that they, too, can get to know.

Having said that, I acknowledge that I have no tithe of a notion of the suffering my fellow inmates caused. Their victims must have suffered hideously and irreparably; their only redress may be revenge and with that thought we are being sucked into a frightening vortex.

# 5

# CHRISTMAS AND NEW YEAR

*England was merry England, when*
*Old Christmas brought his sports again.*
*'Twas Christmas broach'd the mightiest ale;*
*'Twas Christmas told the merriest tale;*
*A Christmas gambol oft could cheer*
*The poor man's heart through half the year.*

Sir Walter Scott, *Marmion*

The document is headed 'Christmas Plans'. I think it has been compiled by the Chaplain. The first page identifies itself by the title 'Memorable Quotes'. I read, 'He that lets the small things bind him, leaves the great undone behind him.' Is this a reference to the misery of colonic adjustment at slop-out or is it a profound truth?

The 'Christmas Message' superficially analyses the Reagan–Gorbachev summit, invites us to imagine that the humble stable could have been in the city where we are currently incarcerated and ends by asking for our 'best hopes for the new year'. It just does not seem like Christmas this year.

We are to see four films over the holiday period. One is called *Loose Screws*. I do not know whether it is about wayward prison officers or about sexual promiscuity. The Clocktower News Agency, our 'main suppliers of newspapers', wishes us a Merry Christmas and a Happy New Year. As I read I am trying to split matches. A blob of sulphur shoots out across the document and lands on the announcement in the programme about a quiz competition. The first prize is £8, awarded by our newsagent. 'What is the opposite of apogee?' 'How do you address a duke?' 'On what date was Princess Margaret born?' 'Who won the cricket championship in 1934?' (This must be a question for a long-termer.) 'When was the National Trust founded?' 'Who was Onesimus?' 'Name first martyr for Christ, with reference.' In fact, everything that the best-informed convicts should know.

36

Ah, but the menus. Christmas Day breakfast is a feast – cereals, bacon, eggs, sausage, tomatoes, fried bread, bread and margarine, toast and marmalade, coffee and sugar. It is the 'and' that is important. As every self-respecting armed robber will tell you, it is the '*et*' in '*et dona ferentes*' that is important. Coffee is a rare treat, but coffee *and* sugar is exceptional.

Lunch will destroy the regulation of my colon for ever. Soup, turkey and all the trimmings, grilled sausage *and* stuffing, roast *and* creamed potatoes, tea *and* sugar. But there is no 'and' between Christmas pudding and brandy sauce!

Tea will bind me eternally. Shoulder (not just any) ham *and* corned beef, mixed salad, bread *and* margarine, trifle *and* pears, coffee *and* sugar. Supper has me groaning in alimentary agony. Christmas cake, fresh fruit, packet of biscuits, tea *and* sugar.

The meals are served respectively at 8.00 a.m., 11.30 a.m., 3.40 p.m. Supper is issued with 'tea'. Lunch is, of course, 'dinner'. The day is broken up thus: 7.45 a.m. Unlock. 8.00 a.m. Breakfast. 8.45 a.m. Exercise – Convicted. 9.00 a.m. Unlock choir. (George Eliot's 'I join the choir invisible' in reverse.) 9.30 a.m. C of E Christmas Service and Blessing of the Crib with Competition (Chapel) results and prizes. A sort of Saturday Night at the London Palladium with Christ as a supporting actor. 10.35 a.m. RC Mass of the Nativity. 10.45 a.m. Exercise – Unconvicted. It seems that our Roman brethren can have either Christianity or Muscularity; there is no time for both. 11.30 a.m. Dinner. 1.40 p.m. Games and Competitions. (We on the rule may not partake of this fun.) 3.40 p.m. Tea. 7.00 p.m. Supper. This last consists of the landing cleaner bringing round a pint of tea.

So, apart from the absence of wife *and* family, port *and* Stilton, we are to be merry.

The above skeleton shows clearly that within the obvious limitations of a closed prison the authorities are doing all they can to make Christmas as pleasant as possible. I can best describe the experience of the Christmas season by quoting from the diary I kept at the time:

*Christmas Eve*

It is 6.30 a.m. and we're waiting for slop out. I don't know why I'm awake and alive so early. I take so long to go to sleep that in the mornings I usually dress when the lights come on and lie snoozing on the top of my bunk. I've even lit my first roll-up; I usually wait until after breakfast. The Aled Jones programme last night was marred by too many interviews. He sounds a delightful boy but I've heard very many better trebles from the Chapel Choir of King's College Cambridge. . . . Just signed for my radio, which I can collect this afternoon. We've a video so I hope they find me because immediately afterwards is the Nine Lessons and Carols from Cambridge. . . . Just been asked by a screw which Trinity School has a lovely choir. He'd seen it on breakfast TV. I suppose it's Trinity, Croydon. Breakfast late today. . . . Just been told by my cellmate that if I go to Leyhill it will be full of people like me – 'Fraudsters and members of the upper classes' – *ex ore innocentium*! He's sure there'll be other *Times* readers there as well as 'lifers' finishing off their sentences and who are, I'm told, very placid. . . . Another bit of officer whimsy. On locking us up after we had collected breakfast the same old boy who was in court with me said, 'One for your chemistry lesson. Analyse that. They'll turn round and say it's synthetic rubber.' I don't know if he was referring to the scrambled egg or to the porridge. I found both acceptable. My cellmate cannot understand the, for want of a better word, 'relationship' I have with the officers. He's just said, 'I don't know what's happening in this prison but I'm glad I'm banged up with you. When you've gone it'll be back to the usual misery.' And he is doing his second stretch in here. . . . Unexpected library visit and then we're going to have our bath today – that plus canteen means all our weekly treats are in one day. Damn. . . . Back to the cell and a Chaplain's visit. . . . the priest has offered to get me *The Times* Jumbo crossword but found that someone had already started it so didn't bother; it was a kind thought, though. . . .

Interrupted for a bath. A marvellous pleasure but with the library it means we have fewer things to look forward to. Failed to get Y-fronts this time as there were none in stock. Been promised them for next week. When changing my shirts one of the laundry cons told his assistant to replace the one he's given me 'and get two good ones'. I still seem in his eyes to be a Very Important Prisoner. Remarkable when one considers how nonces are universally hated.

Straight from bathhouse to canteen where, joy of joys, we were allowed to buy *three* canteen letters. I also bought some matches, cig. papers imprinted 'HM Prisons only', two Biros – the propelling pencil I was lent has nearly run out and one of the sharpened pencils is broken. We are given a £1 Christmas bonus. I've spent that and saved my wages, which will be added to next week's. If I'm careful I could come out with a profit. *Then*, it's all too much. Mail arrived.

Six letters including one from a former colleague who signed himself 'Yorick'. I was hauled before the Censor because my friend had signed the Christmas card 'Castiglione', my nickname for him, and signed his letter 'Yorick'. There was no address on his letter. Did I know him? Where does he live? . . . Disposal of my three letters is tricky. . . . I've received thirty-eight cards and letters so far – to whom do I reply? . . . After-lunch video mildly pornographic; it whiles away ninety minutes but the acres of bare bosom did nothing for me. I still must assume that the tea has been doctored or that I have been. *Times* waiting on my bed after the film. I've not cracked the crossword yet but I've another two days to finish it if I don't crack it tonight. After tea – a rhino chop boiled in oil – I asked for news of my radio and a very kind screw fetched it. Heard most of King's on cellmate's radio. Radio 3 reception is poor but I'm listening to some Tchaikovsky now and eagerly await the Brandenburgs later. . . . the Bach reminds me of last Christmas when I played the concerti at a party. It doesn't feel like Christmas at all. The prison decorations seem inappropriate and apart from the better food we have little to celebrate.

I was going to buy a cigar this morning but decided that without port and Stilton it was a futile gesture. I used the money for the extra letter. Service at 9.30 a.m. tomorrow but as usual we have to enter after it has started and leave before the end. Still, I have had peace of mind in here and don't feel spiritually deserted. . . .

I've just finished *Uncle Tom's Cabin* and must try to model myself on Tom. I now have seventeen Christmas cards. Lovely to be remembered. . . . Much baiting of 43-ers tonight. My 'colleagues' responded by singing carols. I find the insults amusing but don't like being called a 'nonce' – what is it?

Animal? Beast? Nearly 8.00 p.m. and time for the Brandenburgs and my J. I. M. Stewart novel. The cleaner has already
reminded us to put out our Christmas stockings. . . .

*Christmas Day*

Awakened and unlocked about 7.00 a.m. Just in time to hear
Mozart's Fourth Horn Concerto – not Denis Brain, alas. . . . I
regard my radio as my Christmas present and a very welcome
one it is too. All wish each other a 'Merry Christmas'. I grunt
for there is nothing to be merry about. Chapel at 9.30 a.m. and
apart from going out to get the food we are 'banged up' for the
rest of the day. I can't be doing with false bonhomie. Christmas, I've at last realised, is a family time – tho' I'm not
depressed or anything. I just see no point in false bonhomie.
Cellmate wishes every screw in sight 'Merry Christmas'. I
don't know whether it's obsequiousness or crass low-
foreheadedness. . . . Because Jen and the boys are at twin sister's
for Christmas and I don't know her house I can't envisage how
they'll be spending the day. . . . My arrogance finds me wishing
that at an appropriate moment during the day scores of people
will be lifting their glasses to me. I have a long way to go in the
humility stakes. But I raise my coffee mug to 'Absent Friends'. . . .

Just come off exercise after a mere twenty minutes because it
was pouring with rain. Missed chapel for exercise as the two
coincided and as much of the service will be devoted to the
giving out of prizes I see no point in going. Besides which, there
could be trouble for us. The insults were really lively last night
and started again this morning. We even had missiles thrown at
us on exercise. It seems that at this season of goodwill the
frustrations of being incarcerated at Christmas are being
vented on the common enemy – us. I don't find any of this
upsetting – it's rather amusing and I received my fair share of
abuse last night.

Thus on this Christmas Day I shall leave my cell for a mere
twenty minutes plus the time taken to collect three meals.
Should I have gone to church? *No*, I'm not allowed to receive
the sacraments during the service and I don't think prizes
should be given out then. There are games and competitions
for the others this afternoon – that's when all the ballyhoo

should occur. . . . Vaughan Williams' *Fantasia* is on the radio; my recording of it Jen bought me as a Christmas present years ago – perhaps when I was teaching at the Approved School. How funny if I first heard it as a 'screw' and last hear it as a 'con'. If the wheel has come full circle where do I go from here? A Beethoven quartet in a minute then Christmas lunch. I'll keep the prison Christmas programme as the menus are on it. Just had lunch – very good, too, considering the circumstances. Even the ends of the Brussel sprouts were cut crossways! Gave my pud to my cellmate. And now the day is over. Another ten hours to lights-out. It is now 11.45 a.m. and I've had my Christmas 'dinner'. Just the time for an early gin and tonic – my first Bacchanalian thought since coming in here. Reports from the chapel were that the service was not good. I'm glad I didn't go. Chaplain has just entered carrying matches for the Bin Rat. I've already given him one box today and intend to give him hell at slop-out. Chaplain invites us to give our Christmas cards to charity. I intend to keep mine as precious souvenirs, as they surely are. If only the large one, signed by all the pupils, were here. I'm not allowed it for it is a padded one and may contain contraband. . . .

Waiting for tea and listening to King's Cambridge for the second time – bliss. At least I heard the 'Once in Royal David's City' solo before being interrupted for tea – an excellent repast but coming so soon after lunch. . . . For supper – food is supplied with the teatime food, but a hot drink comes round at 7.00 p.m. – I face cake, sausage roll (I've saved cheese for the cake), a packet of four shortbread biscuits and a satsuma. The day from now on will drag interminably. Sad thoughts occasionally intrude, particularly as the rain is heavy outside and I would dearly love to be with Jen and the boys.

Last Christmas was dull on the day but a large Stilton, many mince pies and port in abundance helped things along. I'm sad, too, at the thought of never sitting in the library at my school again and of never seeing the view from our scruffy flat. . . . I hope, my beloved family, you don't feel I've let you down too badly. I shall make it up to you economically but the loss of our combined dream is hard to bear. I'm sure it won't be in a year or two. I suppose another reason for the depression today is that there's no mail or paper – ditto tomorrow, although we have another video and the Chaplain has arranged a Mass for us on Friday. Roll on the New Year; by the next visit I shall feel I have eroded my sentence. I'm damned if I could do six years or even three as some poor devils are.

I've just had my satsuma – my first fresh fruit for a week – and my temporary depression has gone . . . nearly another day over. I'll soon be home. Foot-soak time. I've also got into the nightly habit of airing my socks and shoes on the sill through the bars. I don't know what happens if they fall out. Am now about to turn in. I've just read Jen's sonnet again; I still can't track down its provenance. It has not cheered me; it has reminded me how far I am from the person I love so much. Roll on Boxing Day. It's pissing down here.

The sonnet referred to above was written to me in a letter from my wife. It eventually came to me that it was Alice Meynell's sonnet, 'Renouncement'. Jen had quoted the sestet:

> But when sleep comes to close each difficult day,
>     When night gives pause to the long watch I keep
>     And all my bonds I needs must loose apart,
> Must doff my will as raiment laid away, —
>     With the first dream that comes with the first sleep
>     I run, I run, I am gathered to thy heart.

### Boxing Day

Seems to have rained heavily all night. The news is of floods in Devon . . . water coming over the roofs of cars. It's still raining so I guess we'll miss exercise. That's a bad start. Still I can do no better than quote from the diary extract in *A Feast of Days* – it's by James Woodforde (1740–1803): 'Thank God had a pretty good night last night and I hope for something better.' He feels 'languid and low' so instead of 'one glass drank six or eight glasses of Port wine and it seems to do me much good being better for it.' There you are, Jen, I know what I need.

No exercise. Instead we were allowed (*sic*) to clean our cells. I caused slight banter by inspecting everyone's handiwork afterwards. . . . So without exercise again today the day is going to drag. Tea at 3.30 p.m. – always grimly early but we have a video this afternoon. The cleaner has just been in with the pre-lunch mug of tea. I WAS SOUND ASLEEP. Must have slept for an hour and a half. This has not happened before *and* I had a good night's sleep. Must be the lack of exercise. Lunch excellent but again I could not eat it all because of the lack of exercise. . . .

Appalling video. At the end I got up prematurely and received my first reprimand in front of about a hundred men from a moustached, overweight, macho-screw who couldn't run twenty yards to catch an escapee. . . . Tea immediately after film. It's too much – no exercise and too much grub. My stomach and I cannot regulate my system. Perhaps yesterday's and today's fruit will take effect tomorrow.

Dramatisation of Conrad's *The Secret Agent* on Radio 4 tonight. I'll listen to it. One of our number is laid up with 'flu so I suppose we'll all succumb. It won't be a relief for we lie on our beds most of the day anyway. Tomorrow I'll be in possession of a newspaper and maybe some mail as well. Think I'll write to Jen – where to send her letter is anybody's guess. It's bloody silly not to have sent me her movement plans. I hope she got my pre-Christmas one. . . . Borrowed a chess set and beat cell-mate seven games to nil; given that Tim has beaten me in the past, I find this diversion very boring. So while he waits for *The Archers* on my set – he has very kindly given his to our sick colleague – I am having supper and soaking my feet. Mince pie – oh so horribly sweet – shortbread and an orange. The beverage is coffee – delicious. *Secret Agent* well done though why everyone takes the novel so seriously I don't know. . . .

Crotch smelling and am using the bucket to pee in. Window in the cell is, for the first time, shut as a gale is blowing. It's much colder. We have the choice of icy blasts and the precious Christmas cards being blown around or warmth + stale urine + flatulence + stale oranges + feet. We prefer to be warm! Thank goodness Christmas is over and we are back to normal – apart from special food on New Year's Day. . . .

I'm thinking of coming off the rule again but I think the splendid Wing Officer would think it a bad idea. Technically it's my decision but if I did get into any trouble it might affect (a) to where I am transferred and (b) my parole/remission. My only problem is that I may run out of books before next week's library visit.

I hope Jen and the boys celebrated properly. I do miss them.

So Christmas passed. On Friday 27 December I learned I was going to Leyhill open prison. It remained to get the New Year over and for me to be resettled. Then I could begin my sentence proper.

*New Year's Eve*

Much warmer. Slept heavily and dreamed I was galloping in sandals but stirrup-less. I don't know who my riding partner was but I remember having superb control of the horse. What is happening to my subconscious? What a joy to contemplate the end of this horrendous year. Why we deserved it I'm damned if I know. New Year's Honours include Charles Causley – and Cliff Morgan a CVO – plenty of Celtic awards then. Thatcher says the country is 'bouncing back'. Kinnock talks of another year of 'rack and ruin'. Steel: 'You'll all turn to the Alliance.' Yawn. Yawn.

Asked Wing Officer how to cancel my paper; surprisingly he doesn't know but has kindly said that he would find out from the library. He has confirmed that I am definitely going on Thursday. 'Normal allocation. Open prison. You'll be all right there.' I long to go for an unaccompanied anything. Being escorted everywhere is all right for our protection but it does cramp our personality. There are those in here who want to spend years on the rule. What state will they be in when they come out? I'm currently reading *The Clockwork Image* – subtitled 'A Christian Perspective on Science'. Among other things the author, while advancing the theory of the 'machine-mindedness of our age', writes: 'Even criminals are sometimes robbed of the dignity of being blamed for their actions.' Will a man on the rule for six years ever be more than depersonalised thereafter? The author suggests that if mental illness were the reason given for anti-social behaviour then human beings do become machine-minded. Bob Geldof – Man of the Year. What a surprise! Terry Waite – runner-up. Another shock!

I've not seen a car for eighteen days and look forward rather nervously, to be sure, to seeing one on Thursday. I wonder what else I'll notice. . . . Hope we get a bath today; we won't tomorrow as it's New Year's Day and I'm stinking again and don't want to foul my own clothes which apparently haven't been laundered. . . . Must buy a letter today but I don't know to whom to send it. I don't know where Jen is; she is so vague about times and places though she might like to know where I am! Canteen – bought two letters which I must write before I'm transferred, tobacco and two boxes of matches.

Excellent exercise. . . . my mates say they will miss my 'intelligent conversation'. . . . Then bath. The orderlies made sure I had good clothes – having thought I'd already trans-ferred. One asked me to relay a message to a co-defendant of his in Leyhill. The officer accompanying our bathing party very kindly rang through to admin. to get me Leyhill's exact address to put in my letter to Jen. . . . Then library. Interesting chat with the librarian and his young sidekick who is a friend of my former Art Master. Our chat was short. . . .

I *cannot* cancel my *Times* because of some petty, bureaucratic regulation. Thus I've wasted £2 for nothing. Instead I've transferred it to Doc. . . . Today's *Times* has been brought by a surly screw. I think he resents he doesn't read it and hates to see the crossword completed every day. . . . Excellent lunch – the best soup I've had since I've been here and a tasty shepherd's pie. The only thing that I miss is that my wife hasn't written.

It's amazing how smelly a process peeing into a bucket is. Dear Father Eliot, the Deputy Chaplain, has just come in to say he has written my report for Leyhill. What fun to have an end-of-term report. (Pun intended.)

Much abuse of us tonight. I still wonder if I ought not to have gone on to the landings [joined the main prison population]. Ah well, I shall never know now. I hope we have a final Chaplain's Hour tomorrow. I shall miss all the cons here. Don't feel a bit end-of-year-ish. Just bloody glad we are nearly in 1986. My cellmate wants to stay awake until midnight. Bloody fool. The only liquid for a toast in this cell is urine and none drinks that.

*New Year's Day*

Well, my last day ever, I hope, banged up in a cell. The prison was fairly noisy last night at midnight. Cellmate wished me 'A

Happy New Year' and I'm sitting here this early morning waiting for him to wish the same to everyone in sight. Ugh!! Slept very, very heavily and have a headache and all the symptoms of a cold. Maybe because we kept the cell window shut during the bitterly cold weather and built up a fug. I roll my first fag before 7.00 a.m. I must cut down.

Mild day. I wish Jen had written before my transfer. Now I won't hear before Monday 6th Jan. probably and that's three weeks before letters. . . .

Endured my last stint on the exercise yard. Very cold now and overcast. Head aching horribly and I feel under the weather. I've asked for aspirin but none has been forthcoming yet. Good wishes for the future have been extended by my mates. I look forward to being, if not free, at least at large.

Two men are off on reallocation today. Lucky fellows. My sweet-toothed cellmate got their sugar ration and of course I'll leave him mine. We get a weekly ration but for those with a sweet tooth it never stretches far enough. My cellmate buys extra in the canteen; he can afford to, he's a non-smoker. Today is really like the last day of a holiday; you've got nothing to do and just occupy the time until the excitement of the voyage home.

It's dull and timeless here today. I feel very unwell. Headache no better but the leadenness of the day suits my mood. I just want to get out of this place. Then I will really have started my sentence. . . . Feel somewhat sad about leaving here after all. I hate the cell door being locked. I hate being escorted everywhere as if we were prep school boys. I hate slopping out and the smell of urine. Yet this place has been a haven after the trial. I just hope I don't become too blasé about the new place and hence bored. Then I think the months of imprisonment would be infernal. My feelings are very mixed at the moment. It's the most depressing time of the year and I am further saddened by not having had a letter from Jen and the boys. It is the moment of stasis for me. I look forward to the dynamic of Leyhill.

A priest comes in and asks about the closure of Truro Cathedral School. He teaches at Exeter School. . . . He asks if I'm coming back here as he's 'sad' that I'm leaving just as he's getting to know me!! Chaplain's Hour was with the wonderful

Father Eliot. Communicated but with no wine. He spoke at length about the significance of Christian names. . . . anecdotal, standard analogies etc. but he has a sanctity and venerability impossible to ignore. He wishes me well. . . .

I'm as restless as hell at the moment. I just want to start my life at Leyhill. . . . *I am* missing Jen and the boys. Just turned on Choral Evensong. It's from Winchester College. On the memories of that place! I hope there is a reason for all the current anguish. My career: Winchester College – Deputy Headmaster – Headmaster – sex offender. There is no easily discernible pattern, is there?

I've just packed – i.e. taken down eighteen Christmas cards. I even felt sad as I normally do after such a deed and the cell looks bare. All my belongings fit into a small brown paper bag. Indeed were it not for the two books I've been given I'd only have a few letters, cards and notebooks.

The Christmas decorations have been taken down in the prison and now that this Bank Holiday is drawing to a close an air of normality will prevail. I've just had what I hope will be my last public enthronement! If Leyhill is as discreet as I'm given to understand it will be quite strange using the lavatory in private. I'm a bit apprehensive about tomorrow – perhaps latent signs of institutionalisation. . . . I look forward to regular conversation; here we talk only on exercise and association. Cellmate and I rarely converse as we have nothing to say to each other. He has just turned on the most sickening tape of religious songs. I went spare and he has graciously turned them off. I think much more of his company would turn me desperate. . . .

Well, I've just soaked my feet for what I hope will be the last time. I'm hoping it's possible to get a daily bath at Leyhill. Still interested to note my libido is virtually non-existent. Should I worry about this? Halfway through Stewart's *A Memorial Service*. I have two and a half hours to finish it before lights out. I think (hope) I've just had my last pee in a bucket. This cell really is multi-purpose. Was it Donne who wrote, 'And make one little room an everywhere'? Literary quotations flood into my mind. The influence of Stewart's very cultivated young heroes, I expect. . . .

# 6

# PRISON OFFICERS

*'Bolt [him] in, keep [him] indoors.'*
*But who is to guard the guards themselves?*

Juvenal, Satire VI

Fully acclimatised prisoners regard the officers as furniture. At worst the inmates maintain a ritual hating of the 'screws'; at best, a relaxed relationship prevails. My own experience of the custodians at Exeter was almost totally pleasant. I felt very different at Leyhill.

During my trial I encountered several officers as they sat in the dock – initially I was surprised to see them. On the second day of my trial I was admonished by the judge after a prosecution complaint that I was distracting the main witness against me by making 'snorting noises'. That these noises existed in the dock was true, but they emanated from an overweight, none too young officer who had a heavy cold and was sucking lozenges the whole time. This man was not entirely untypical of the physical condition of many of the officers. Generally these men treated me with courtesy and friendliness. On my last entry into the dock to hear the verdict I was 'frisked' by a man who was to become a firm favourite in my memory. He was the Mr Evans I have referred to before. It was this man who, after my conviction, asked me the many questions and filled in the various forms while I was in the cells; he and another colleague were splendidly sympathetic to Jen and Jamie when they came to see me after the verdict.

As we waited to go on to the coach to take us to prison I remember noticing how relaxed, almost carnival, an atmosphere existed between the cons who were obviously accustomed to prison and the officers. I found myself surprised by the swearing of the officers – not surprised that they swore, but that they swore in front of the convicts. I suppose I was still thinking like a schoolmaster and regarding the officers as 'staff' and us as their 'pupils'.

# Prison Officers

I have already described how, in the coach, one officer pulled the curtain across the window beside which I was sitting to prevent the press taking photographs of me. It was an act for which I was grateful. The journey surprised me. I suppose I had expected a grim atmosphere as if we were on a tumbril heading for the guillotine. Instead conversation was animated and the officers laughed and joked all the way. I did envy them their cigarettes but already was feeling somewhat at ease.

I have explained that the Reception officer was rather harsher but I think that not only was he harassed by the late arrival of so many men but he may, too, have been giving me a crash course in acclimatisation. Later I was to learn that officers in white shirts were senior or principal officers and that blue shirts denoted the lower ranks. Now all officers wear the impractical white shirts. At this time, also, I learned of the existence of assistant governors who were addressed as 'Sir' by the other officers. They wore civilian dress and it was one such who escorted me to my cell on Rule 43. As I have said, he was friendly, almost solicitous in tone and arranged for food to be brought to me. So far, then, my vision of Dickensian turnkeys was proving false.

On my first morning I came into contact with my Wing Officer, Mr Thorner. At our first encounter, when he called me out for interview, he addressed me as 'Mr Bettsworth'. Later he rarely used my surname. He seemed to treat me with a respect and diffidence which he did not use towards the other inmates. I do not think it was my imagination but I felt that the majority of officers treated me as if I were an oddity. It is true that a number who had been in court believed me to be innocent, but I think my type was a rarity and an even greater rarity on the rule.

Their courtesy was one which I was determined to match. I resolved to be obedient, co-operative and courteous. This policy paid off for I was told later by the Chaplain that 'The officers are impressed by your humility'. I suppose they were expecting me to act as the autocratic headmaster of their youth – indeed, it was said to me on more than one occasion that not only may the jury have been prejudiced against me because I was a headmaster but so too might other inmates associate me with unpleasant memories of the past. I found this idea far-fetched but on reflection can see its force.

It was some time before I concluded that prisons were totalitarian regimes and that inmates had no rights. Accordingly I acted initially as if my every want should be instantly supplied. For example, I had no writing implement and asked for one. The Wing Officer, during my first interview, searched for several minutes in his office and finally produced a red ballpoint pen which I have to this day. There was no necessity for him to find me a pen at all. I keep the implement as a souvenir of one of those 'unnumbered acts of kindness'. Later Mr Thorner opened the library just so that I could have reading material; he arranged for the collection of my radio and had two long chats with me in the form of 'interviews' which really need not have been as long. He argued that I should stay on the rule – 'It's easy for a tea urn to be accidentally spilt.' In short, this officer made my life in prison as acceptable as it could humanely be. And his attitude towards me was indicative of the attitude of many officers at Exeter. In many ways I regarded him as an ally.

The Censor, too, was a man with whom I struck up more than the most casual relationship. It was he who brought me the pupils' Christmas card on Friday 20 December:

While waiting to go to the library an officer unlocked the cell door and curtly ordered me outside. Initially he seemed surly; he was burly and bearded. He had brought me a huge padded Christmas card, signed by most of the pupils and some of the staff. I'm not allowed it in the cell as it's padded and may contain contraband. I had not time to read all the inscriptions and a huge lump came into my throat and I was close to tears. One girl, whose charge against me had been dropped when she changed her story to the truth, signed, 'With love and apologies'. . . . Another wrote, 'With every inch of my love'. A third signed, 'I'll never forget you', and a fourth, 'I think of you every day'. It's the closest I've been to tears since Jen asked me if I was 'all right'. I would give *anything* to have that card in my cell. Instead I've signed for it and it's in my property. It's the only thing in my property for I deliberately entered this hotel with nothing. Now I have 'property' which is more valuable to me than words can express. As I write in my cell I am fighting back tears. . . . I still feel deeply moved by the Christmas card . . . [it] has affected me deeply.

Thus my diary extract about the card. I do not know whether the officer was obliged to bring it to me but he certainly appeared to know that it would be a precious object and I am grateful to him for bringing it.

Later, this same officer had a reasonably long conversation with me. Occasionally this happened with officers and it was always a cause of comment by my cellmate. I am not, perhaps, being fanciful when I say I thought I was being treated slightly differently. This particular conversation I recorded on Boxing Day and it typifies the relationship I generally had with Exeter officers (Leyhill was to be very different):

> Just had my most civilised chat yet with an officer – one of the censors. *Inter alia* I learned that he censored about a thousand letters a week. We discussed the state of education; he told me he had been to a public school and named it. He deplored co-education but was proud of his own schooling and of his vocation (*sic*) as a prison officer. . . . He suggested I open a tutorial college in Birmingham or somewhere suggesting that once I'd made a name for myself the money would come rolling in. I said tutoring was soul-destroying and the conversation ended. Apparently this officer is not known to be gregarious. I enjoy these little chats for they keep me in touch with a sort of normality. His final words were, 'It's a pity to waste your education.' His words were not patronising, though given that we are automatons obeying every instruction and with less independence of thought than a seven-year-old prep school-boy, the officers must instinctively feel superior to us. Thus I am in a very odd position. I am better educated and more 'book learned' than anyone I've met in here yet I am their inferior. It makes for subtle niceties in relationships. . . .

Perhaps the most moving encounter with an officer occurred when I was told that Jen had phoned. I have already recorded that even to this day I hear his soft, sympathetic voice saying, 'She's all right. She sends her love.' Just as I shall never forget the forty-minute conversation I had with Mr Evans the day before I left Exeter. I can do no better than quote from what I wrote at the time:

> Long conversation with Mr Evans – the officer in court on the last day. He came to give valedictions and to ask about Jen. He

wondered why I was still on the rule and said that Jamie's swearing in front of his mother had not impressed him [Jamie had got lost in the warren below the courthouse and, suffering as I have said from acute claustrophobia, had panicked somewhat]. We talked miscellaneously for over half an hour – apparently an unprecedented thing. What a wonderfully unexpected orchid of humanity. I am most grateful to him for his concern.

He wished me well and hoped things would turn out successfully. He said the majority of people at Leyhill were 'of your class. Bent chief inspectors, solicitors and bank managers. . . .' We talked of the basic humanity there was in here. He *implied* the staff take extra trouble for those they feel sorry for. Again, it seems I am not the child molester of tabloid fame. He was certain, though, that I need not have gone on the rule. But I was put on it and told to stay on it. I feel now as if I've been cowardly but he was gracious enough to say that officers got peace of mind by my staying on it. What a remarkable experience this is all turning out to be. He agreed that my being in here was, *per se*, a useful experience but that being on the landings would have broadened my knowledge. He reckoned there was an almost nil chance of my not getting parole and that Friday 13th June 1986 would be the date and not Monday 16th June. I would love that.

In the event Mr Evans was wrong but the effect of this talk was enormously cheering. He had explained that a number of the officers were ex-sailors who had retired back to the West Country and had great experience of life – hence their attitude to prisoners was generally tolerant. This theory seemed sound enough to me.

But the most compassionate act was done by an anonymous officer. After Tim's and Jen's first visit with Jay, one officer told them that he thought I should not be here. It was one thing for Jen and even the two older boys to hear that opinion; for Tim to hear the unsolicited words from an officer was an experience of such great magnanimity and *caritas* as to defy belief almost. I have many a time and oft wished to identify this man.

So there were many reasons for me to respect and like the officers at Exeter. Indeed, their concern even continued in the bus which took me to Leyhill. An officer who had just been posted to the prison lent me his paper to read. It does not sound much but it is indicative of a concern, of a fellow feeling, which I found largely absent at Leyhill. This is not to say that there were not decent men there or unpleasant coves at Exeter.

I have no idea what makes a man or woman want to become a prison officer and I did not ask them. There can be little doubt that some will have entered the service with a genuine belief that they would be helping their fellow man. After all, the censor, not an uneducated man, had used the word 'vocation' about his own position. To others the idea of job security and, despite recent publicity, good pay is an attraction. I cannot think that any job which pays its lowest grade £15,000 a year including overtime is lowly paid. My wife and I aggregated 220 hours' work per week and our combined income began at £8500 per annum and had not risen to more than £15,000 after three years. I have never earned that amount in my life despite having a good honours degree and three additional years of professional training to add to my twenty years' experience. Thus pay must be an attraction when one considers that entrance qualifications are virtually nil.

Some officers were former policemen who either did not like or could not cope with policing. Incidentally and, to me at least, inexplicably, there was no love lost between the two professions. I imagine other men liked the idea of being in a disciplined force and enjoyed their uniforms. Some wore their hats squashed into the archetypical Gestapo shape or wore their peaks low over their eyes to resemble guardsmen – which some of them had been. I am sure others joined the service to give hell to the prisoners – men who believed in exemplary punishment for offenders. It is not insignificant, for example, that polls about capital punishment reveal that the majority of prison officers – and policemen, too – favour the penalty.

What I cannot understand is why human beings wish to spend their working lives locking up other human beings. It's like the traffic warden. His or her function is to spy on his fellows with the sole object of making sure that his fellows are fined for trans-gressing parking regulations. It does not seem like a job for a man. Yet I would not, in the main, accuse prison officers of being unmanly for there is no doubt that at times their job is dangerous and at all times potentially so. Some of the long-termers I met in Leyhill must certainly have been very hard to control earlier in their sentences. It is also true that I was in an allocation prison for a very short time only and then went to the relative cushiness of an open prison. I am sure long-term prisons challenge the mental and physical resources of the warders. But none of this answers the central question of why people become prison officers.

There is virtually no rehabilitation in prisons and such as there is is done largely by civilian staff. Princess Anne called the prison service 'the forgotten profession' and she is right. It is forgotten because society wishes to sweep its existence under the carpet. It is also unmemorable because it is not seen to 'do' anything, and I do not think it can be.

I spoke above of kindnesses to me. I think it is a mistake to think that all prisoners received the courtesies which I had at Exeter. None was directly abused but some were tolerated less than I. From this one may deduce that I was *rara avis* but also that it suited the officers to find a *modus vivendi* with us all. There were enough causes of tension in prison without extra, gratuitous ones being added by the staff. This makes sense. It comes, therefore, as something of a surprise to record that some officers seem to think that abuse of prisoners is a *sine qua non* of their job. My first experience of this I recorded in my diary:

> Just met my first graceless screw. A face like a baby's – looks about fourteen but hides behind an absurd moustache. At tea I courteously asked him how one went about sharpening pencils and acquiring notebooks and was told by him that he had a home to go to and couldn't help. I finally asked for permission to go to the 'recess' and was told 'two seconds'. When I came back, without irony I thanked him only to have the door slammed in my face with the words, 'He's a right fucking Jack the lad, isn't he?' Well, my theory of officer courtesy has finally been tested by this simian exception.

Not an earth-shattering encounter but it was unnecessary and it unsettled me. He had a home to go to. So had I. He could go to his. I could not go to mine. Several people, including the probation officer at Leyhill, told me that the officers were serving a 'life sentence'. What an absurdity. They went home each night; they saw their families; they made love to their wives; they could enjoy a pint. I suppose they rarely thought that we, too, had loved ones or that our sex drives were like theirs. That we felt and laughed and cried. Perhaps such a thought would have made it impossible for them to do their job. Certainly those on the outside who advocate a harsh regime for prisoners forget not only that prisoners are sentient beings but also that they have a family which goes through an ecstasy of suffering.

I did not take kindly to be addressed as part of a group of 'fucking cunts' by a member of staff. My whole professional life had conditioned me to speak with great respect to my pupils whatever their situation. It took me some time to accustom myself to the 'unprofessionalism', in terms of man-management, of some officers.

The man who wore his heart most on his sleeve had spent eight years at Leyhill and had hated every minute of it. When I was called to the Assistant Governor's office to be told that I would be going to Leyhill this man was told to give me information about the place. The session would occur on the following Monday morning. I looked forward to it for when I was escorted back to the Chaplain's office by this officer – my 'call-up' had occurred in the middle of Chaplain's Hour – he told me he had not liked Leyhill for he hated a prison 'run by cons for cons'. I wrote of our *al fresco* encounter on Monday 30 January:

Spoke to the officer about Leyhill while on exercise. He hates the place. 'I don't like prisons run by inmates.' He says I'll be in a dormitory cubicle. Everyone there is a Redband – a Trusty. All are expected to be responsible for organising their own affairs. They have to be at the right place at the right time or, as he gleefully told me, 'They go back behind the wall. Many's the time I've put them in the van and put them back behind the wall.' He is, as you will have gathered, a most enlightened gentleman. Visits are of three hours' duration but not at all on two days a week. The place is a mile from Junction 14 on the M5 – 'Turn right over the motorway.' Apparently a new prison is being built there. He advised me to cancel my paper and told me that private cash would take a fortnight to be transferred. As Jen can't send money in advance I'll have to phone her when I'm there – permissible, I'm told. . . . My January 10th visit will be honoured. Despite the dislike the officer has for the place it sounds all right to me. There's a farm, carpentry and print shops, a market garden, library and education service as well as the usual orderlies' jobs. I fancy the market garden *in the spring* – but the library holds no fascination.

I mentioned this officer to people at Leyhill when I got there. One of the civilian instructors, Peter Quick, about whom I shall have something to say later, remembered him as a man who found it totally impossible to get on with inmates. Even at a closed prison this officer had been attacked.

It would, though, be inaccurate to suggest that I *knew* the officers at all at Exeter. My acquaintanceship was casual in the main and my impressions may pervert the truth. I do not think I am wrong to feel that there was a disinterested concern for me by most officers at Exeter. I shall be forever grateful for that. At Leyhill we were to know the officers considerably better and I cannot say that the knowledge reflects well on many of the staff. Suffice it to say here that I changed from being a man prepared to do his time as co-operatively as possible to one who would do anything to subvert the authority of the staff. The system won but I had a good run for my money and look back with horror at the downward path I was taking.

Of the higher echelons I knew nothing at Exeter. The Governor had confirmed me on the rule but even now I could not describe him. The Assistant Governor – one of a number – escorted me to my cell on Friday 13 December and interviewed me about my move to Leyhill. All I remember about that interview was his telling me that at Exeter 99.5 per cent of the men were not like me, at Leyhill 95 per cent were not my sort. He told me my speech and manners would give me away, and that he was sticking his neck out in sending me to Leyhill; I was, he explained, a Category C prisoner going to a Category D prison. Apparently if I absconded 'the department could be embarrassed'. Additionally, he emphasised, if any sexual assault occurred near the prison my 'name would be in the frame'. I listened with disbelief at first but soon realised only too well what he meant. Anyway, he said, 'I am going to slip you quietly into Leyhill now that the publicity has died down.' I was to grin wryly when I recalled this phrase later, for my reception at Leyhill was anything but quiet. But first I had to get there.

# 7

# TRANSFER AND OSTRACISM

*Many have fallen by the edge of the sword: but not so many as have fallen by the tongue.*

Ecclesiasticus

My diary records that I slept well and that I was recovering from my head cold during my last night at Exeter on Wednesday 1 January. New Year's Day seemed to me to be an appropriate time to embark upon a new adventure but it was with some trepidation that I set to to pack up my few belongings after my hot roll and porridge breakfast.

I had no idea when I would be called to Reception and so I sat listening to a radio programme – ironically about prison reform. The presenter was discussing a concept called 'self-surrender'. The essence was that a convicted person would not be whisked straightaway to his cell in a state of shock. Instead he would be allowed to put his house in order and to take proper farewells of his family and friends and would be 'called up' to prison when a suitable vacancy arose. This struck me as pre-eminently sensible. Even assuming that there would be a number of people going AWOL, the overall effect on the bursting prison system and the suffering of families would be drastically reduced. Presumably only those who were considered dangerous enough to be held in custody on remand would, if convicted, go straight to prison. Further ideas included the greater use of hostels and the possibility of privately run prisons on the American system. These ideas emanated from the then SDP and were, naturally, rejected by the Prison Officers' Association.

At last I was summoned. I picked up my huge bundle of bedding and books and followed an officer to Reception. My bundle was deposited on a table while an officer went through it. The booklet containing Prison Rules was unfortunately removed; I regretted that for I wanted it as a keepsake. My diaries were examined but I explained, half-truthfully, that I had the AG's

57

permission to keep them. I believe the position is that one may keep a diary in prison but not bring it out. I did both and am not the first to have done so.

I was placed in a narrow, doorless cell similar to the one I had entered a lifetime before on 13 December. The same old lag who had quoted John Donne at me was there, telling me how much I would enjoy Leyhill. I was given my own clothes to put on. I was very surprised to see they had not been laundered but had been stuck in a box to fester. I took little pleasure in putting on dirty clothes but I did enjoy wearing a tie again and being in a suit. It could have been worse for I was told later that at one time a prisoner's clothing was put into a bag of mothballs and left there until his final release.

I waited and waited until I was called with three other men to the 'desk'. I was handcuffed to a stranger and waited while the others were similarly restrained. Soon it was clear that all was not well. The 'system' had put another man into this particular consignment and there were not enough officers available for the escort duty. We waited. Finally, the momentous decision to allow me to travel unhandcuffed was made. It struck me as absurd that I was going to an open prison in handcuffs. We climbed aboard a mini-coach and waited for the 'off'. An officer came on to the bus and required me to move to a different seat; apparently the seat in front of me was to be occupied by a second officer and his colleague was concerned for his safety. The second officer came on and I was told to move again. Finally we drove out of the prison gates and I felt all the excitement I had experienced when I had first flown.

Even after so short a time it was novel to observe cars and to see women and children. We dropped the other men off at Taunton Police Station; they were waiting for Crown Court trial that day. Two of the officers went into the rear entrance of the Police Station leaving one with me. I was given the opportunity to get out of the vehicle to stretch my legs but asked instead if I might see my padded Christmas card, which was in a box with my belongings. It was handed to me and I read and reread the inscriptions. How I missed my beloved pupils and my school.

The journey was resumed. I was given the *Daily Express* to read by a new officer who, with his colleagues, spent the whole time talking about the 'tied' accommodation at the prison and the state of decoration. I was left to my thoughts and apprehensions. After about an hour and a half on the motorway we turned off at Junction 14 and drove through the gates of Leyhill.

I was conscious of a huge building site and remembered that a new prison was under construction. It had been raining and mud and huge puddles are the sum total of my first impression. I was taken to reception by impatient officers who by now wanted to go to the Officers' Club and get rid of me to my new guardians. The only conversation that passed between the Exeter and Leyhill staff concerned the whereabouts of the bar and the fact that I had got my 'memoirs' with me. 'We're not interested in those,' was the response and I thought, mistakenly as it turned out, that my diary was safe and legal.

The inmate orderly, a lifer, was sent to get me some lunch. I was given a plate and cutlery to wash up first and sat down to enjoy food. What I ate I cannot remember but I think I was given a choice. Certainly the food at Leyhill was generally excellent, but on this first day, alone and pretty palely loitering, I had little interest in gastronomy. Afterwards I filled in forms, was stripped, issued with clothing – including an odd pair of shoes which I was told I could change the next day. In fact I determinedly kept the odd shoes for the whole of my sentence for reasons which will emerge.

Eventually the Reception orderly, not an officer, escorted me to Ward 2. I met a tall, handsome, moustached con who was the ward cleaner and who was to show me my cubicle. I made my bed, put out my Christmas cards – but not the padded one – and sat down wondering what the hell to do. I had to see an officer at 2.00 p.m. for a tour of the estate but beyond that I was left to my own devices.

Soon the members of my ward – about twenty-five men – came in; it was lunchtime and their midday break of about an hour. I came out of the cubicle and studied, for about the fourth un-necessary time, the noticeboard. One of the notices displayed the price of tea, sugar, fruit and so on which could be purchased from the prison canteen. I wondered when I would have any money. I had been told the canteen would open for me but when I went there it was locked and deserted. I regretted not buying more tobacco in Exeter; I could have afforded to.

No one spoke to me. I was called by the Principal Officer of our wing. The prison was divided into two wings. He gave me a preliminary interview and very kindly tried to contact Jen by phone. There was no reply. I was in a new prison and my family did not know where I was and I did not know where they were. They had gone north for Christmas and could have been staying with any of a large array of friends and relatives in Yorkshire or Lincolnshire.

I returned to the ward to face, for the next few days, the most unpleasant time of my life. I can do no better than quote my diary entries, written, it must be said, by a man totally alone in a hostile environment. Unbeknown to me at the time, Thursday was national movement day in Her Majesty's Prisons. Most reallocations occur then. Very occasionally did inmates come to Leyhill on a Tuesday and they were regarded, in the jargon, as 'a bit iffy'. Most arrivals come to the prison in a largish group and use the local Women's Prison at Pucklechurch as a staging-post. I came in alone and not via Pucklechurch. I came in on 2 January – just after the New Year when movement was slack. I was slipped into Leyhill with such quietness that the sound was deafening. I *had* to be an oddity. Before the lunch break was over trouble was brewing; it erupted later that night to such an extent that I was shaking like a jelly the following morning: when I went to collect my breakfast, the contents of my plastic tea mug were spilled on to the ground before I returned to the ward. This is what I wrote at the time:

> Very friendly and helpful Reception officers. One warned me not to leave my tobacco lying around or to give my name and address to other cons. My name? I was allowed to keep my memoirs as the Exeter officer called my diary. . . . I have a cubicle in a ward. Ward 2, Cubicle 3. I've already been 'made'. I heard two cons read my name on a list in the ward. One said, 'He's the headmaster, I think.' His companion replied, 'What? The nonce?' They've gone off to work while I wait for a tour of the place. I'll see them later I hope. I don't want trouble or I'll go back behind the wall. It seems I am entitled to a Reception Visit. Thereafter visits are fortnightly. The place is rather scruffy but there is a new prison being built adjacently. I've got temporary clothes on at the moment but should get permanent issue later. Library, TV, table-tennis, snooker etc. seem to be

available daily out of working hours and one can bathe or shower daily. Having been recognised so early I hope I can contain any nastiness. The power of the media seems great.

In the pouring rain and unprotected I was given a tour of the estate and shown the bounds. I am the only new inmate. Rather confusing but lovely to be in the open air and free. 312 cons here I'm told and never more than six officers on duty at a time. Regular 'tallies' – i.e. roll calls – a sort of 'stand to your bed' affair, literally. I have to see the Censor at 6.00 p.m. tonight and the Medical Officer at 7.30 a.m. in the morning. Then at 8.00 a.m. I report to the Farm Office to see where I shall be working. (All new cons have one week's induction on the market gardens before their permanent job is allocated.) I see the Governor at 11.00 a.m. Some time I have to tour all the workshops to see what goes on in them. Then I choose a job and am eventually allocated. . . . There seem to be dozens of clubs here with which to occupy one's time. I will feel more relaxed when I have sorted out the two who 'sussed' me. I hope to settle our differences tonight.

The ward cleaner is an excellent chap. He's due out in May after doing five years for, I think, a violent crime. He is an ex-soldier who was unkeen to identify the two with whom I wish to speak. 'Prison makes everyone selfish. Let it blow over,' was his advice. I choose to ignore it. It's not my way. The general population here is very mixed. I may be in the new prison eventually; the officer who took me round the place says it's due to open in May. [In fact it opened in November.] I'm told I can get an immediate visit – thereafter fortnightly. Hurrah. The second visit in the month is known as a 'privileged visit' and can be withdrawn at any time. Perhaps Jen can come at the weekend.

Everything here is entirely self-reliant; one has to be on the spot, on the dot, but it does seem very slack.

I'm lurking in my cubicle waiting for tea and listening to shouts, directed at me, of 'Nonce,' 'Dirty, fucking bastard,' 'I'd hang the cunt,' etc., etc. I suppose I'll have to grin and bear it until the novelty wears off and they get used to me. I identified the two who had recognised me at lunchtime. One is a lifer with a large mouth and a small brain. I've decided to tackle him first. I went to his cubicle and said I wanted to talk to him. He was standing up doing something. He faced me and said he did not talk to 'beasties'. He told me to go away as he did not have truck with animals. I remonstrated to no avail. He told me I was trespassing on his 'home' and 'private territory' and that I was to go away. I persisted and eventually he said, 'This is my private domain. Go away, please.' I went. I did not win the encounter, but I didn't lose it either. This fellow hunts in a pack – he's the leader. He says he'll talk to me later. Certainly he was nonplussed by my direct approach. I feel horribly vulnerable and isolated. I'm surrounded by freely moving people but it's as if I'm confined in solitary. I suppose it can only improve. Eaten my curried beans in my cubicle. We walk to the dining room and can choose to eat our food there or bring it back to the ward. The dining room is cold and as I know nobody. . . . My 'enemy' has just gone to play squash, I think. There are so many activities here but I hardly dare go out. I think I'll lie low for a few days until the others get to know me and I know the routine. I hope after a week they get used to my presence and I can settle down.

I have to see the Censor in twenty minutes and then I'll go to the Quiet Room next to the library, read *The Times* and get some books out. It's a massive irony that I can walk out of the prison with ease, yet I am self-confined to my cubicle. At the end of the ward is a dart board and recreation area. In the prison there are three separate TV rooms – one each for BBC 1 and ITV and a third for BBC 2/Channel 4. I'm in no mood to go to any. There are two full-sized snooker tables and a table-tennis room. Apparently outgoing mail is randomly censored and incoming mail is opened in front of the recipient. Outgoing letters with enclosures have to be left unsealed. Written a short note to Jen. Seen the Censor.

It's now 8.00 p.m. and I'm back in my cubicle. I spent an hour or so in the library and then there was an emergency tally. Apparently someone had disappeared. After it, I went into the library to read the papers. The 'heavies' are laid out for us each day. Strolled to a TV room but couldn't settle down because of the hostility. Came back to hear the lifer discussing my case with a bunch of cronies. 'Did you see what was left on file?' There was a yell of 'Dirty bastard!' The insults flew and flew. This went on for some time until I could stand no more. I thought about what to do. There were about five of them at the end of the ward enjoying themselves hugely at my expense. If I do nothing it'll never end. What do I do?

I left my cubicle, went to the bottom of the ward where they all were and told them if they wished to discuss my case they had better do it (a) to my face and (b) in full possession of the accurate facts. The lifer asked me if the papers were lying. I said if they were his source of reliability he'd better think again. He told me I was not in prison for being 'a good boy' and indicated with his thumb that I should return to my 'cube', saying he would speak with me later. I went back – again having neither won nor lost. I await developments but I don't like the atmosphere at all. At least, though, I've given them something to think about in that I've challenged them all. I just hope they soon get used to my being here; it's a very unsettling start, though. I get the impression that the others who witnessed the encounter were vaguely embarrassed. Clearly my presence has raised tensions here. I suppose the others will take their lead from the 'star' lifer. This place could be so marvellous but at the moment I'd rather be back at Exeter and I don't want to skulk in corners. I can avoid them all until 9.00 p.m. – at which time we all have to be back in our wards for the rest of the night – but six months in solitary is rather long. Perhaps it will improve but I've yet to discover how. I reckon I've just got an unlucky ward.

After tally. 'You're fifteen, you're beautiful and you're mine' has just come floating towards me. 'Dirty fucking bastard!' 'Report to the headmaster immediately and he'll give you six inches of the best.' This last remark caused me to grin to myself. I am lying on my bed pretending to read Asa Briggs' *Social History of England*. I've read the first paragraph about ten times and can't remember a word. The abuse is just pouring in on me from all sides. I am *miserable*.

'Let's put him on trial again' – that's a sinister development. It's certainly not the case that the cons here are of my 'class'. The cons at Exeter were far better.

After the 10.30 p.m. tally I climbed into bed a nervous wreck. The abuse did not abate and I expected any moment to be attacked. In a way that would have been better. The place is such a contrast – earlier I had seen a con withdraw *The Penguin*

*Book of Love Poetry* from the library but now I was surrounded by a pack of animals.

A marvellous end to the day. The two inmates who recognised me initially were Jim and Brian. As I was in bed, feeling desperately alone and miserable, Jim came into my cube, shook hands, introduced himself and told me not to worry about the verbal abuse. We had a brief chat. I told him I was prepared to face anybody at any time which, I continued, was why I had waded in earlier. He knew of my confronting the group and encouragingly said, 'I heard about it. It takes a good man to do that.' I told him I was used to open discussion and had nothing to hide. He told me that during my trial people in here had read about it and said it was 'a load of bollocks'. I said I'd settle things as quickly as I could. He left me by saying that if the situation got even worse he'd wade in on my side. He advised me to use my radio earphone – I'd been given one by the authorities because its use was mandatory at Leyhill – to block out the noise. God moves in a mysterious way his wonders to perform. I am much heartened and hope that when people see me for what I am I shall start to enjoy being here.

My diary the following morning opens with the words:

I was subjected to about two hours' very nasty verbal abuse last night until after midnight. It was without doubt the worst experience of my life – so nasty, in fact, that I could not believe it was happening to me. And I had no defence. When twenty men are insulting you – and one bastard insulted Jen – in the dark and from twenty different cubicles, there is no way of getting back.

I think I was in a greater state of shock than I had been when the jury had consigned me to oblivion. I went round in a daze hardly daring to leave the shelter of my cube except to walk around the large playing field. It was not that I feared a physical attack; naturally I did not relish the thought of pain, but I remember thinking it would be preferable to the stinging verbal insults which assaulted my psyche. I could not retaliate in any significant way for I had no allies and there was no way the staff could sort out the problem. I knew now how some wretched schoolchildren feel when they are ganged up upon. Staff could not make them popular or fight their battles for them. I was at a total loss but the routine had to be gone through. What made matters worse was that I was the *only* new arrival. Had there been just one other man to go through the reception procedures with me it would have been easier.

My diary of Friday 3 January records the following:

Eventually I slept and woke at about 6.30 a.m. Had a wash and shave and am now waiting to go to breakfast, then medical, then Farm Office, tour of departments, equipment issue and Governor.

Maybe today the abuse will die down a bit but it's all pretty nasty. One remark about Jen was very hurtful but I retaliated not at all. All those people yelling from their beds is not easy to handle. They've assumed I'll be given a cushy job in the kitchen or library. 'The bastard ought to come and plant trees with me.'

'Yeah, we can hang him from one.' The first remark assumes that I am not used to manual labour – an irony, for I lost count of the number of trees I personally planted on the school estate.

Just had my medical. 'Trousers down. Cough. Do you take anything for your wheeziness?' 'No, I've just got a slight cold.' 'All right, thank you. You can go.' In twenty minutes I go to the Farm Office and then on a tour of departments to see about choosing a job. Keep bumping into my tormentors. Went into the Clothing Exchange Store (CES) to collect my kit at 8.15 a.m. but was sent away until 9.00 a.m. by a Welsh tormentor from my ward. It seems I'm not expected to work until Monday.

Returned to CES at 9.00 a.m. where they were 'waiting' for me. My Welsh tormentor, a long-haired oriental-looking shit, was reading aloud from an article about my case in a West Country newspaper. The article must have been at least a fortnight old. Where had he got it from? I was given my kit in silence. It was all old, ill-fitting and obviously the worst they could find. [It is a feature of prison life that nonces are 'fitted up' in every way possible. Thus odd shoes, torn shirts, dirty bedding are supplied to them by their fellow cons. It was very different for me at Exeter, as I have recorded.] All the while the article was being read to me, I congratulated the Welshman on his ability to read and left the hall in silence.

Later Jim offered me comfortable words saying, 'Let them get it out of their system.' He agreed that it had been best not to try and retaliate last night.

Just been taken aside very conspiratorially by another inmate of our ward. He told me to take no notice of the abuse; he had reported it to the staff and they were going to deal with it. But, this saviour went on, 'I don't want to be seen talking to you or they'll start on me. I'm not a nonce. That's why I keep my "deps" on me.' Many prisoners I discovered kept their legal depositions with them so that if there was any doubt about their actual offences they could prove to the others they were not nonces. I just hope my detractors don't think I've been running to the screws. A third man has just come up and told me not to take too much notice. As with the others, I've thanked him and given him some details of my case from my point of view. It may get better; this con reckons it will last two or three days – I am, he explains, the current scapegoat (*sic*). Once someone else comes in he'll get it. I somehow doubt that because of the amount of publicity I got.

I've just done a tour of the departments and met some very friendly departmental heads. All except the kitchen staff are civilian employees. Each has signed my sheet of paper to indicate that I've been to see them. A number of nudges between working cons occurred as I went my solitary round; so the word is out about me. Mind you, I came into this prison on my own so stuck out like a sore thumb. So much for my being 'slipped in' here quietly. I don't know where I want to work. Only the printer and woodworker offered me employment. I will be doing manual work for the first week as I've already said – unfortunately my main tormentor is at the same place. . . .

I've enjoyed a stroll around the estate; it's a beautiful morning but I am rather tense. If the worst comes to the worst I suppose my possessions will be interfered with and garbage thrown on to my bed. If things get bad the culprits can be put back behind the wall. There is no chance of violence – in a way that would be preferable for it would clear the air. Verbally it's no good as one of my abusers is a Welshman. One of last night's complaints was about the shortness of the sentence – intelligent minds would, perhaps, think that that fact said something. . . .

# Transfer and Ostracism

Off to see the Governor in a minute. He may have already heard of the trouble; we'll see. Waited nearly an hour for the Governor; he didn't appear so I didn't see him. Came back for lunch and Jim very kindly took me under his wing. On the way back from collecting my meal yet another con told me to ignore the attacks. Jim said that last night's vociferous Geordie – a man who suggested I should be tried by a kangaroo court – had been *defending* me in the afternoon. At 1.00 p.m. I forgot to report 'off' so a screw came looking for me. As I wasn't 'on' anything I was surprised! . . .

Mr Owen has rung home again. No reply. Where the hell is my family? I need them now.

Taken my labour forms to the Labour Office and was asked to choose two jobs from a list. I chose Works Department and said I could paint and decorate, and Laundry because Jim works there. I go before a Labour Board tomorrow at 2.00 p.m. Now I have two hours to kill and will, I think, go for a walk. At least I'm enjoying private and convenient use of a lavatory.

Just done two laps of the playing field; the screw who conducted me round said it was a mile in perimeter. I think it's much shorter. A bitterly cold easterly wind but a very bright sunny day. I saw a cat and three dogs! It's amazing how I relish these little things. The field has a soccer and rugby pitch, four grass tennis courts, a scrummage machine, sandpit, bowling green and four hard cricket nets. Trees bound the area and it's just so lovely walking in the open air. Unfortunately I was reminded of my first winter stroll through the school grounds and a few sad memories came over me. . . . I will feel better when I know what work I will be doing and what my workmates will be like. This hanging about, though pleasant, is getting to me slightly.

The above extract is reproduced as it was written. It has an essential dishonesty, I now feel, for I dared not put down the intensity of my feelings – not least of all because I wondered how deeply I really was being affected. Like Macbeth, I feared to be afraid and even though I thought that I, too, dared to do 'all that became a man', I wondered. For the first few days I relaxed not one minute. I suffered continually. Certainly if my tormentors knew how successful they were being I would have had no rest. It was interesting, too, to notice that all those who gave me words of comfort wished to remain anonymous.

I am certain that this early reception at Leyhill – so different from what I had been led to believe – affected my subsequent attitude and conduct. It affects me still in some ways. My wife was subsequently to comment on how I was 'changing'. Certainly I resented the whole judicial process; I loathed the police officers who had conducted my case – with several complaints and two reprimands. Above all I hated the eleven members of the jury who had found me guilty.

That moment – two days into Leyhill – was the nadir of my life. I had lost my school, and I had loved it as much as life itself. I was separated from my family, whose support had never wavered. Society had made me an outcast, and even in the prison society of outcasts I was alone. It's hard to describe, to anyone who has not been in the position I was in, what it was like. The articulation of the experience does scant justice to the feeling. The opprobrium that had been poured on us at Exeter was distanced by Rule 43 – besides which I was one of a group there. Here, I was face to face with uninhibited hostility and I was utterly, utterly alone. There was no way that I was going to run from the experience – I am not a coward – but there was no way I could cope with it. And I still had to get to work on Monday.

# 8

# KITCHEN DRUDGE

*O, how full of briers is this working-day world!*

William Shakespeare, *As You Like It*

I heard no abuse on Friday evening and woke early on the Saturday. There was no work for anyone so few stirred before 9.00 a.m. I rose latish, had a shave, broke my razor and faced the first crisis of the day. Here was I, an ex-headmaster, worried about the fact that I had broken a plastic razor. I shaved holding its head in my hand and managed to cut myself all over! My 'crisis' was that I had to find who issued razors so that I could replace my broken one. I knew that razors were issued on a one-for-one basis but would a broken one count? Would whichever con who controlled distribution give me another one or would a simple broken razor be the basis upon which another attack would be launched? I record this trivial detail not only to indicate my state of suffering but also to demonstrate how it is the trivial things in prison which assume gargantuan proportions. I need not have feared, for Dave, the ward cleaner, was also the ward representative and kept the razors.

There was a Governor's inspection on Saturday mornings and much activity went into cleaning out cubicles and in tidying the ward. When I had dusted and swept my little home I went to the library to read the papers. While in there, a tall, ramrod-backed man entered and called my name. He was the Assistant Governor of our wing, reputedly an ex-SAS man, called MacAllister. He took me to his office and asked how I was settling in. I told him that I was. He asked me if I was having any trouble. I replied that I was having none that I could not handle. He said he had heard things and did not see 'why you should take shit from that lot. I'm going to move you.' I protested that such a move might make matters worse if the others thought that I had complained. He was a no-nonsense Scot and ignored me. I had forgotten that prisoners have no rights.

69

# Marking Time

With a heavy heart I went back to the full ward to gather up my things. All the others were doing their tidying-up. I went to Dave and with a bravado I did not feel told him I had been ordered to go to Ward 6. I hoped to be able to gather up all my belongings in one go and disappear from the ward for ever. Unhappily that was not possible and as I was escorted by MacAllister to Ward 6 I dreaded going back to fetch the rest. By the time I made my second journey my pillow had disappeared and I could not find it. With my tail well between my legs I scurried back to Ward 6 – one of four wards outside the main complex. I was introduced to the ward cleaner, an ex-detective-sergeant, who helped me to get another pillow and settle in.

My new cube was filthy but there were ready hands to help me clear it up. I felt as if I were in paradise. I could talk again, albeit carefully, and I could walk around the ward. Sadly this euphoria was short-lived. A few minutes after a fellow had offered me a cigarette (I declined: one did not smoke others' precious tobacco) I heard the word 'nonce'. I did not know if it referred to me but my heart sank. (And it's worth stating that hearts do sink, just as mouths run dry and tears do prick the backs of eyes.) Lyn, the ward cleaner, gave me tea and milk but was immediately told off by a large, red-haired man called Ginger. 'Don't give him anything. He's a fucking nonce. Dirty animal.' I went straight to this man and challenged him. He pushed me away with an oath. 'Here we go again,' I thought. Lyn looked at me and shrugged his shoulders.

Later that evening I spoke to several men who told me that Ginger was 'an animal' and that none knew why he was in an open prison. But my torment by him was short-lived. I heard him enter the ward and state that it was now known as a nonce's ward throughout the prison and that he had applied for transfer to another ward. So he went out and I had virtually no trouble in the ward for the rest of my sentence.

At work it was to be an entirely different matter for many weeks.

I spent a fairly relaxed Sunday and found most of my new companions very congenial. I was lent a bar of Lifebuoy soap 'until pay day' by an utterly charming lifer, enjoyed an excellent lunch and then joined the rest of the ward in an after-lunch snooze before doing three walking laps of the field. I felt calm and confident while watching, with three others only, *Songs of Praise*, but then a mood of depression set in. I am sure it was to do with the uncertain day that lay ahead. I feared that I would get trouble, not least because I had moved ward but also because a number of those who had given me a hard time worked in the market gardens. I prepared my dungarees and jeans for the uncertain morrow, putting my dungarees on back-to-front initially. Matters were not helped by cries of, 'I'd personally hang every nonce with piano wire.' It would have been more bearable if I had had contact with Jen but the Christmas holidays had put paid to that.

Monday morning filled me with dread. I had had a breakfast of porridge without milk or sugar, boiled egg, toast and marmalade. I did not want it and only went to the dining room to persuade myself that I was not going to skulk in corners.

The dreaded eight o'clock came and with a very, very heavy heart I laced my battered boots and went to sign on at the Farm Office. I felt, quite wrongly of course, that all eyes were on me. I reported to the civilian instructor, who told me to stand and wait. After a few minutes another con was told to escort me to the market gardens. This man, a chap of very few words, appeared hostile towards me. As we walked the quarter mile or so up the hill towards the 'Killing Fields', as the gardens were known, he told me he was an ex-soldier doing life for shooting someone. His tone was gruff and hostile. I was to discover that though he was outwardly tough, inside he was really rather an unintelligent, harmless, likeable inadequate. But this I learned long afterwards.

We arrived at the office, in which a number of cons were lingering. I reported again and was told to wait. I had understood that my task would be to stand at a conveyor belt and cut the stalks from cabbages. This was all right provided I was in no way interfered with. After about ten minutes' waiting I was told to go to the kitchens for the day; a washer-up had reported sick and they were a man short. To me, this was even worse. I had gradually got accustomed to being in the market garden. I had observed other workers and had not detected any hostility; the others were as indifferent to me as I was to them. But now, to go to another place was almost too much.

Even with the 'status' of headmaster I had never enjoyed strange environments or meeting strange people; I was happiest on home territory. This whole business was proving to be very trying. I did not even know where the kitchens were – I could only vaguely remember the position of the dining hall and assumed the kitchens would be behind them. I set off back down the hill. As I went down my main tormentor came up chatting with his cronies. I feared an encounter but he walked by, much to my relief, without a word to me.

I arrived at the kitchens, saw the officer in charge, was directed to get some kitchen whites from the kitchen store and to return changed; I rushed back to my ward to change. When I got there, Lyn, the ward cleaner, told me to calm down and take my time.

Finally I returned to the kitchens and was taken to the washing-up room where I started to work with a Rhodesian. As I walked through the main kitchen the word 'nonce' was bellowed. 'Oh God,' I thought, 'not here as well.' I went into the wash-up and found one of the bakers, a lifer called Tony, saying to the Rhodesian, 'I feel sorry for you, working with a fucking nonce.' I went to the lifer and told him he had better make any comments he had to my face. Ignoring me, he shouldered his way past. I apologised to the Rhodesian that he was having to work with me and explained my side of the story to him. He seemed sympathetic and conceded that all stories have two sides and that he was indifferent to the offences of others. He said he was in for drunken driving.

My first job was to scrape out a huge baking bowl; it was bigger than a bath tub in volume. Thereafter, I had to scrape out porridge dishes, huge cylinders in which custard was made, baking trays – in fact to wash up everything that had been used for the preparation of three meals a day for over three hundred men.

The waste food – and there was much – was sluiced down a huge drain by a hosepipe. Many was the morning in the pitch dark and with snow lying on the ground that I froze with my hosepipe. The inmates preparing the vegetables and the bakers and the 'cooks' brought in a succession of filthy dishes. None spoke a word to me. At about 9.30 a.m. I was called to the Education Department for an interview with the Education Officer. I was asked if I had O-levels, a question which surprised me given that my academic and professional qualifications were already on file. It was finally decided that I did not require 'Education'. I was asked if I would act as a stand-by teacher in the evenings. I refused, saying that I would be happy to work full-time in the department but that I was not prepared to work all day in the kitchens and again in the evenings. I had, by this time, learned that survival in prison is precarious enough without volunteering to work for nothing.

I returned to the kitchens in time for a mid-morning cup of tea. My workmate escorted me to the small, kitchen-staff restroom and we sat and chatted. He dunned a smoke from me, a constant habit to which I eventually put a stop. Others came in but I was totally ignored while conversations about 'nonces' were held all round me. We went back to work. I was happy enough working alone and hard. I hated it when there were lulls for, unlike the Rhodesian, I could not go into the main kitchen and chat with the others. I remained in the wash-up or slipped outside for a quick smoke. The novelty of the first lunch-time made it a passable experience.

An hour before main lunch we queued up for our food and took it to the restroom. For the first day or so I accompanied my workmate. Soon, though, he was to realise that fraternising with me was 'not on'. So for three months thereafter I sat in the small restroom at a table by myself while the dozen or so others enjoyed an animated and amusing lunch break. The same routine pertained at breakfast- and tea-time. Never have I felt so utterly alone. The longer lunch session was only bearable because generally I received at least two letters every day and could occupy my time by reading them. Some of the kitchen cons took their food up to the main dining room. I decided not to as I regarded that as a defeat for me and a victory for my enemy. But how I dreaded meal-times. This ostracism went on for about three months and it took many forms.

Among the very few perks for kitchen staff was the receipt of a loaf of bread each night. For the first few days I was not given mine. Later I did receive it but not personally from the baker – it was left on the drying racks. A number of illicit perks – stolen milk, sugar, butter and so on – were shared among the staff, but never with me. Indeed, when prisoners were occasionally discovered to have stolen something I was sometimes thought of as the one who had 'grassed them up'.

Despite all, I was reasonably content to remain ignored and obscure in the wash-up. However, my assignment to the kitchen was for two days only. On Wednesday the 'boss', Mr Ryan, told me to report back to the market gardens the following day. I had already discussed this with the Rhodesian who was happy for me to work with him. I told him I did not want to leave the kitchen. He spoke to Mr Ryan who thought there would be a job for me after the Labour Board met on Thursday. This was no good to me; I had learned from the Rhodesian that a group of hostile inmates were just waiting for me to go to the market gardens and had prepared a reception. This was to take the form of a barrage of nail-filled potatoes. I did not relish that prospect. What could I do? It is probably not too much of an exaggeration to say that by this time I was desperate to remain in the kitchen – better the devil you are coming to know than a hostile, faceless monster.

Mr Ryan had a deputy, Mr Knight. I went to see him when his boss was off duty and asked if I could remain in the kitchen and forgo the pleasures of the market gardens. Happily he allowed this and I remained in the kitchen for the rest of my sentence. But I was not out of the woods yet.

The verbal abuse – and, even worse, the ostracism – continued. One day a huge, ex-SAS fellow came into the wash-up and asked if I was having 'hassle'. I said I was receiving 'verbal' but nothing I could not handle. He told me to ignore it and said that he would sort out anything if necessary. I thanked him and felt once again, as I had in Ward 2, that there was someone somewhere keeping an eye on me. I was delighted to learn later from someone else that this man, 'Big Pete', had said that I had got 'bottle' – I suppose because I was not retreating in the face of enemy fire. This 'courage' probably stemmed more from the fact that there was nowhere to go than from innate 'intestinal fortitude'. In fact, Pete was not the only ally. One morning a huge, heavily tattooed chap came into the wash-up. He had just been on Home Leave. I expected trouble and was surprised to be asked, 'Are you getting hassle?' I gave my standard answer, only to be told, 'Don't let the stupid bastards get to you. They're a fucking sight stupider than you are.' I felt enormously cheered.

Even the officers became involved. One morning Mr Knight called me into the office and told me that he had heard that I had been getting trouble and would help if he could. I told him the trouble was minimal and that I could handle it. In the office with him was another officer, who followed me from it when Mr Knight had finished. This man turned out to be our ward officer,

# Kitchen Drudge

Mr Vallender, who also offered to help. At no time did I go to the authorities, for I grew heartily to loathe them – and the feeling was mutual. The fault was entirely mine. The exception was Mr Vallender; he was a thoroughly decent man whose relationship with the cons was informal and unobtrusive. There were some inmates who did not trust him but I have nothing but pleasant memories of him. I suppose he was a bit slack and he had not been in the service long – a redundant engineer, I believe. He did not bully or despise us. I liked him greatly.

Eventually the honeymoon period in my relationship with the Rhodesian came to an end. It happened like this. Whenever Mr Knight was officer on duty there was a rush at the end of the day so that he could leave. One afternoon the Rhodesian had a visit and did not bother to return for the afternoon session. I washed up on my own but did not finish all the tea dishes before Mr Knight was ready to go. He told me to finish off in the morning.

The following morning came and with it a complaining Rhodesian. I explained that I had been ordered to leave the mess. He refused to listen and our argument became more heated until finally I pushed him through a door, whereupon he went straight to an officer and complained. I was hauled before Mr Ryan and given a stern talking-to. The incident worried me in three ways. First, that a fellow con had rushed to an officer for help. Second, that the officer was not really listening to the facts. And third, that the Rhodesian's support had finally been lost to me; he went to the other workers after the incident and poisoned them all the more against me. Again, I say, the event sounds trivial and it was childish, but there is nothing more unpleasant in my experience than working in a totally hostile and alien environment. I loathed it and dreaded each working day.

Eventually the Rhodesian got a job in the main kitchen and I was set to work with a boastful, overweight Liverpudlian. He and I worked together splendidly for a week or so before he, too, was moved into the main kitchen. He was replaced by a Welshman whose hatred of me was sovereign. The inimical attitude I could stomach; his laziness I could not and I had a blazing row with him eventually. He called me a nonce and threatened me with violence. I told him, crudely, that I had 'seen dogs shit better stuff' than him and he stormed off. The upshot of this was that he got the sack from the kitchen – after an absurd rota system imposed on us by Mr Ryan to ensure that the Welshman and I rarely met!

Before he was sacked I was, again, summoned by Mr Ryan. I was told I was a trouble-maker whose sense of humour 'was different from everyone else's'. I asked what he meant by this and was told that I had made a remark about pigs to Mr Knight which was not funny. That, to me, was the last straw. If these people thought they were going to arbitrate my sense of humour . . . I was told I would stay in the wash-up until I had proved I was capable of something better – 'The only thing you're fit for is washing up.' I replied, 'I'm sorry if I am guilty of any solecisms but I have found everyone's attitude to me so inimical that I find it hard to be calm.' The effect of this pretentious mouthful was as I hoped. The officer understood not one word of what I was saying and let me go. It is no exaggeration to say that no officer at Leyhill felt easy in my presence for they, like many inmates, feared my tongue. Two cons on separate occasions were later to tell me that they 'wouldn't like to cross you'. My final workmate in the wash-up was another Welshman called Bryan. He had been in Exeter Prison and told me that 'none of the lads' thought I was guilty and wondered why I had been on the rule. I worked gladly with this ex-alcoholic, practical joker for many happy days.

Finally I was offered the chance of becoming the dining-room cleaner. I accepted this job after consultation with Bryan and spent the remainder of my sentence sweeping and mopping floors and tables. Without doubt my new job was the cushiest in the kitchen, if not in the prison. I worked from about 8.00 a.m. to 9.00 a.m. and again from 12.30 p.m. to 1.00 p.m. and served the food out on alternate evenings. My new workmate, Trevor, was a jovial 'Brum' whose case was an absurd mixture of ignorance and incompetence. I do not feel he should have been in prison for three years and was shocked to learn after my release that he had been given a one-year 'knock-back'. My affection for him was limitless; I will not sour my memory of him by making any reference to his case.

Weekends were the same for us, of course, except that the days started a little later and on Sunday mornings Trevor and I went to the Anglican service. Eventually we instituted a rota system whereby only one of us came in on Saturday mornings. For this seven-days-a-week job I was paid £2.65. It was enough for my needs, as I was always 'topping up' my supplies with illegal consignments of tobacco and the extra food I could bring from the kitchen could always be bartered. Many other inmates were paid more for a five-day week but I preferred to work at weekends. It helped to pass the time more quickly.

As the weeks and months passed I came to be regarded as a useful and amusing member of the workforce; all my detractors became friends and towards the end of my time I was elected their spokesman whenever they wanted to air a grievance. At no time, though, was I offered promotion in the kitchen. I was not trusted by the authorities for reasons which will emerge. I was, in any case, more useful as the lowest of the low.

# 9

# SEX

*It is amusing that a virtue is made out of the vice of chastity;
and it's a pretty odd sort of chastity at that, which leads
men straight into the sin of Onan.*

Voltaire, Letter to M. Marrott, 28 March 1776

Whether Voltaire is right in declaring that the vice of chastity leads one into the sin of onanism is a matter for moral philosophers and theologians. That enforced separation leads men to masturbate is a simple and not very surprising fact. That sex is a constant topic of allusion in prisons is only to be expected.

I was not conscious of sexual feelings myself all the while I was at Exeter Prison. I suppose partly I was reacting to the horror of being sentenced for a 'sex crime' but also I was coming to terms with my new environment. Besides which, it was virtually impossible to gain relief in private short of soiling one's own bedding. At Leyhill things were different.

I suppose the first thing I was conscious of was the proliferation of 'girlie' magazines. They flooded the prison and were plastered on the walls of the majority of cubicles. I think it is true to say that in my ward there were only three cube walls free of 'dirty' pictures – mine and those of my two neighbours. For many weeks I poured scorn on these magazines, feeling that even if I were to get aroused there was little I could do about it that would satisfy me. Eventually, after my first experience of smoking cannabis – it made me feel vile – I succumbed to the pictorial delights. Certainly the effect of the unaccustomed drug was enormously arousing and I could understand how people advocated that drugs and sex were a potent mixture.

My ward formed what they called the Cock Book Club. Membership was restricted to those who gave their magazines to a central 'library' and who promised not to abuse the magazines while abusing themselves. I was never a full member but was granted honorary 'status' in return for a number of favours. It was a source of constant wonderment to me that so many men could spend so much time looking at photographs of what we were all thinking about the whole time. It was not just the young men who succumbed either.

One of the paradoxes of the place was that although the Governor would allow these magazines into the prison, he had a hatred of pictures showing pubic hair adorning men's cubicles. I could never understand this but he always wanted pudenda covered. I was always reminded of a sex manual that had been sent to a contemporary of mine at school. We were both about thirteen and my friend's father was an army officer in Singapore. He sent a yellow-covered booklet to his son explaining the 'facts of life' in question-and-answer form. One question, 'Why do ladies have hair around their vagina?' elicited the response, 'To keep flies off them when they are in the jungle.' Perhaps the Governor thought Leyhill not enough of a jungle.

Anyway, girlie magazines did help the sexually repressed convict to pass the time; they served as aids to onanism as they did in a boarding school and they gave promise of what was to come. Apart from masturbation there were few ways for inmates – heterosexual ones – to obtain sexual relief.

A number of younger men would indulge in what is euphemistically called 'heavy petting' at visits. I remember one stranger telling me that he had lost five days' remission and had been threatened with a ship-out for, and I quote from my diary, 'having a finger in my wife's twat while she was wanking me.' Like Milton's Satan, I knew not what to answer.

Certainly visits were a tremendous sexual 'wind-up'. There at a table next to you is the woman you love and with whom you have slept for perhaps twenty years and yet as far as the sexual delights of marriage are concerned she might just as well be on the moon. And people of Jen's and my generation are far too long in the tooth to wear our hearts on our sleeve. Even kissing before and after each visit was a restrained, unnatural experience, even more so for Jen than for me – I, at least, was on home ground. All we could do as time went by and release approached was plan a sexual orgy – much better than a honeymoon because we were old partners. We had not slept with each other before we were married but the new 'marriage' would be even more exciting sexually precisely because we did know each other sexually. Thus a daily dream for most of us was the time when we would make love to our wives again.

The only other relief available to inmates before the end of their sentence was that obtained by risk or patience. Risk involved going over the wall by prearrangement with one's wife or lover and having a passionate hour's action in the back of a car. Some men did this and came back looking much happier. The patient man would wait for his Home Leave and dream meanwhile of all the sexual fantasies that aroused him in the expectation that his wife would oblige. Calculations of fiendish complexity about menstruation occupied many men. I can remember no heterosexual returning from Home Leave who did not complain that he was sore. 'We had the last one in the bath we were both so fucking sore' was not an infrequent comment. The rest of us gritted our teeth, not so much in envy as in anticipation.

That sexual deprivation was an important aspect of our lives was recognised by the prison magazine, *The Leyhill News*. This appalling journal was edited by a pretentious con from a position of superiority; he would write, to his limited mind, 'learned' leaders exhorting us to join this society or support that event and invariably used as his moral lever the fact that we spent 'too much of [our] time developing thick right wrists'. Why he assumed we continually masturbated or used our right arms, I do not know!

Even the officers used sex as a source of amusement. When a charming negro who worked in the kitchen told Mr Knight that he had a sore throat, the officer's shameful response was, 'You haven't been gobbling anyone, have you? Deep throat?' The same officer did amuse me, though, by saying that a sexual problem which long-termers particularly encounter on release goes something like this: Wife to husband, 'Come on, darling, let's make love.' 'Sorry, dear,' is the reply, 'I've just had a wank.'

That men had to gain sexual relief was recognised among themselves in a disarmingly open way. Many a time, reasonably late at night, I would enter another's cube only to be told the following morning that I had disturbed the man 'having a wank'. For all that, though, it is not natural that men should be segregated for so long. I understand that the situation in women's prisons is even worse; there, lesbianism is rife and a high percentage of the officers indulge, according to the wives of two men who were in prison at the same time as their husbands

# Sex

Strip-searches, too, in women's prisons are infinitely more frequent and improper than those in men's.

There is no easy answer to the sexual frustrations of the heterosexual male. Certainly mixed prisons would not be an answer to the sexual problem nor would 'conjugal visits'. It would be possible if wives could visit for a weekend, perhaps, but the idea of, so to say, booking into the conjugal cell for one's statutory session would have as much appeal as copulating with a donkey. As with everything else in prison the knowledge that one will eventually be released keeps things in a reasonably tolerable perspective. Lifers, of course, do not have this knowledge, as will be seen, and I often wondered how the young men who were sentenced to life imprisonment when they were fifteen – there were three at Leyhill – would cope with the sexual side of life when they were released at the age of thirty or more.

For the homosexual population life was very different. Some men paired up and remained faithful to each other. One couple, both lifers, enjoyed a chaste 'love–hate' relationship and seemed happiest quarrelling. I remember one calling the other a 'bitch' when I was serving tea one evening. The one was in for killing his homosexual lover; his friend was convicted of stabbing a girl in the vagina with a broken bottle and watching her bleed to death. He obviously found women a threat.

Another man in our ward was a convicted homosexual. He had received eight years, reduced to six on appeal, for homosexual acts with adolescent boys. He was a member of the homosexual community at Leyhill but was not very active. I helped him to write his parole submission and felt inordinately sad as I read what he had written: 'And I hope I shall never go with men under the age of twenty-one again and when I've had my treatment that I won't go with male persons ever again.' I have total sympathy with the homosexual population; I do not regard the condition as treatable nor do I feel there but for the grace of God go I. This man needed friends and was happiest in the company of other males. It strikes me as monstrous that homosexual acts by and with those under the age of twenty-one are illegal. It is high time the law for homosexual males was the same as for heterosexuals.

One particularly unpleasant old man was desperate for sex apparently. It was rumoured that he would pay inmates half an ounce of tobacco if they would allow him to masturbate them. I have no direct evidence for this but do know that he was caught buggering another man. His 'victim' worked in the kitchen and, it turned out, was a homosexual. The old man rarely shaved, did not wash very much – I know this for I was in his ward for a time – and was as natural a sex object as a bucket of maggots.

Even nastier was an incident of homosexual rape. The victim was a homosexual. He was a young man, rather effeminate in manner and looks, who seemed to keep himself much to himself. One night he was attacked by an extremely brutal man, bisexual, bald and 'an animal'. His age was hard to determine – perhaps he was in his mid-thirties. He had spent a considerable time in prison; it is believed he had been sentenced in all to over forty years' imprisonment in his life. He was known to be violent and had, on one occasion, bitten off someone's ear. It was also held that he had performed a mastectomy with his teeth on one of his victims – he was a rapist, among other things. It transpired that he was forcing his attentions on the young man in his ward after dark. The victim had been an acquiescent, if not willing, partner until the attacker went too far. The victim complained to the authorities who shipped out the rapist and, eventually, his victim. It was rumoured that criminal proceedings were to be instituted against the bald assailant.

One of the lifers in my ward recalled a similar incident at Wakefield Prison; the attacker was fined £1 by the prison Governor. Once again, I say that prisons are totalitarian regimes where the Home Office rules supreme. It would be easy to gauge the reaction of the general public if a sentence of £1 for homosexual rape were imposed in the criminal courts. Fortunately this was the only attack as such, but homosexual love caused a disaster for one man.

I remember going into the kitchen one day to find a new face in the wash-up. I was then working in the dining room and went into the wash-up only to wash my own utensils after meals. At first I thought I had seen a rather pretty woman with long blonde hair. I was not wearing my glasses and this part of the kitchen was always steamy. What in fact I had seen was a new convict; he was a young man with hair down to his shoulders who, it must be said, was very pretty. As time went by I got to know him very well and liked him enormously. He was a drug addict whose craving got him into all sorts of trouble. On one occasion he returned from Home Leave stoned out of his mind. He was finally sacked from the kitchen for general bolshieness and, sadly, was shipped out to a closed prison before my release.

In the kitchen, at the same time, was an arsonist serving a life sentence and into his thirteenth year. It was clear to me that the second the youngster came into the kitchen, Bill, the lifer, fell for him. He followed the boy around like a lapdog and I noted in my diary that trouble would eventually come. It did with great force and a carving knife.

One afternoon Tony, the youngster, who by this time had had his hair cut short, came to me to say that Bill had 'touched' him and that he, Tony, had told him to 'fuck off'. I told Tony that I believed that Bill was in love with him and that he, Tony, had done little to discourage him. Tony agreed that Bill was 'after' him and said he felt sorry for him. He further said that he had told Bill to stop courting him, as it were.

A few days' later Bill, who was deeply in debt for tobacco, was taken to the prison hospital for some form of sedative treatment. He returned to the kitchen early one morning demanding to see Tony. The officer on duty was serving breakfast and had, unusually, left his office unlocked. In the office the knives were kept. Bill helped himself to a knife and ran amok in the kitchen. Tony sprinted outside for safety and the rest of us scattered. Eventually Bill was cornered, sedated and shipped out. The 'affair' was tragic from start to finish. Bill was eminently likeable and friendly to me – mind you, he left owing me three ounces of tobacco! He was doomed to spend an indeterminate time in hospital and as a result of his latest act had probably delayed his release by at least seven years. It was easy to see how after such a long time in prison he had become homosexual or had had his homosexual tendencies confirmed. I suspect Tony played the part of the innocent child in Bill's imagination and that the affair was more Platonic than otherwise. I did learn afterwards that Tony, despite his protestations to me that he was 'straight', managed to guarantee his supply of cannabis by offering his backside for others' pleasure, but I saw none of this side of his character.

Naturally nonces at Leyhill – unless they had enjoyed the publicity which I had had – were less obvious than they had been at Exeter. One man, a cripple, was convicted of assaulting young children with dildoes. To speak to him was to speak with a sane, educated, 'ordinary' man. Another nonce was, to me, the most interesting man of all.

He had been educated at Harrow, was clearly a man of substance and influence. I spoke to him but rarely; I was told by his workmate that he rather regarded me as a threat. The man told his whole story to his colleague; his colleague relayed it all to me. I wanted to learn as much as I could about the man for his type intrigued me.

It was strongly rumoured in prison that the man was one of the founders of the group Paedophile Information Exchange (PIE). I remember, as a headmaster, receiving circulars warning about the organisation which, as I recall, advocated virtually any form of sexual encounter between adults and children. Their aims were disgusting and unbelievable. I vaguely remembered the trial of some members of the organisation and wanted to see what made them tick. The man was, of course, universally loathed. He was probably the most hated man in the prison.

It transpired that he was doing seven years for buggery and that he was not a member of PIE. When I had proof of this I tried to put the record straight with a number of cons, but I failed. It is a fact that cons believe what they want to believe. Nonces fulfil a useful function for the rest of the population in that the sex offenders give the other convicts a feeling of superiority; they feel that if there is a group upon which they can look down, then perhaps their offences are not so terrible.

The man, whom I shall call Alec though that was not his name, believed that the age of sexual consent for males and females should be reduced. I think he believed that fourteen ought to be the age and not the current sixteen for heterosexuals and twenty-one for homosexuals. None could find this view totally without merit – and I do not say this merely as one convicted of having an affair with a fifteen-year-old girl. The sexual maturity of modern young people is apparent; their sexual experience, too, is shockingly obvious. This man had been married and had sired sons. His family had totally deserted him. He claimed to have been in solitary confinement for many months because his predilection was for fourteen- and fifteen-year-old boys.

When he was arrested he was in bed with one but he claimed that this was with the parents' knowledge. He claimed, too, that he had often educated boys from poorer backgrounds with the full approval of their parents who knew he was sexually abusing the boys. Be that as it may, the man's whole aim in life was to have the age of consent lowered.

More interesting than all this were his post-release plans. He was to go to Brazil where, I understand, boys are readily available. Certainly he was a man of property and he was well connected. One of his visitors, a bishop of the Church of England and known to me personally – not the Bishop of Truro who had visited me in Exeter – was implicated by Alec in some of his homosexual activity. Another visitor, a well-known member of the House of Lords, had himself been in prison for homosexual acts many years before. Alec, like many lonely and vain men, was a great talker and boaster.

He claimed he was part of a group which supplied boys to an Arab sheikh and that he was connected with 'Boys' Town' in Colombo, a section of the city reputed to be a ghetto of young males whose sexual favours are bought for export. He boasted contacts – for the procurement of boys – with a veritable Who's Who of British society. The list of names he bandied about would cause one of the great sensations of the century and I could not see that he had anything to gain by lying, particularly as he thought he was talking in great confidence to one other man only. Indeed, my informant was told by Alec that he was the only man he trusted and spoke to; that was a true enough statement for all to see. The two men worked alone at the Officers' Club and Alec dared not leave his own room much during out-of-work hours for fear of being attacked. There were two occasions to my knowledge when he was attacked at Leyhill while I was there.

The story was fascinating and incredible enough to be true. He showed some documentary evidence of what he was saying to my contact and my knowledge of his episcopal visitor confirmed much of what he said. Perhaps one of the most extraordinary facets of the whole story was that Alec himself was an incredibly ugly man with foul teeth. The thought that he could fascinate young boys struck me as absurd and yet he was having an affair with a young cleaner from another ward.

I can vouch for their liaison – not least of all because one evening when the prison was showing Olivier's *Richard III* Alec and his boyfriend were the only others in the audience with me and they disappeared to his room for what I had been told earlier was their 'nightly buggery'. Shortly before my release I spoke to the cleaner, who confirmed his homosexuality.

That sex is a topic high on the cons' agenda of thought is certain. It plays a central, negative role. That is, like the concept of freedom, it is uppermost in the mind for most of the time. It is something which is regarded as an eventual goal whose constant presence in the imagination operates like a perpetual torment. Instead of taking its rightful place in the order of an individual's life it is promoted to the status of an obsession. Given, as I said earlier, that it is a powerful instinct, it should not be so powerfully promoted. Again, I am sure the hardliners would regard this sort of unnatural deprivation as part of the punishment; I wonder if they would accept that it is part of the punishment for wives on the outside.

One wonders, too, whether or not sex lives are affected adversely after a man is released following a long sentence and whether, as is sometimes claimed, heterosexual men and women are, *faute de mieux*, turned homosexual by the experience. As with much else to do with prison reform this is not a question our legislators have addressed their minds to. The usual attitude of puritanical hypocrisy which has ruined this country prevails. The wrongdoer must be punished. The wrongdoer is not like us, therefore he cannot experience as we do. We love our families and would hate to be parted from them. He is a malefactor and would not understand our love, therefore he does not need it. We enjoy sexual intercourse because we are 'normal'. He is 'abnormal', therefore either he cannot know its true nature or, if he does, he will pervert it. Better, then, that he is deprived of it.

I may seem to exaggerate but I know of no truer statement of penal policy than the following remark from a book called *A Man of Good Abilities*: 'Prison is no deterrent; it is a system in which the well-to-do impose their will on those incapable of receiving it and call it treatment.' It goes on: 'Prisons are, after all, only bastions of unthinking inefficiency, administered usually by men steeped in traditions of privilege and class, many of whom think as their predecessors did fifty years ago, that "bad" people can be made "good" by character training, and that crime is really a matter of sinfulness and redemption.' The underlying belief is that habitual offenders could give up crime if they really wanted to, as others give up smoking, by making a 'real effort'.

# Sex

The same applies to sex. We can give it up if we make a big effort. What of food and drink – life itself?

Sidney Smith once wrote that there are three sexes – men, women and clergymen. I think he meant men, women and convicts.

# 10

# LIFERS

*Thou shalt not kill; but need'st not strive*
*Officiously to keep alive.*

Arthur Hugh Clough, 'The Latest Decalogue'

The taking of another human life has long been regarded as the most appalling of all crimes. If the life be that of a child then the murderer is the most reviled of all people. This viewpoint is not one that I have strongly held and my experience of lifers confirms me in the view that there are more terrible crimes. The common revulsion to murder seems not to stem from a Christian viewpoint which would argue that all life is God-given and sacred – 'The Lord gave and the Lord hath taken away' – for many who feel passionately about the murder of a child are quite happy to cry out for the death of the perpetrator.

Given that the majority of murders are committed in hot blood and within the context of close bonds – either within lawfully constituted families or within groups of people extremely well known to each other – this common revulsion is hard to explain. Fear, I suppose, is one source of loathing, a kind of 'There but for the grace of God go I' response which smacks more of selfishness than of brotherly love. The few murders which are greed- or sex-motivated rightly cause a reaction in society but, again, one cannot see what the purpose of society's reaction really is. That the murderer has been deterred by judicial execution is beyond dispute. But history proves that no one else will necessarily be deterred. That the murderer should be 'punished' is the commonest reaction. The problem is how this punishment should be effected.

There is no easy answer to the problem because every case is different. Some men kill because they are 'sick' in the mind. If they cannot rationalise the horror of their deed then they cannot understand the nature of their 'punishment'. On the other hand society must be protected from their dangerous actions. This

88

protection takes the form of lengthy incarceration in prisons or in high-security institutions like Broadmoor or Rampton. Society is happiest when the 'evildoers' are out of sight.

Eventually the time comes when the malefactor may be considered 'cured'. A brave decision is made to release him or her. Sometimes he or she kills again and society has a major problem. Not only has it made a terrible 'mistake' in relation to our, now, double killer, but it also has to consider similar cases. In short all those who are in custody for murder have had their chances of release reduced by the 'mistake'. The circle closes with an inevitable reappraisal of how such killers are to be treated. Prison is the alternative to death. In prison the killers do not generally kill again and after a passage of time they are considered for release. But no one can be sure they will not kill again. Only two actions are possible. Continue to incarcerate the malefactor or release him and hope he does not reoffend. It is a nasty choice for those in authority, particularly when they must satisfy the twin public demands of safety and the desire for retribution.

My own introduction to lifers came at Leyhill. I had heard in Exeter Prison that they were generally quiet, uncommunicative people who kept themselves to themselves. They had been years in the system and liked to 'get on with their bird' without the distractions of short-termers. They were natives; we were immigrants. Like all generalisations this was only partly true. Some lifers were withdrawn; others were as extrovert as anyone else. Some seemed to enjoy the aura of having killed; others still could not understand the nature of their past misdeed. Some became close friends of mine; others hated me from the day I arrived and, if anything, intensified their hatred as time went on. Generally, though, with rare, noisy exceptions, lifers tolerated nonces more than the rest of the population.

The general prison population seemed to regard them as very special – almost heroic – figures, because of the length of time they were doing. I, too, regarded them as very special but for a slightly different reason. I served fewer weeks than many of them had served years in prison. Therefore, I constantly felt an enormous compassion for them. I loathed the weeks of separation from my family and friends and the hardships of deprivation and loss of freedom. How much more, I felt, must they be suffering. I had the knowledge of a certain release date. By law I *had* to be released by a certain time. They knew not from one year to the next when they would be released.

Lifers – and everyone else for that matter – wait for a 'date'. Those with determinate sentences are given three dates when they enter prison. The first is Parole Eligibility Date (PED), the second Earliest Date of Release (EDR) and the final one Last Date of Release (LDR). Lifers have none of these. Their cases were regularly reviewed. The system, put simply, worked like this. A lifer would receive a review. The result of that review would be made known after about twelve months – twice the length of time I served. The result may be that the lifer would have his case reviewed in another twelve months. Thus from the time of the first review to the time of the next and its answer at least three years would pass. And the second answer may give a date for two years hence – a total of five years would have passed before the man was released.

The process is slow and tortuous. I suppose it has to be, but the prospect of a six-month knock-back broke the spirits of short-termers; to us, the prospect of a five-year knock-back was incomprehensible. I lost count of the number of short-termers – by which I mean those serving six years or less – who told me they would 'top themselves' rather than do a life sentence. I knew what they meant but knew equally that if they were faced with a life sentence they would cope. Probably most of us would agree with Nietzsche's statement that 'The thought of suicide is a great source of comfort: with it a calm passage is to be made across many a bad night'. Perhaps the thought is – the action would be dismissed out of hand by most.

As I have explained elsewhere, the first person to give me hassle in the ward was a lifer; the first person to give me hassle at work was a lifer. Their actions were untypical of lifers – some of whom, it must be said, were nonces but had, through the sheer passage of time, lost that label. The kitchen lifer remained an enemy for several months. Suddenly he became a friend and his conversion was a source of tremendous happiness to me for two reasons. First, it meant that my days at work would be less tense – even though by the time he and I spoke I was well established in the kitchens – but it also meant that I could speak to him about his crime and its effect on him. The reconciliation happened un-expectedly and simply.

# Lifers

For some days he had been suffering from a bad back and I had said to him that I sympathised, for my wife similarly suffered agonies from a spinal weakness. I made my remark *en passant*, as it were, when he walked past me wincing. Several days later he pointed out to me that the menu blackboard, which Trevor and I had to fill each day, contained a misprint. They were the first unsolicited words he had ever spoken to me. I quipped that I should be able to alter the menu because writing on blackboards was a thing I had done before. This exchange of banalities caused disproportionate mirth in both of us and the ice was broken.

Long afterwards I realised that, if I had earlier extended the hand of friendship, it would have been taken. At the time, though, I was more concerned to let them know I did not give a damn about their hostility and that if they wanted it to end *they* would have to proffer the olive branch. Stupid really!

Shortly after this breakthrough the lifer, Tony, asked me about my case. Together we sat in the deserted staff room and I spent an hour giving him full details. It changed his mind about me completely and I think it is true to say that he felt shame about his earlier hostility. We became firm friends even though shortly after our conversation he left the kitchens to work in the market gardens.

In return for my story I wanted to hear his. I had heard rumours that he was the victim of a judicial mistake but then, I suppose, all of us claim to be innocent, and those wretches who are, are disbelieved with those who are palpably guilty but who maintain their innocence. Before I left prison I had read Tony's depositions and also an account of the murder and trial which he had specially written for me. I have promised him that some of the things he wrote down would remain strictly confidential, but these things were very personal and had no bearing on the murder, for which he was sentenced to life imprisonment at the age of about nineteen. He had served twelve years, more or less, when I met him and was still protesting his innocence.

His story is simple. He and a more senior guardsman left their barracks for a night on the town in London. They returned in the early hours of the morning and while walking home accosted several people for a light for their cigarettes. One of them was an elderly man who refused to give them a light and walked on. He was pursued by Tony's companion, who beat him up so severely that the man died. In the terror of the moment and under the threats of his older companion, Tony says he was forced to help the murderer carry the body to a stream, where it was hidden. Fearing himself to be the next victim, Tony obeyed his companion's order to say nothing. They returned to barracks and a week later were arrested. Their movements had been charted from the time they caught the tube in London to the time they were 'clocked-in' at their barracks. Both eventually confessed, but Tony says fear of the police was his main motivation. He is unshakable in his claim that it was his friend who beat the man to death.

I have no way of knowing the truth, but I find it hard to believe that the man I met was the man who had killed. Perhaps he has changed in prison. I do not know. Certainly the Tony I know is a dignified and efficient worker – an excellent baker and co-operative inmate. I say this of a man who for many weeks followed the pack in making my life hell. He obeyed all 'authority' and I can believe that he was under the influence of his senior colleague on that tragic night – a man whom he has never seen since the day of his conviction, incidentally. I cannot conceive of the panic and shock he would have undergone realising that he was involved in so brutal an assault. He does not excuse his part in the concealment of the body; he denies that he killed another human being. He has nothing to gain by the denial.

Tony got married while in prison and, sadly, divorced, too. He was having problems in gaining access to his child and suffering additionally because his parents were finding it difficult to visit him. In May 1986 he told me that he hoped to be released within eighteen months. Quaintly, to me at any rate, the charge partly reads, 'did murder Mr X Against the Peace of our Sovereign Lady the Queen, Her Crown and Dignity'. Few will think that he has not paid the price for his crime and should be allowed to be released soon.

And release for lifers is a very tenuous concept. They are on licence for life and can be brought back into prison at any time.

There was an Irishman at Leyhill who had been released on life licence but who got into a brawl in a pub. He was sentenced to twelve months for causing an affray or some such offence, but the judge did not revoke his licence. He served his time in Kingston

Prison and three days before he was due for release the Home Office revoked his licence. That act occurred six years ago and he is still waiting for a 'date'. This splendid Irishman hated the authorities, did the minimum amount of work but seemed never to lose his sense of humour and to have come to terms with his foul lot. I can think of nothing more cruel than keeping a man dangling for years. I found it bad enough waiting to hear if I had got parole.

But the Irishman's lot was not as harsh as that of Little Ernie, a quiet, rather pessimistic double murderer. Ernie first came to my notice as the star of a sketch in the prison show, a mixed entertainment held in the early summer. He and several other lifers performed an amusing sketch of no substance. I learned afterwards that Ernie had killed his first wife and been given a life sentence. He was eventually released on licence, remarried and killed his second wife. The second murder had occurred over twenty years before. Now, after working his way through the system twice, he was at Leyhill where he had a proper expectation to be released in a relatively short time.

One day I saw Ernie being taken to the Reception area. He was not in handcuffs but it was obvious to me that he was being shipped out. I was told later that he had just received a three-year knock-back and was going back to Kingston Prison. Ernie suffered from cardiac disease. His knock-back meant, in effect, that in three years' time his case would be reviewed. The answer to that review would come after twelve months. If he got a date it would be for a year to two years thereafter. In short, Ernie had just received the certainty of at least another six years in prison. This may not seem too harsh for a man who has killed twice. It is torture of the most barbaric kind when one considers that Ernie had been allocated to Leyhill, a Category D prison from which every offender reasonably and rightly expects to be released. One draws an uncomfortable conclusion. I believe Ernie was sent to Leyhill to buoy him up so high that when his knock-back came he would fall so low that despair, coupled with his faulty heart, would kill him. After all, who would risk releasing him? He cannot be hanged; he cannot be released. He had served over twenty years and humanely might be regarded as having some hopes of a merciful release. The circle spirals viciously and only Ernie loses.

It may be that in six years Ernie will still be alive but so enfeebled by imprisonment that he can be released in time to die on the outside. One man was thus treated. He had served at least twenty Christmases in prison for, I think, more than one professional killing. He was reputed to be a hitman for the Kray twins. When I knew him he was a spent force, but clearly he had been a huge power to control. He was a broad-shouldered, tall, tough-looking Geordie. He had suffered terribly in prison, through his own fault. He had led riots at Parkhurst in the 1970s and the scars still remained. By now, though, he had lost a lung and suffered from chronic heart disease. He hated time spent in hospital for his earnings were reduced to £1 per week – considerably less than he had been paid years before in a high-security prison. But the price lifers paid for going to a Category D prison was the loss of some of their long-term privileges. The man was obviously dying. He was given forty-eight hours' notice of his release. Within a week of leaving prison he was seriously ill in hospital. I left shortly afterwards so did not hear what happened to him. I am prepared to bet that, as I write, he is lying buried in a northern cemetery. The system had beaten him and protected society.

I further suggest that not only are prisoners sent out, having been broken by the system physically, but they are, in some cases, reduced to the mental state of a cabbage by the administration of drugs. This assertion was initially made to me by a lifer who had served eighteen years and claimed to have seen it many times. I accept the hypothesis on the basis of experience in Leyhill.

The lifer whom I knew as well as anyone had served twenty-five years. I had got to know him because he was a writer and had, among other things, written a play with Leslie Grantham, which had been performed when they were both in Wormwood Scrubs. When I met this man he was busy writing short stories, plays and television scripts. I promised to help him to get them published.

In the course of our many conversations I told him that I wanted to publish his life story. It seemed to me that a lifetime in prison would be an interesting subject for a book and the more we talked the more convinced I became that his story was fascinating. He told tales of the escape of George Blake, which he reckons was arranged by the authorities. He spoke of more famous murderers whom he had met, of the Krays, Richardson and the Great Train Robbers. The more he talked the more I became intrigued. We finally decided that I would tape-record his life story. A machine was 'acquired' but after he had recorded only about three hours' worth the officers found the machine. However, I managed to get the full tape out with me. Unfortunately it does not explain the man's crime, and here there is a mystery.

It was rumoured in the prison that he had raped and killed twice. The second woman was alleged to have been the wife of another convict whom the man was asked to contact when he was out on his initial release. He vehemently denies the second murder and I believe him. Yet in our conversations he admitted that there was a sexual assault on his file from early days and he once used the word 'reoffend' in connection with himself. I suspect that he had a history of sexual deviancy which culminated in a nasty murder, and twenty-five years later he was still in prison. The duration of his sentence suggests a more than ordinary crime. Constantly during our chats he mentioned the psychological aspects of his case. Clearly over the years he had come to rely on psychiatric explanations for his conduct and was exculpating himself through their medium.

Often I said to him that the interest in him as far as a book was concerned rested with the horror of his crime and the deep experience he had of prison life. He persisted in explaining away his – to me unspecified – conduct. He blamed a motor-cycle accident in his youth. He blamed drink. He blamed an inherited personality disorder. For years Home Office psychologists and psychiatrists had fed him with different theories. Generally, though, he was prepared to believe that a final explanation would be given which would result in treatment or release. This belief notwithstanding, he was sure that because he was at Leyhill, he had high hopes of a reasonably speedy release.

The weeks went by and I helped this articulate, fit man in his fifties prepare his entry to the Laurence Olivier Competition. I read his short stories and advised him on his scripts for television sit-coms. During the day he worked on the market gardens and in the summer he ran the bowls. He was a non-smoker who very generously bought me some tobacco in appreciation of what I was trying to do. I mention all these things to indicate that not only was he mentally very alert but that he was, also, physically in good shape. Then the change came.

He called me to his room one evening. It was on the day that he had been given yet another psychiatric examination by a Home Office specialist. He excitedly told me that his condition had been diagnosed and could be treated with drugs. His joy was almost unlimited. My dismay was as profound. He started taking the drugs. By the end of the first week he had taken a day off work – the first time ever, he said. He spoke of not feeling himself; he was incapable of writing and was gradually becoming more and more lethargic and 'not with it'. In the second week his drug intake was doubled. Slowly and surely he was being turned into a junkie before our very eyes. I asked him to get me a pill so that I could smuggle it out for analysis. He refused for two reasons. First, he believed that if he was caught in such an action the 'treatment' would stop and he would not be 'cured'. Secondly, he did not want to deprive himself of any pill in case the treatment was affected. It is true that it would have been difficult to get a pill for it had to be swallowed in front of an officer, but my pleas for even a grain of the stuff went unheeded.

I had been asked to keep an eye on him by another lifer who was preparing to go to the authorities to demand that they stop the 'treatment' because the man was being turned into a mindless addict.

There will be some, no doubt, who find my reaction fanciful and hysterical. I merely state that I find it impossible to accept that after twenty-five years in prison the 'cure' had suddenly been found to a man's mental problems, or, further, that this cure reduces a once articulate and literate person to a state of almost gibbering imbecility. Doubtless by now the man's system has accepted the drugs and the more extreme symptoms have worn off. I suspect that he will remain on the drug as long as he lives and if he is soon released it will be into an institution like a hostel which will ensure that he remains on the pills for life. So, again, his release will be 'safe' for the public.

I offer no solution but find that our society will release men to die or will send them out of the system dependent on drugs which take away their mental faculties. Echoes of the Soviet Union are not a Siberian wind's distance away.

The lifer who had expressed concern about his fellow's drug treatment was a remarkable little Irishman with a huge shock of curly, grey hair. He was, because of his diminutive size, known as 'Inch'. He, like the man undergoing drug treatment, was in my ward. He was a new arrival so did not yet have a room. Gradually he and I became friends and eventually no day was complete unless we had played several games of darts. We had a weekly ration of games to play and though I was useless at the game I looked forward to its nightly absurdity.

As our friendship blossomed so I learned more about him. He told me he had served eighteen years but that recently new evidence had been discovered which suggested that his conviction was unsafe. I took that news with a pinch of salt as I did his assertion that a Home Office conspiracy was keeping him in prison and preventing his return to his native Ireland. However, I once again found it hard to accept the truth that this extremely jovial little man had killed, though he certainly had a temper which generally came to the fore over trivia. Once, for example, another inmate hid his food. Inch went wild and when the food was retrieved refused to eat it. He loved an after-lunch nap and was furious if he was ever disturbed. To this day, I am not sure if he killed a man or a woman – I suspect it was a woman. Indeed, more women-killers were in the prison than men-killers.

An interesting sidelight into his morality was shown by the drug treatment his colleague was receiving. When Inch came to me to enlist my help in keeping an eye on the other man, I acted Devil's advocate and suggested that if the drug were repressing murderous or other violent tendencies then surely (always a dead giveaway, that word) the treatment was justified. If it stopped the man from killing another woman, who could deny the wisdom of the action? The response surprised me. 'What's a fucking woman in a box?' Inch asked. 'The woman could have been my wife,' I protested. 'No it couldn't. Your wife doesn't sleep around,' replied Inch. Even assuming that subconsciously Inch was justifying the action of murder, as he might well have been, given his own conviction, it is an interesting observation that he also implied that 'loose women' are reasonably fair game for killers.

But Inch was much more interesting in his own right. He was a highly skilled craftsman who had won many prestigious awards for his ability to make models in matchsticks and wood. When I first met him he had won gold medals in international competition for his work. At the time his model of the *Mary Rose* was his *chef d'oeuvre*; it had featured on television and I remembered seeing a photograph of another of his ships on the back page of *The Times* when I had first come to Leyhill.

Most of his spare time was spent preparing for the 1986 Wembley Model Engineering Exhibition. He was modelling, in a variety of hardwoods, a ship called the *Great Harry*. Every piece of wood and material he seemed to have to scrounge. I remember stealing string from the butcher so that he could deal with the riggings and other embellishments. He fashioned the guns and the decoration with an ingenuity which I found staggering. All he had to copy from was an indistinct postcard which he pinned above the hull of his boat. He had a special room in the woodwork shop but as time went on he moved his model into his cubicle so that he could work on it after 9 p.m. For relief he made jewellery boxes for convicts to give to their wives. Mentally he was preparing further work and had decided to concentrate on making Viking ships after the *Great Harry* was complete. He came to me one night and was disappointed that I did not have the dimensions, design, use and other information about them. 'You're a fucking schoolmaster, aren't you?' he moaned.

Part of his work was devoted to raising money for research into leukaemia. He had befriended a young girl who had died of the disease. His models were in possession of her family who displayed them to raise money. When I knew him, I was told that he had raised over £70,000. Certainly this remarkable man has a future when he leaves prison. I tried to persuade him to write an instruction booklet about how to make matchstick models, but the written word was not his *forte* and the plan was shelved. Certainly he was well known in the modelling world and the range of correspondence he had received over the years showed that he was held in high regard. What was most remarkable about the whole enterprise was that he was given no special privileges by the Prison Department. It would be a perversion of the truth if any were to think that the 'system' had reformed and motivated him. He was a man who had learned to survive years of incarceration through his own guts and skills. He was universally liked.

The same cannot be said about some of the murderers whose crimes defy belief. One such was an Asian who was employed in the Labour Office. His job was as a sort of filing clerk to the officer responsible for allocating work. Over the years this inmate had clearly worked himself into a position of some influence and power. One or two cons even called him 'Mr X'. He was a small, superior-acting, rather oleaginous man who certainly had delusions of grandeur. His crime? He had murdered his children and served them up to his wife as curry. She became suspicious, so the story goes, on the discovery of curried knuckles.

The man learned one day that I was hoping to publish my prison diaries and came to me for advice about publication. He was, he said, writing his own life story. I suspected that he had been sent by the authorities to discover if I was keeping a diary, so I denied all knowledge of everything. (I had recently been caught smuggling and had a number of other such charges levelled against me.) When I learned of his crime, I remembered with amusement what I had been told at Exeter about the Leyhill inmates being like me.

An equally repulsive creature was known throughout the prison as 'Dig 'em up Dave'. He had been convicted of the rape and murder of a woman, whose body he had interred. Some little time afterwards, he disinterred her for the purpose of sexual intercourse. Like the Asian, he had spent a considerable time in prison. He was a jovial man who drove a tractor. Often on my afternoon run I saw him dumping manure on the midden and wondered if the mechanical digger he operated daily was some form of therapy. His presence in the prison was tolerated humorously by most inmates. He was one of the main attractions. I did not enjoy speaking to him. Among his responsibilities was care of the small aviary. He shared this function with Trevor, my work companion, and often told him of his life in long-term prisons.

I vividly remember a tale of summary inmate justice at one prison. The necrophiliac was concerned with birds there too. One day a number of the birds were discovered to have had their legs ripped off. The culprit was found and nailed to a door. The authorities, naturally, did not discover the perpetrators of this foul deed. An interesting sidelight is again thrown on prisoners' attitudes. The suffering of a few birds is more important than the crucifixion of a fellow human being. Indeed, a number of the lifers kept cats as pets; food for these animals was on sale in the canteen and I often saved scraps from the kitchen for them.

The crimes of the above two men are as unfathomable to the rational mind as the murder, by an ageing Welshman, of his grandchildren. This man, a practising homosexual in the prison who would pay for his own sexual gratification, carried his victims around in a suitcase for several days after the murders. I once spoke to this man in my early days in Ward 2 about Welsh rugby, little realising at the time what he was in for. Once I knew, I did not avoid him – it was not necessary, for he lived in a world of his own for the most part – but I did not try to speak with him.

What is, perhaps, the most noticeable aspect of being in the company of killers is that one soon accepts their presence as the norm. I remember my mother asking after my release if I had been scared because there were over eighty murderers at Leyhill. The question struck me as absurd. Twelve months previously the idea that I would be having afternoon tea with men who had killed would have struck me as appalling. To me they were fellow prisoners of a particularly unfortunate sort. I do not condone their actions, largely because I cannot explain them. Some murderers, however, killed for very understandable reasons.

One man in my ward had shot his wife, having found her in bed with another man. I think his action to be extreme; his reaction can be understood by any happily married man or woman. This man lent me his soap in my first days at Leyhill so I always held him in affection. As time went on it transpired that he and I had mutual interests and contacts. He had been one of the foremost sports parachutists and knew people I had come across when I indulged in the sport years ago. He appeared in a classic book, a copy of which I still possess, called *Alone in the Sky*. He was a man in his fifties who was very anti-smoking and who ran miles each day to keep fit. Additionally he was a great reader and it was he who gave me, among other volumes, a copy of Nietzsche's *Also Sprach Zarathustra*. He had served twelve years or so – far too many in my view, but those who had known him a long time said he had always bucked the system.

On one occasion he and another lifer in our ward – a man convicted of killing his father's girlfriend – mounted a protest because the authorities turned off the gas heating in the rooms. A search had revealed that a number of the gas jets had been tampered with. In the interests of safety they were turned off and the occupants of the rooms offered the chance of a temporary cubicle or permanent hypothermia. As lifers they felt that they were entitled to keep their rooms and that the authorities should sort out the problem quickly. In protest these two men packed their belongings and prepared to march to Bristol. In the event they did not, but they did refuse work and were fined £1.50 each. Happily, the parachutist was released exactly a week after me, and his companion, whom I liked enormously, the following September.

There was, though, a lifer in our ward whom I loathed and despised. The feeling was mutual. He was a Scotsman, called 'Jock' of course, who had stabbed a man in a pub, I believe. Jock was an evil-looking man with a moustache, close-cropped grey hair and a vicious expression permanently on his face. Certainly there was an aura of evil about him and he was treated with great respect by everyone else. I never knew why. He was captain of the rugby team but played the game like a girl. He rarely entered a scrummage and I did not once see him tackle. His greatest asset was his mouth. He was, without doubt, the most opinionated windbag in the prison. To his credit he kept reasonably fit and entered all the 'fun runs' held in the prison. I suppose I hated him most because he hated nonces. In this he was unique among all the lifers at Leyhill with whom I spoke – and that was the majority. One day a mock petition, headed 'Hang All Nonces', was pinned to his door and, I am appalled to say, signed by a number of people in the ward who regarded themselves as my friends. This indicates the power the man seemed to command.

There came a crisis in the rugby team when his replacement as captain was sought by the players. I remember going to the bottom of the ward to practise dart-throwing one evening when Jock was in secret conclave with the team coach – a half-caste who had conned £48,000 from an old woman who, as a result, had attempted suicide (a vile crime which Jock could accept). The coach, who came from another ward, asked me to go away as he was speaking privately to Jock. I refused and elicited the reaction from Jock, 'Well, what do you expect from fucking filth?' I stood alone at the dart board for another half-hour deliberately annoying the two men. I expected the 'tough' Jock to react later. At no time did he. In fact, he kept a wide berth, though occasionally I would annoy him by offering him some of my bread ration. Shortly before I left I heard that he had received a 'date'. Even though I despise him, I am glad he is no longer in prison. And he did amuse us all one night by smuggling in a bottle of whisky and getting gloriously drunk.

This brief catalogue of lifers would be incomplete if I failed to mention Charlie. He was my prize character, to whom I can do little justice in words. Were I to be a chat-show host, Charlie would be my permanent guest. He had a broad Cockney accent and used the words 'fucking' and 'cunt' as naturally as the rest of us breathe. He spent his time going through the motions of sweeping the paths of the prison. In reality he was a collector of cigarette ends and seemed to live for that. My diary records that in a conversation with me – I was privileged to be one of the few with whom he would stop and talk – he mentioned that he had not meant to 'hit her'. I gathered that he had been a dosser and that he had killed a dosser. From what our conversations produced I learned that he had killed a mentally ill woman whom he had looked after for years. 'I'm no fucking murderer,' he would say. Certainly he resented not having been given a 'date' after fourteen years' imprisonment and quoted chapter and verse many others convicted of far worse crimes who had been released on licence. He was particularly resentful of sex murderers who served fewer years than he had.

He always shouted when he spoke – a trait which stood him in good stead when he appeared in the lifers' sketch during the prison show. He played the part of a Texan, wearing a huge stetson which he had made himself out of paper. He must be the only Texan, real or imaginary, who in a broad Cockney accent called his pardner a 'fucking cunt' on stage. My enduring memory of this lovable man was his asking me how he could contact his probation officer. I found it odd that I should be telling him about prison administration. After all, he had many times told me of his pleasant life in Parkhurst and elsewhere. I told him and received the reply, 'Good, 'e 'asn't been in touch for over free fucking years. I'm gonna write and say, "Are you fucking dead, you cunt?"' I repeat, the written word does no justice to Charlie. I hope he is out now, but I suspect he is not.

When I was a little boy, I used to pray that if I were going to kill someone it should happen before I was eighteen. That way I would not be hanged. This rather ghoulish piece of infantile imagining stemmed from my consciousness of the Craig–Bentley murder case. Craig had, at the age of sixteen, shot and killed a policeman. I remember the case particularly well, for the policeman was the uncle of a schoolfriend of mine. Bentley, aged eighteen, was hanged, even though he did not pull the trigger. Craig was, as they say in the trade, 'HMP'd': detained according to Her Majesty's Pleasure. I learned what that meant at Leyhill.

One day, I met a young man of about twenty-five and asked, in the course of conversation, when he was due for release. It was a common question. He told me he was a lifer and had been in custody since he was fifteen. There were several men under thirty whose adolescence and early manhood had been spent behind bars. They all awaited a 'date'. I cannot conceive of their future lives. They have reached and passed full maturity and probably never gone out with a girl. They had never enjoyed the wonders of sexual intercourse. I hasten to add that none seemed a homosexual. All were as happy as could be expected – not surprisingly, I suppose, given that they knew no other 'home'.

It boggles the imagination to write down a list of the 'normal' things they had, as adults, never experienced – like driving a car, owning a house or, at least, having their own front-door key. They had never travelled abroad or even been to a football match. They had never seen a television programme after 9 p.m. or had the opportunity to do so. They had never visited a pub or enjoyed parenthood. All had done more than ten years in prison.

One was convicted of throwing a stone at a prostitute. The unfortunate woman had died. I am in no way condoning their actions but cannot help wondering what sort of people they will be when faced with the realities of life 'on the out'. Certainly, prison is not preparing them, for despite the occasional outings they got into Bristol, they were never there long enough or independently enough to taste responsibility. More often than not they would return dazed by the size of shops or overwhelmed by their pint of lager in a pub.

I look back upon the companionship of many of these killers with affection and regret. I no longer regard murder as the most horrible of crimes and know that many murderers are as likeable as any other people. Most killers are not like the Moors Murderers or the Yorkshire Ripper. They are like you and me.

I recognise the hugely difficult job the authorities have in deciding whether or not to release a man or woman convicted of the crime. I accept that there may well be a category of murderer who should never be released – not only for the sake of public safety but also, as perhaps in the case of Myra Hindley and Ian Brady, as a symbol of the permanent abhorrence of their deeds. However much this smacks of the Russian attitude to Rudolf Hess, I think the action can be justified.

After all is said and done, there can be few human beings who have never uttered the words 'I could have killed him', in a moment of stress. Happily, our nation no longer executes felons and in that we may be said to have made a start in the proper treatment of some offenders. If only we could separate the revulsion we feel about a crime from our response to the criminal.

# 11

# RECREATION

*He brought an eye for all he saw;*
*He mixt in all our simple sports;*
*They pleased him, fresh from brawling courts*
*And dusty purlieus of the law.*

Alfred, Lord Tennyson, *In Memoriam A.M.M.*

My isolation on Rule 43 in Exeter Prison necessarily separated me from whatever recreational activities went on there. Apart from my concentrated reading, desultory chess matches and daily wrestle with *The Times* crossword, I indulged in no 'simple sports'. My one attempt to be allowed to use the gymnasium was turned down by a lady Assistant Governor on the grounds that the facility was overused.

At Leyhill opportunities were enormously varied. There were facilities for a wide range of indoor and outdoor recreational activities. I resolved, once I was settled in, to participate in many of these; I reasoned that time would pass more quickly and that, at least, I would be released in reasonable physical shape. I had trained years before as a Physical Education specialist and had been coaching team sports up to the time of my demise. However, things did not turn out quite as I had expected.

I had intended to use the gymnasium regularly. In the event I entered its ancient portals but once, when I was summoned by the officer in charge of sport. The interview I had with him replaced the main Reception board's which, because I was the only new entrant on my draft, did not occur. I spent but a few minutes with this man, who, among other things, asked me if I would return home after my release. I resented this question as it had nothing to do with sport or with him, so I told him to mind his own business. Much later, I learned that he was the wrong officer to cross and that my subsequent troubles – reported elsewhere – may well have stemmed from him.

He asked a number of impertinent questions and some relevant ones. Arrogantly, I gave him to understand that I had been qualified to teach PE since almost before he was born and that I was well aware of the nature of exercise, having co-written a book about exercise and cardiac disease. We became instant enemies. I learned, too, that because I was over thirty-five years of age I would have to undergo a medical examination to pass me fit for sport. It was one of the absurdities of the system that those who wished to play bowls at that advanced age had to have a medical but that kitchen staff were required once a week to haul enormously heavy trailer-loads of supplies up a hill without any such examination.

I resolved not to use the gymnasium, partly because I loathed this man but also because most of the kitchen staff used the place during their time off in the afternoons and, as I have explained, they were my arch-enemies for many weeks.

Thus my early days consisted of lone walks around the playing field in the afternoon. There was a dusk curfew each day so it was not until early summer that we could enjoy the magnificent sunsets and splendid views from this large field. I believe that my daily walks in all weathers contributed as much as anything to my remaining reasonably sane in prison. In part this was because I enjoyed the freedom of the open air and some tempestuous weather, for the winds at Leyhill are powerful and exhilarating. In January and February I wore jeans, overalls, donkey jacket and sweaters in an attempt to keep warm. When the snow came men wore towels as scarves until the practice was banned by the Chief Officer. But I also enjoyed the walks because the views of the surrounding countryside were so splendid. Below the prison was a huge lake beyond which was the M5, whose traffic sent a steady hum of hope towards us.

There had been a time when inmates were allowed to visit the lake – indeed, so had their visitors – but, I believe, incidents of *al fresco* copulation had put paid to that privilege. Yet the lake was there as a symbol of freedom; it was just beyond the wire and down in a valley. As the months passed, I enjoyed watching it freeze over, to be used as a skating rink by the birds. Its thaw heralded the spring, and as April turned into early summer the growing foliage on the trees obscured it from view more and more, until I calculated that the total disappearance from view of my escape symbol would herald my return to the 'free' world.

From another border could be seen rolling hills, on top of which was a huge obelisk. I have forgotten what it commemorated – possibly something to do with Cranmer. The lake and the obelisk became significant talismens for me. Very many times did I look over the wire and weep my time away – particularly after a visit or when a particularly moving letter had been sent to me. I was never tempted to go over the wire.

The time came, however, when a three- or five-lap stroll around the thousand-metre perimeter failed to satisfy my desire for physical exercise. I needed to run. My problem was that I had no kit and had not been passed fit. This second difficulty was easy to overcome. I would not have a medical; I would just run and see what happened. The kit problem was solved by another prisoner, who kindly 'acquired' for me a set of running shorts, vest and plimsolls from the gym. My first run – three laps into a strong wind – revealed to what physical ruin I had slumped. I enjoyed the experience enormously but suffered afterwards.

From late January until the day of my release I ran every week-day afternoon. There was a time when deep snow prevented me from doing so, but even then I walked daily. And many other inmates ran too. The prison from time to time organised 'fun runs' but I did not enter these. I did not participate, deliberately, in any activity that was organised by the authorities. This stubbornness derived partly from my resentment at being in prison at all and partly from my loathing of the appalling regime under which we existed. True, I had fallen foul of it through my own fault but, then, survival in part depended upon acting with a degree of independence. Thus I ran 'unofficially' and tried to buck the system in other ways. It seemed to me at the time that I was retaining my dignity in this way.

Eventually, my running attracted flattering attention. One old man so boasted to a friend about the combination of my advanced years and speed of running that I had to settle a bet between the two of them and come clean about my age, which was forty-three. The old man told me, 'You've got to be careful. You shouldn't go round so fast.' Even the rugby club coach remarked to me shortly before my release, 'You've got a good body on you and are very fit. May I ask how old you are?' I had, the previous day, overtaken him when we were both on a training run. A third man also admired my body – but I think for no sinister reason. I say all this less to boast than to indicate that my accumulated physical skills held me in good stead in my attempts to survive in prison; my grey hair belied my ability to run. My small stature did not suggest an ability to stand up to the nonce-bashers, as I had done. On one marvellous occasion, I was challenged to a race by a man twenty years my junior. I won and elicited the response from him, 'You surprise me every day, Mr [*sic*] Bettsworth.'

These pathetic feats were part and parcel of my mental exercise, too. When the wind blew and the rain lashed down it was extremely difficult to persuade myself to run. At no time did I not run because the weather was bad – save in a foot of snow, when I thought I might do myself harm. My wife, to whom I relayed these incidents as a means of assuring her that I was in good trim, took a marvellously iconoclastic line. When boasting of my victory over flush youth, she said, 'You'd rather die than be beaten.' But all the same she was, I am sure, relieved that I was not vegetating in a cesspit of self-pity. Tim, too, who throughout the ordeal regarded his Dad as a hero, was much cheered by my athletic vaingloriousness.

The organised 'fun runs' – much supported by the Deputy Governor, himself an able marathon runner – had the carnival atmosphere of a school sports day, and as such I loathed them, just as I loathed the euphemism 'camp' for prison. We were in prison and no amount of name-changing would alter that. A prison by any other name would smell as foul. (The summit of labelling I encountered in an article in the *Prison Officers' Journal*: prisoners were referred to as 'clients'.)

For those who did not enjoy the solitary discipline of running there was much organised sport. In the winter the gym was open for weight-training, although from what I heard it was more weight-lifting and extremely badly supervised. In essence it was an opportunity for the young bloods to assert their strength and masculinity and to undertake extremely demanding circuit-training. Certainly its function was sublimatory; much excess and potentially harmful energy was burned up by the gym sessions. Others played badminton or volleyball.

Outside, the soccer and rugby teams enjoyed a full season of home and away matches. Occasionally they won; more often than not it was the competition in the bar afterwards that seemed to bring out the most skilful play on the part of the rugby team, who rarely returned home sober. The soccer players seemed to be more abstemious. Certainly coaching of the teams was a part of the responsibility taken on by the two gymnasium officers, though both knew little of how to coach and nothing about how to control men. The soccer coach, an elderly officer known as Fred – it was interesting that the two gym officers were called by their Christian names – took more interest in his black labrador but seemed to have a heart of gold. He was liked rather than respected, I suspect. The rugby man was my old adversary, Roger. He spent a great deal of his time at matches calling his players 'fucking cunts' and hence leaving an indelible impression on the curious visiting teams.

There can be no doubt that sport was a valuable therapy and that fitness in general was an important part of the prisoners' routine. Even matches against the police – potentially very explosive affairs – were conducted with good heart by the players, though the spectators were less than courteous to our opponents. Of course, when the POA strike was on it was the sports programme that was the first to suffer. However, as a means of welding together our heterogeneous group and giving it an object and a talking-point, the soccer and rugby played a large part.

In the summer it was the cricket which reigned supreme, with bowls coming a close second. I intended to play cricket if I did not get parole but happily this option was one I did not have to take up. I watched all the home cricket matches and often found it hard to believe I was in prison. On the few sunny afternoons that there were, I took my tea and cucumber sandwiches to the far side of the field and, while sitting under a blossom-laden tree, enjoyed the traditional sights and sounds of the English summer.

The standard of play was variable but the atmosphere was tranquil and except for the presence of a peak-capped officer one could have been anywhere. Occasionally visiting cricket teams brought their wives or girlfriends. I remember a number of us objected to this, as we did to officers' families parading on the field. In the presence of women and children treating the place like Hyde Park, it was hard to remember that we were prisoners.

Just as the cricket captain was in our ward, so too was the bowls captain. This game still remains a mystery to me, but I much enjoyed watching overweight middle-aged men join forces with the young, fitter inmates, to pull the heavy roller over the green.

The sight, too, of men in shorts, carrying radios in one hand and a wood in the other, was equally memorable. Dozens of inmates partook of this mystery to the evident enjoyment of all. Bowls in the foreground, cricket in the middle-distance and runners round the perimeter of the field belied the nature of our institution. The sight and sound of so much activity diluted the effect of separation and lack of freedom. Paradoxically, too, these traditional pastimes reinforced the profundity of our bondage and loneliness.

For me, an ex-schoolmaster and sports master, the experience was all too like a busman's holiday. The playing field became that of my school. The players were beloved pupils and team teas seemed unnatural because my wife was not serving them. I think to any schoolmaster the summer term is the most enjoyable of the year. Leyhill was no substitute school but it reminded me daily of the life I had lost.

In May one of the officers offered to supervise a rambling club for the over-forties. He volunteered his services and for that must be given credit. I did not join this group because by the time it was formed I knew I had got parole and did not want to take up the place of another, less fortunate inmate. Outings were to be monthly affairs. The first trip was an unqualified success – I think the hiking was rather less strenuous than I had been used to on Dartmoor, but the men who went certainly enjoyed themselves. And it is worth noting that the kitchen boss, Mr Ryan, ensured that the group was well provisioned. In fact, it was over-provisioned and I enjoyed, among other things, large quantities of jam which remained after the first walk.

The tennis courts, too, were well used and as much care was taken in preparing them as in making sure the bowling green was properly rolled and the cricket square in good trim. Several of the estate's inmates seemed to have full-time jobs in cutting and rolling the acres of grass. And there was no shortage of specialist equipment. Expensive grass-cutters and lawn-mowers abounded. Strimmers whirred daily and the smell of new-mown grass combined with the fragrance of early blossom to cause all but the hardest hearts to soften in the bitter–sweet joy which is early summer in England. It was the 'Oh to be in England, now that April's here' syndrome and it made imprisonment very hard. It came as no surprise to me that closed prisons became more and more explosive during the summer months. And the cause is probably less to do with heat and overcrowding than with the renewed hope we all feel in summer; to convicts this renewal of aspirations is a cruel lie unless, like me, they have imminent release to look forward to.

For those who were less keen on outdoor pursuits, table-tennis, darts and snooker served them well. Constantly there were competitions for the beloved tobacco or money prizes. Even Scrabble became an inter-ward sport. Those with intellectual pretensions participated in the Debating Society meetings but the motions for debate were so dull that I forwent the pleasure of reasoned argument. I joined the chess club and played in three matches – only one of which did I enjoy.

Our opponents were students from Bristol University. It seemed to be my lot to play against a monosyllabic, unshaven physicist who always thrashed me. I hated the thrashing but liked even less his loutishness. His only conversation seemed to be to boast of criminal damage and to try to impress us. There was, though, one glorious occasion when I played against a boy and a girl. He was a history undergraduate and she was reading English. We spent several happy hours discussing the poets of the six-teenth and seventeenth centuries and the Norman occupation of Sicily. It transpired that the young man knew several former colleagues of mine and that one of his best friends at public school had been Jamie's best friend at preparatory school. I loved this evening, for it was the only time in prison when I completely forgot that I was in jail. That I won my matches was an added bonus but entirely irrelevant. I was just relieved to know that I could still conduct a civilised conversation and that there were still people in the world who punctuated their syntax without the word 'fuck' or the sound of farting. The only tricky moment occurred when the young man asked me what I was in for. I refused to tell him at first; he had committed the unpardonable sin of asking the unaskable question. However, when his girl-friend left us I did tell him. It stopped the conversation stone dead. Later that evening, he was to tell me he was thinking of becoming a priest; presumptuously, I advised him to make sure of his motives. It struck me that he was of the 'shining light' brigade, who have the potential for doing as much harm as good.

On the strength of that encounter I eagerly awaited the next match. Sadly, my new-found friends were absent and I was, again, at the mercy of the uncivilised physicist.

Of the other societies in prison I know little. The Leyhill Amateur Dramatic Society (LADS) mounted two very good productions while I was there and woodworkers and bird fanciers followed their separate activities with a will. Even amateur gardeners were catered for in that invitations to apply for an allotment were extended to us in spring. Most takers were Asian but the digging and delving, planting and pruning were followed with a frenzy truly English.

But my delight on a Monday night was to make soft toys. It came about by a happy accident. A Welshman, nicknamed 'Spock' for reasons unknown to me, came to my cube one evening for 'tiffin'. The word was one I had introduced to the prison as part of my eccentricity; we used the word loosely, to mean an informal meal, afternoon tea or any organised meal. He arrived on this occasion bearing an impressive pink-and-blue elephant. He asserted that he had made it himself. So impressed was I that I reasoned that if he could make elephants I might be able to make smaller animals. The idea seemed very appealing, for, at that moment, I resolved to make a soft toy for every girl pupil who had written regularly to me in prison. I did not want to work alone, so I recruited Trevor into the scheme.

The two of us enrolled with the soft-toymaking class, but had to wait two or three weeks before being taken on officially. My problem what that at that stage I had only six weeks to go before my release and I had set myself the task of making twelve toys. We were allowed to transfer £10 per term from private cash for the purchase of materials and once we were on the class we received a grant of £6. No official tuition could be given until we were officially enrolled. In the event, the charming lady who ran the class so skilfully and tactfully helped us before we were fully paid-up members of her group.

I had resolved to tell none of my family and friends about the project in case I failed to deliver the cuddly objects of my attention. In fact, I did tell Tim the secret at one visit as a means of cheering him up and of letting him and only him into a secret.

Trevor, who turned out to be a remarkably skilful seamstress chose to make a koala bear while I undertook a polar bear in white and pink. Progress was made and despite much ribbing from my ward-mates – many of whom had made soft toys in the past at other prisons – the time came to stuff my beast. (Eventually I persuaded the class that 'season' was a more dignified word than 'stuff' and this refinement was universally adopted.) Sadly, my polar bear had all the appearance of a polar rat after I had seasoned it and I was rather disappointed. Trev's koala, though, was a magnificent beast and I resolved to try to make one. My first effort was sufficiently encouraging for me to decide to make another eleven, which I duly did. All my spare time, apart from the dail run and read of the newspapers, was now devoted to sewing. Fewer things gave me greater pleasure than sitting in my cube after my run and bath, taking afternoon tea with Trevor while we listened to Radio 3 and sewed with all the concentration of Tennyson's orphaned girl. We used the 'mail-bag stitch' for the general sewing and the 'ladder stitch' for closing up.

In the last six weeks of my sentence I made twelve koala bears, one polar bear, two seals – for Tim – and four mice, three of which were blind as my cash allowance would not run to my buying the eyes. Trevor made koalas, kangaroos, badgers, Care Bears and dogs. How I envied him his skill. At every visit his granddaughter would commandeer the next toy he had made. My problem was that I was stock-piling these fluffy delights at such a rate that I would be unable to take them all out with me upon my release. Or rather, I did not wish to take them out with me as I had resolved to leave prison as I had entered it – in the clothes I stood up in.

Thus the time came to tell Jen to prepare to take out a batch of toys. She seemed impressed by my handiwork, for when she collected them she commented, 'They're not bad.' And that was praise indeed from her! Unfortunately there was an administrative slip-up at the last moment, which meant I had to bring the final consignment out with me on my final morning, so I did not quite leave prison as I had entered it. The countless hours of sewing paid off; all the girls who received a toy expressed as much delight as surprise and the anticipated mirth at the headmaster sewing gave me real joy.

So it was, then, as time went by, that I entered a routine of activity which did ensure the fruitful passage of time, so that June came with reasonable speed and with it the longed-for release.

It would be hard to imagine a more constructive timetable of events than there was at Leyhill and yet the existence of the clubs and societies in another sense did nothing to alleviate the stress of prison. I suppose this was because everything one did was done 'with permission' – there was no freedom, for cons organised very little and even where societies were controlled by inmates the control was, inevitably, more notional than real. And one could as easily fall foul of the authorities by participating as by not, as I shall show.

I discuss illegal activities and entertainments in another chapter. For the moment I will leave recreation at Leyhill with the final thought that provision for constructive activity was plentiful there. Not even the most churlish would deny that we were well catered for and even if, as seemed often to be the case, the authorities tolerated rather than encouraged the activities, there was ample opportunity to learn new skills or indulge in rusty pastimes.

# 12

# A POLICY OF HUMILIATION

*The object of punishment is, prevention from evil; it can never be
made impulsive to good.*

Horace Mann, *Lectures and Reports on Education*

The object of prison is punishment; it follows that those imprisoned are prevented from evil. Or does it follow? Assuredly
those in prison, unless they escape, are prevented from offending
in the outside world, but it does not prevent them from misbehaving, from being evil, in prison. If an inmate breaks the rules he is
punished. Punishment for the transgression breeds resentment
which causes him to reoffend and to be repunished. This absurd
cycle of events raises the question of the nature of imprisonment
as a punishment. Is the prisoner sent to prison as a punishment or
to be punished? If it is the second, then certainly one can claim
that the system of internal sanctions helps greatly in the pursuit of
the aim. If, on the other hand, the act of sending someone to
prison is the final punishment then the nature of prison discipline
runs in the face of the absolute aim because even the best-
behaved prisoner is subjected to further punishment once he is
inside.

Loss of liberty is a terrible burden. The burden is sometimes
made intolerable because it is, necessarily, accompanied by a loss
of individuality. A prisoner ceases to be a person; he becomes a
number. This loss of individuality – a substantial extinction of
personality – means a loss of dignity. Once an individual's dignity
is lost he is nearly destroyed. Humiliation and deprivation of
all kinds have commonly been tools of the torturer. Taken to
extremes they result in the complete disintegration of the individual. There is little difference between this absolute state and
that which pertains in English prisons. The difference is a matter
of degree not of kind.

Loss of liberty means loss of choice. Choice is the essence of
democracy. Prisons offer no choice for inmates; they are, hence,

totalitarian institutions. I have never been in an environment where such absolute control by one group of human beings has been exercised over another. The situation is made worse when one remembers that the officers in authority are largely semi-literate members of what used to be called the 'lower orders'. They are, in short, the very last people who should exercise absolute control over other human beings.

If the function of prison is the temporary prevention of evil, then, in the main, it works. If prison's object is to deter offenders from committing further crime upon release then it fails absolutely. Reasons for this are many and complex and I wish to examine some in a later chapter. Here I am concerned to report the nature of the prison experience in the light of prison discipline, to demonstrate the 'truth' of some of the above remarks.

One accepts that prisoners have been found guilty of an offence and for the sake of my reporting I will concede that they were appropriately sent to prison. (In reality my concession is an absurdity.) Let us further assume that being sent to prison is the punishment; one is not being sent there to be punished. So far, then, a twofold purpose is achieved. The prisoner is losing his liberty for breaking the law and appalled society is being avenged and protected. So far so good. But now the problems occur. A method has to be developed which feeds, houses, occupies and generally looks after tens of thousands of men and women – some of whom are very dangerous.

Just like the armed services or schools, prisons have to have routines. So one accepts that meal-times, bath-times, recreation periods and so on have to be regimented. Security has to be maintained and reasonable levels of sanitation and health reached. So far so bad, for in our regimentation no heed is paid to the individual demands of thousands of very different people. In the army one needs a single fighting force with each individual pulling in the same direction to achieve a common goal. The same applies in schools or police forces or fire brigades or cricket teams. Prison populations are heterogeneous. The regimentation is bound to cause problems, even for the most co-operative inmate.

Let us go back to the beginning. A man or woman is found guilty and sent to prison. He or she is the one to be punished. In reality his or her family, friends and acquaintances are all adversely affected. It could, of course, be argued that prisoners should have thought of that before they committed their offence, but this consolation is a bleak one for the innocent inmate. It is bleak even for the guilty whose imprisonment might be argued to be inappropriate, unreasonable or downright unjust. I think it is far more striking to state that the punishment is not being *in* prison but being *out* of home and society. Yet for the time being let us consider the going to prison. What does it seem to mean?

Well, the going is the punishment. It entails a loss of liberty, loved ones and livelihood. Loss of liberty takes away all freedom of choice and movement. The physical restriction for those brought up in a western democracy is initially appalling. It manifests itself in a thousand random ways. The inmate becomes aware of the lack of daily noises – motor cars, dogs barking, trains, children's voices, washing machines, telephones, letters dropping through the mail box, running water, female voices. He becomes conscious of visual monotony. He does not see grass, multi-coloured clothing, friendly faces, shops, buses, roads, pubs, policemen, children, animals, trees, churches, houses, traffic signs. His tastebuds forget home-cooking, alcohol, butter, coffee, chocolate, his wife's lipstick, and his sense of smell adjusts to the loss. And even if some of the commodities are available, their availability is irregular and random – depending upon the state of the prisoner's weekly finances. The nose loses some scents and picks up strange stenches – human waste, sweating feet, institutional disinfectant, mass cooking and the bodily odours which accumulate before the weekly bath.

All the above would be bad enough if the inmate were free to move around the prison at will and converse with the other inmates. But the experience of being banged up for twenty-three hours a day compounds the misery. Even the decision about when to use the lavatory is decided by the authorities, as is the time you will eat, sleep, rise, dress, bath, receive letters, post your weekly letter, exercise, associate once weekly with other prisoners. Thus every decision, however insignificant, is made for you. The denigration is complete and so far I have ignored the pain of separation from your loved ones.

This loss of loved ones is, of course, the hardest thing to bear. To someone who has been happily married for twenty years, as I had been, the stress is great. It is not initially the loss of sexual activity which is hard. That deprivation, that unnatural situation, that denial of a God-given sacrament, is bearable to begin with, but the custom of sleeping by oneself has to be relearned. The ritual in every family of the goodnight kiss for one's children, for example, has gone. It is as if one had no family. Until the incarceration the 'man' of the family has had a responsibility which has given his life some purpose. This final loss of a labour of love completes the process of individual destruction. The prisoner, in effect, is dead to the world. I speak elsewhere of the effect on one's family and friends.

To many, being sentenced to prison automatically means a loss of livelihood. The dignity of labour is gone. The purpose of that labour was to provide for one's family. At a stroke, though, not only is the ability to provide for a family gone but the family is gone and the freedom to make temporary plans to help one's family to survive is also gone. There are no phones. In Exeter Prison I was allowed two letters a week. Their content was censored so even the uninhibited expression of deep and private sentiments was taken away from all but the boldest. It is as if the prisoner is not allowed to write – and hence think – thoughts of love to his wife and family. As for writing about business or finances, that is forbidden by prison rules. I was told at Leyhill that I could receive a visit from my accountant but that we were not allowed to discuss financial matters. But over and above all these deprivations, it is the inability regularly and necessarily to communicate that I found the hardest. One is not only at the mercy of a totalitarian regime, but that regime to all intents and purposes holds the prisoner *incommunicado*.

I do not know what the man-in-the-street understands by the expression 'He's been sent to prison.' I suspect he does not even think about what it means. He may have some vague notion that the prisoner's family will suffer from the separation and that there will be financial hardship. I daresay that he will not have the wildest notion that the man in prison has ceased to exist as anything except an automaton at the mercy of an arbitrary system run by those who have no notion whatever of what the experience is like for those who receive it. One wonders if the First World War would have been conducted differently if Field Marshal Haig had manned a rifle in the trenches on the Somme or at Ypres.

# A Policy of Humiliation

I have sought to show that the loss of liberty, loved ones and livelihood is made more acute by the indignities of the daily routine and essentially by the inability to communicate with the outside world in anything except the most superficial way. The total effect is one of degradation and humiliation. And even the few privileges a prisoner is granted are offered in a way the effect of which is precisely the opposite to the one intended.

It is regarded as necessary for the prisoner to receive visits. The strict prison rule is that each inmate is entitled to one half-hour visit every twenty-eight days. In practice the visits are often longer but not more frequent, except in, for example, open prisons, when a 'privileged visit' every fourteen days is allowed. Thus, under the most liberal parts of our system one is allowed three visitors every fortnight. One can understand that chaos would be the result of daily visits – the proper lot of remand prisoners – for the entire population, but the notion that it is a privilege for one's *innocent* family to see their husband or wife, mother or father, twice a month is risible. It would be made more bearable if the visits were private. Instead, and of course necessarily, an artificial conversation is held between people under stress in a crowded and noisy room in which uniformed guards gaze alike on prisoner and family. I am not saying the system can easily be improved; I am merely defining the experience and would invite the reader to imagine seeing his or her spouse and children once a month for two hours in the presence of scores of strangers and a few uniformed warders.

Visits are, perhaps, the most exciting things to look forward to in prison apart from one's release day. In practice they are the most terrible disappointments and cause several days of depression after they have occurred. So strongly is this the case that many inmates prefer to have no visits – and no letters for that matter – and both my wife and I enjoyed the loss of privileged visits which I experienced from March to May after I had been caught smuggling. Note that I include my wife in this sentiment. The visits were as stressful to her as they were to me.

Thus the attempt to make the lot of the inmate more bearable results in a typically unsatisfactory English compromise. Strict application of the rules would permit a prisoner to see – not touch and certainly not make love to – his loved ones for a total of less than seven hours in a year. About sixty seconds a day. Those with long sentences would see their loved ones for the equivalent of one day every four years. The strains on relationships are acute and many marriages end because of a prison sentence. Divorce is traumatic at the best of times; to the deserted automaton languishing in a prison cell for months, let alone years, the effect is catastrophic because, despite all deprivations, the prisoner can be sustained by looking forward to release and reunion with his loved ones. If that hope goes then life itself becomes full of sound and fury signifying nothing. And prison ruins many marriages. Does this stark fact ever strike the mythical man in the Clapham omnibus or the judge or the prison officer?

If visits, then, are the monthly or fortnightly highlight of the convict's life, and I have expressed reservations about that, then what constitutes the alleviation of the daily round? (I ignore the necessity of occupying one's time, which varies from prison to prison: in Exeter there was virtually no work for anyone; in Leyhill all prisoners worked.) Here I am still concerned with the cosmetic attempts to retain some normality in the lot of the unfortunate inmate.

Letters punctuate the periods between these visits. All incoming mail is censored, as is outgoing mail. As I have described, at Exeter one issue (second-class) letter was given out weekly and one could buy a first-class one from the canteen. There was a limit to the number of incoming letters one could receive, though over the Christmas period it was not applied to me. At Leyhill one could send out six letters per week and receive any number. In fact I received on average thirteen letters per week for every week I was in custody. This number excludes 'special' letters to solicitors, probation officers and certain other categories. There were two problems which caused anguish among letter-writers.

The first was that because the telephone and the general decline of literacy had caused the art of letter-writing to sink to a trivial pursuit it was very difficult for the average prisoner to express his sentiments cogently and within the allotted space. Even I found it hard to say precisely what I wanted to and I had the advantage of having spent the whole of my professional life dealing with language and literature. The second problem was that there were often lengthy delays between letters so that information was frequently out-of-date when the letter was received. Occasionally an injudicious or more often carelessly expressed phrase would cause great upset. One received a letter which caused concern. One misinterpreted the offending phrase and wrote a reply accordingly. A week might elapse between the reception of the letter and one's reply being received. Further time would pass before the reply to the reply was delivered, by which time the prisoner would be frantic with worry about something that his wife or whoever had long forgotten. In the outside world such misunderstandings would probably not occur and if they did a quick phone call would put matters right. I lost count of the number of times men went through agonies of this sort. In extreme circumstances, it would sometimes be possible to have an emergency phone call, but the success or not of the request depended entirely upon the whim of the officer. More often than not 'stiffs' were despatched. These were smuggled letters which were sent out on visits.

Thus, again, the system of written communication was sometimes a source of great stress. And let me hasten to say that what appears, perhaps, to be trivial when one is free becomes grossly significant to the hapless, helpless inmate. So the two devices – visits and letters – which are part of the penal system in this country combine to cause as many problems as they are designed to prevent.

The third official medium of communication at Leyhill was a card payphone. Once more the provision of this exciting facility was a source of more trouble than peace. I ignore, for the moment, the difficulty of apportioning time to each call and of the prisoners' attempts to defraud British Telecom by trying to cheat the machine. Naturally, a limit was put on the number of cards one could have at a time, and very quickly they became a source of currency anyway. The discontent stemmed from the inequality of the system. I, whose home was near Land's End, had the same £2 card as the man who lived ten miles from the prison. Arguably my need to phone home was made more acute by the greater distance which separated my wife from me. Reverse-charge calls were not allowed any more than were operator calls or the use of the phone book.

The kindergarten mentality existed here as well as elsewhere and the phone became as much a 'wind-up' as visits and letters. One phone for over three hundred men was available for short periods daily. If every man had wanted to phone for his allotted ten minutes he would have been able to use it about once every three weeks. Inevitably the selfish motive came to the fore. Men argued that the phone was there for them. Thus they were entitled to use it willy-nilly and would damn well do so by hook or by crook. This attitude will find few defenders but it indicates what, to me, was the root cause of the major dissatisfaction in prison.

I can best illustrate my point by going on to the next device aimed at improving the inmates' lot – the prison canteen. This is the shop at which certain articles can be purchased from earnings and fewer articles from private cash.

All inmates, whether they work or not, are paid. In Exeter I received £1.19 per week. At Leyhill, for working a seven-day week, I was paid £2.65. At Exeter I was not allowed to buy toiletries from private cash. At Leyhill toiletries could be purchased or brought in by visitors – though this last 'privilege' was nearly taken away by the Governor. (Note then that it is a privilege to receive soap and toothpaste from a visitor.) Certainly tobacco could not be bought from private cash but had to be bought from earnings, as did letters, stamps, fruit, confectionery – in fact, all the things which were essential. The exceptions were newspapers, a radio and radio batteries.

In the context of the many stresses which I have outlined above, it might be reasonable to assume that prisoners should be allowed to smoke. After all, at the moment I am arguing that the act of sending a person to prison is the punishment. He is not going there to be punished. And the deprivations and strains I have described are compounded with the loss of the three Ls – liberty, loved ones and livelihood. Perhaps the risk of drunkenness rightly outlaws alcohol – although conduct in the Officers' Mess at Leyhill would suggest that inebriation was a sacred rite. So the man who is accustomed to unwind at the end of a day with a whisky cannot have that. But he is allowed to smoke. Prison regulations allow him two and a half ounces of tobacco in his possession at any one time. I am a pipe smoker and do not know how this amount compares with tailor-made cigarettes or with the amount of rolling tobacco an 'average' smoker would consume in his civilian life. As for me, I found that it was a very generous ration when I came to roll my own cigarettes, *but only because I never had that amount legitimately.*

# A Policy of Humiliation

Look at the economics. One ounce of tobacco costs, say, £2.10. Two and a half ounces cost £5.25. Add to that the cost of matches and cigarette papers, and the total approaches £6. Thus, by right, a prisoner is entitled to £6 worth of smoking materials. He is paid a third of that sum. He is allowed to buy a letter or five per week – another 90p. And to someone receiving over a dozen letters a week he will wish to buy the maximum number of letters. He will wish to buy birthday cards for his family – provided he can give the three weeks' notice in advance to the authorities and sign the silly registers. He will wish to buy milk for his tea, for at Leyhill tea and sugar rations were distributed. In effect, each prisoner received a small quantity of tea about once a month. The authorities provide tea-making and some cooking facilities. It is assumed they are there to be used and it follows that their use depends upon the prisoners' ability to acquire the necessary ingredients for use. Say another 50p per week.

We now have a picture which Mr Micawber would deplore. Income £2 per week. Expenditure £7 per week. Something has to give. Yet there is nothing in our expenditure list which smacks of the profligate. It is not unreasonable to wish to reply to letters or to brew a cup of tea. It is far from unreasonable to expect the man who has smoked for thirty years to wish to continue to do so. After all, the narcotic effect of nicotine is needed more in prison than elsewhere, particularly when the twin delights of alcohol and sex are denied. But the system succeeds in making sure that the inmate is always short of tobacco at the same time as it taunts him with the legality of having far more than he can afford.

We are back at the root cause of dissatisfaction in prison. It is that the system in theory allows many privileges but in practice ensures that these privileges cannot be attained by the prisoner however hard he tries. If he is allowed two and a half ounces per week why is he not paid enough to buy them? Why should he decide between the craving for tobacco – shared by many a judge and jury – and whether or not he can afford to write to his wife or buy half a pound of tea? He has not been sentenced to give up smoking. And remember, I am still speaking of the act of being imprisoned as the punishment. Does it not now appear that this fact of incarceration, this going to prison 'as a punishment', is in reality going to prison 'to be punished'? I would regard it as semantic hair-splitting to say that if going to prison entails such conditions then such conditions are part and parcel of the going 'as a punishment'. I have amply demonstrated above that the deprivation would be less severe if each prisoner were allowed to have his full allocation of daily necessities. I cannot for the life of me understand why visitors cannot bring stamps, tobacco and other necessities to the prisoner or why he cannot buy them out of private cash.

I suppose it will be said that such generosity – I use the word ironically – will encourage the black market and that anyway prisons should not be 'too comfortable'. If, after all I have said, this view pertains then I despair of humanity, and the prison system is doomed to perpetual strife. Even without these daily stresses the experience of prison is, as I have tried to show, hellish. Besides which, if every man had his basic needs of tobacco and so on supplied, there would be no need of a black market.

But the simple alleviation of the daily scratching about for a dog-end – and on a number of occasions I myself picked up cigarette ends from the floor of the dining room as I swept it – will not easily be relieved in this country. We prefer to say 'no' rather than think of why we should say 'no'. We love what Bernard Levin calls the 'single-issue fanatic' who is trying to deprive us of a pleasure and of our right to choose. It does not matter if it is the anti-smoking lobby who presume to decide our physical condition or Mrs Whitehouse who dares to censor our television viewing. In prison this historical legacy rules supreme.

The ones who win are those who are tougher, cleverer, braver and who control the illegal supplies of tobacco, drugs, alcohol. I will come to them later.

So far I have suggested that many of the pleasures of prison turn, because of the system, into pain. Visits, letters, canteen, telephone, all can cause as much stress as they are designed to relieve. But what of the luxury of Home Leave?

Certain categories of prisoner are entitled to the privilege of Home Leave if they are serving a determinate sentence of about two years or more. I did not so qualify, of course. There is an institution known as pre-parole Home Leave and another which grants Home Leave to prisoners who have passed their Parole Eligibility Date. Sometimes the leave is for a weekend; sometimes it is for a week. However, to qualify for this leave an inmate has to have behaved himself and to have saved £2 from earnings. There are other stipulations relating, for example, to suitable home circumstances.

The economic survey which I have outlined above becomes even worse for an inmate hoping for Home Leave. If he has to save £2 before he can be considered then necessarily he has to forgo either tobacco and/or letters and/or tea, and so on. If he is an addicted smoker then he will almost certainly not be able to give up the habit at a stroke. Therefore he will get into debt in order to make the saving which will grant him the vital fillip of Home Leave. It is to be assumed that Home Leave, like mail and visits, is designed to maintain his contact with his family and the outside world; it is an aid to readjustment. However, as with all else in prison, the rules – at least at Leyhill – collude to ensure that it is as difficult as may be to qualify. If he is to qualify financially, the prisoner must suffer stress which ensures that the object of relief from stress which a Home Visit should give is not freely obtained.

In any case, it seems to me that the Home Leave system is an absurdity. If a man who is serving, say, a nine-year sentence fails to be granted parole he has to wait three years for Home Leave. A man similarly denied who is serving thirty months has to wait ten months. A man with a twelve-month sentence is released after six or eight months. Does it follow, then, that there is a proportional relationship between length of sentence and the need to see one's family and the outside world? Is there an automatic mental adjuster which persuades a nine-year-termer that he can survive without going home for three years but that a thirty-monther needs to see his family in under a year? It is absurd. The system is, of course, based upon incentives. The more serious the crime the longer the incarceration. However, it is hard, as it is in many spheres of life, to accept the position at which the line is drawn.

Matters are even worse when one considers the disparity in sentencing policy.

I have sought above to indicate that the experience of going to prison as a punishment turns into an experience where every day suggests that one is there to be punished. I have sought to show the distinction to be more than semantic and to suggest that even the 'carrots' which are dangled before the prisoner's eyes disguise unexpected sticks.

The inmate, then, is kept short of tobacco and other necessities. He earns less than he is permitted to buy and even being allowed home according to the rules deliberately causes hardship, and hence resentment. The process is self-defeating and does accord with what seems to be a deliberate policy of denigration and humiliation. The policy is not, as Horace Mann wrote in 1845, 'impulsive to good'. This is so because even the most co-operative and law-abiding inmate is subjected to these pressures, which are designed to make his lot harsher than it already is.

# 13

# BREAKING THE RULES

*Necessity hath no law.*

Oliver Cromwell, Speech to Parliament, 1654

By now it will be clear that the superficial notion (if any) about prison that is held by the layman is not quite the simple 'loss of liberty' that he may envisage. When the fact of tobacco shortage is added to the frustration of inadequate communication with the outside world and to the strictures of the puritan ethic it is soon clear that the prison experience must cause resentment. Rarely did I find convicted felons resentful about the fact of being in prison. They resented the unnecessary additional burdens that were added to their already stressful lot. It soon became obvious that the surest way to survive was to tackle these problems of inadequate supplies head on. And I was amazed and awed by the ingenuity with which men thwarted the authorities. Each day was a struggle to overcome and to survive into the next.

The legitimate ways in which one could ensure an adequate supply of tobacco depended upon selfishness and an oriental skill in bartering. I found it took me some time to learn to say 'no' to requests for tobacco unless I knew that the favour would be reciprocated. There was one lame man in my ward at Leyhill who was a past master at the art of dunning anything. He played upon the fact that he was lame, unable to work and had commensurately low pay. However, after he owed me about half an ounce of tobacco, great quantities of tea, sugar and milk and I discovered that he had overflowing supplies of all, I ceased to share my goods. Indeed, I was repaid only when I threatened to expose his stocks to the rest of the ward.

Bartering, though, was the *modus vivendi* of all inmates. I was lucky in that I worked in the kitchen and received certain weekly perks which I could use for exchange. I also learned how to steal extra cakes and occasionally fresh mushrooms and other goodies. It seemed the most natural thing in the world to help oneself to anything left lying around. A friend and fellow kitchen worker once remarked that 'Prison's turning you into a thief, Mike.' I remember grinning happily in reply. On another occasion a colleague managed to steal a catering tin of coffee while bringing stores from the storehouse to the kitchen under supervision. He lived most comfortably for a long while thereafter and kindly shared his booty with me.

Legitimately, though, I could always guarantee tobacco and letters – the two most vital commodities as far as I was concerned – by swapping yoghurts or milk or fresh fruit with other inmates. And it was not only goods which were bartered. Services were also paid for. Thus, for example, men who were skilled artists would produce wonderfully painted birthday cards for payment in tobacco. The skilled soft-toymakers would run up dogs and bears and elephants for generous quantities of tobacco. Those who could model in matchsticks or wood made jewel cases and other objects for payment. I had no skills until the end of my stay, by which time I had mastered the art of making toys and made a koala bear for a friend who did not offer payment (nor did I want payment from him). My most regularly used service was that of letter-writer and legal adviser to many men, and even though it often took several hours to prepare a man's appeal or Home Office petition I never sought payment. I hasten to add that this was not merely out of a feeling of altruism. I was somewhat green to the ways of the prison and by the time I was 'street-wise' I had no need to supplement my supplies in this way. Besides which I was genuinely angry about what many of the men had to endure under our system of so-called justice and wanted to do all I could to help them, because my lot was much more palatable.

In prison the line between the illegitimate and the legitimate becomes very blurred. It is for this reason that I think I will classify the bartering of prison property as legitimate. Thus, for example, one could ensure a well-laundered supply of new clothes by paying for the services of an inmate who worked in the laundry. Illegal phone calls could be made if one knew the right orderlies and was prepared to grease their palm.

In fact, a thriving economy existed legitimately within Leyhill, and I am sure it did at Exeter but I was there for too short a time to discover it. Even so, I managed to receive large supplies of tobacco via remand prisoners while I was there. Psychologically this undercurrent of wheeling and dealing was an excellent boost to morale, even though I am certain the authorities knew far more about what was going on than they revealed. But they did not know everything despite the system of informers which prevailed. But I will talk about the 'grasses' later.

It was also possible to supplement one's wages by selling goods on the black market. This was against regulations, of course, but could not be stopped. Thus the non-smokers would sometimes use their wages to buy tobacco for resale. From what I said earlier it will be readily apparent that non-smokers were the most affluent members of the community. It was possible to be paid £10 in private cash for three ounces of tobacco – retail price less than £7. At peak times the price went up. And it was very easy to increase one's stocks to make quite a healthy profit. For example, it was a common occurrence to lend out tobacco at a high rate of interest. Half an ounce of tobacco lent out for a week would bring back three-quarters of an ounce. Often it was the case that those saving for Home Leave, for instance, had *faute de mieux* to borrow in this way. The problems of repayment, given the financial status of inmates which I have described above, are obvious. It is worth repeating that this risky system of bartering or borrowing would have been wiped out at a stroke if the authorities had allowed each man to have the maximum amount of tobacco which regulations prescribed.

When I was first in Leyhill, tobacco was still a major currency. Within a few short weeks it was the possession of cannabis resin which ruled supreme. In fact it is probably fairer to say that tobacco was the currency for buying drugs which then became the real currency. When the telephone was installed, illegal phone cards were added to the currency. Thus there were four major commodities with which to ensure a comfortable life. The fourth, which I have not yet mentioned, was cash itself. Leyhill swam in money. Many is the time I saw £50 notes and I know of several men who regularly sent out several hundred pounds on visits.

I have already suggested that the system itself encouraged irregular behaviour. On the one hand, the deliberate policy of keeping men short of essential items which they could legitimately possess encouraged them to find other means of acquiring them. On the other hand the system of degradation and humiliation channelled men into covert activity as a way of maintaining an individuality and self-respect which the system was doing all it could to erase. But there was another motive in my case. I was indescribably bored in prison and wanted to concentrate all my energies into beating the system. At first this was a game which I played for fun and in relatively simple ways.

For example, I was always able to smuggle four ounces of tobacco and twenty tailor-made cigarettes from a visit. The system was that one declared to the officer on duty what was in one's possession before a visit. This inventory he entered on a form. If the inmate was taking tobacco into a visit the amount was estimated and entered on the sheet. During the visit it was a simple matter of stuffing the contraband into one's underpants in such a way that the cursory body-search we all endured at the end of each visit revealed nothing. There was always a risk that the officer would find it, but that only added to the juvenile excitement. If, of course, one was given a full body-search, then all was lost. This happened to me, as I shall relate later.

Unfortunately, my early successes were accompanied by a naive boastfulness and generosity, so too many knew of my supplies. It took me several weeks to learn to operate on a 'need-to-know' basis; in the early days I assume all convicts were loyal to each other. Later I learned that our real enemies were the other cons. However, my happy game turned into a vendetta when I fell foul of the blatant injustice of the system. I record the fact in my diary on Saturday 1 February:

Sent Trev off early as he has a visit. Finished the cleaning on my own at 1.35 p.m. Went straight to the Small Business Course which starts at 1.30 p.m. At 1.40 p.m. a huge and – to quote Betjeman – 'large and most unfriendly rat' of a screw known as the Honey Monster 'nicked' the Rhodesian and me for missing the tally. There is a 1.30 p.m. tally but because we were both working late we should, apparently, have clocked in at the Unit Room. We have to see the Governor on Monday. This is bizarre because (a) no one told me of this procedure, (b) I was legitimately at work, and (c) I had been told by the Education Officer that during the course we could tally at the Education Centre.

Our absence delayed the whole prison and made people late for visits. I do seem to be doing well and to cap it all the person who can vouch for tallying in Education is away on leave. Knight, the kitchen screw, will not square it for us, saying, 'Only the officer who nicked you can get you off. Not even the Governor can.' Typical of this two-faced inadequate. So I see the headmaster on Monday – perhaps he'll expel me. To make matters worse the security screw was in the visiting room today searching everyone very thoroughly; one is usually given a cursory rub-down. I shall have to be careful tomorrow. . . . Got Lyn, the ex-copper, to frisk me thoroughly as I am practising for tomorrow. He frisked me twice and found nothing – so short of a full strip-search I should be all right tomorrow.

I conclude the entry for this day by writing:

Visit tomorrow, Hurray, hurrah!! As long as I can get tobacco. . . . I'm beginning to think less and less like me.

Indeed I was beginning to think like a criminal, or at least I was beginning – and I emphasise beginning, as I did not really regard the smuggling of tobacco as a cardinal sin – to change my lifelong outlook. At the time I did not even realise that my conspirators were breaking the law. Besides which, I argued, no one was being harmed and I shared my tobacco at this stage. In fact, I undertook no transaction in prison which resulted in any advantage for myself. On the one occasion when I tried to make a profit I came unstuck, as I shall duly record.

By the time I had seen the Deputy Governor on Monday morning, I had resolved to take the authorities on full tilt. The diary for Monday 3 February contains the following entry:

I collected my summons at 9 a.m. I appear before the Governor at 11 a.m. I am told many are on report including two who were caught smuggling tobacco on a visit. How very naughty of them! The procedure is as formal as the appearance in an outside court. One enters a plea of guilty or not guilty. Witnesses may be summoned by either side and we are allowed time in our ward to assemble our defence. I'll plead guilty but with mitigation. Knight reckons I will get a caution. . . . I was fined 50p today by the Deputy Governor – a slim, tall, rather supercilious long-distance runner called Chapman. My mitigation was ignored. My fine is generally regarded as heavy punishment for the offence. The Rhodesian went in before me and was fined 50p so my fine was a foregone conclusion. So you do extra work to let a pal get ready for his visit, you then go straight to a prison-run course and obey the tally instructions of the department which runs the course, you fail to get support from your departmental screw, you get punished. I have drawn my own conclusions from this example of prison discipline. . . .

I had not been intellectually prepared for the crass stupidity of the exercise of 'justice' in the prison. I would have accepted the fine, which because of my smuggling activities did not affect my supplies of necessities, had I been guilty of a deliberate offence. My 'crime' was that because I was a new boy and decided to listen to instructions I had fallen foul of the gap between the right and the left hand. I resented the punishment almost as much as I resented being in prison in the first place. I vowed all-out clandestine war. The authorities won – but in an unexpected way.

My earlier generosity with tobacco had given me the reputation of being a supplier. There was an occasion in February when the canteen was closed early because of snow. Thus the majority of the prison were unable to buy their weekly supplies. Within the space of an hour thirteen strangers had come to me wanting to buy tobacco on the black market. This worried me greatly and I denied having any. In fact I could, at that time, have dealt in about seven ounces. However, I was afraid that too much attention would come my way and I was planning two major coups.

I knew that keeping a daily diary was frowned on by the authorities. I had no intention of losing it and managed to smuggle completed volumes out of the prison – sometimes on my own visits; sometimes by using other prisoners' visitors. The method depended upon how 'hot' I was in any particular week. For some time I became very hot indeed, as I shall describe. Thus anything which would prevent the safe egress of my diaries was to be prevented.

But the second reason I was concerned to keep a low profile was because I was planning to smuggle a tape-recorder and a camera into the establishment. The second was so that I could have a unique photographic record of the inside of the prison. In fact, things became so hot for me eventually that the camera idea was abandoned. The tape-recorder plan, though, was a priority.

I had become, as I have described, extremely friendly with a ifer (the writer) who had served twenty-five years. I was keen to write the story of his life in prison and to hear his first-hand account of his crime and trial. He was a fascinating man of mystery. We hit upon the notion that if we could smuggle a tape-recorder and tapes into the prison he would talk for hours into the machine and I would have his talks typed up in readiness for me to turn into a book when I was released.

Everything went according to plan and after a couple of weeks of coded letters, detailed arrangements, etc. – none of which my wife knew about at the time, incidentally – the machine and three tapes 'arrived'. It was a major triumph and one which gave me overweening and unfounded confidence. By this time it was common knowledge in my ward that I was keeping a diary. I did not hide the fact from them because they often marched straight into my cube and saw me writing. When they asked what I was writing I told them. I still did not realise that the prison was full of inmates who were prepared to trade information with the authorities in the vain hope of a favourable parole report.

Sometimes during the course of these conversations, or when I spoke to my partner in my paper-thin cubicle, I had let slip the fact that I had a tape-recorder. Stupid boasting or carelessness – I do not to this day know which. The result was that a week after the tape-recorder had been brought into the prison my co-conspirator's room was searched. He was sent for and asked by the security officers if there was anything in his room which there should not have been; he knew from his long experience of prison life that the question's correct answer was already known by the authorities. He confessed to the tape-recorder, saying that it had been offered around the prison at Christmas time and that he had bought it to help him with his writings.

Unfortunately, we had not yet had time to find a permanent hiding place for it, so the authorities got it. But, quite brilliantly, in the act of handing the machine and two loose tapes over to them my partner managed to empty the full tape from the machine, palm it, hand it to the ward cleaner, who gave it to me. (When the search was made there was just the cleaner and me in the ward. All the other inmates were at work.) I sent the tape into hiding where it remained for several weeks. I found out later that it had been hidden in the Officers' Club and had finally gone out of the prison as official mail. This last act of emission cost me much tobacco but the tape is safe and sound with me now.

My partner was fined £1.00 for the offence. Despite several anxious days my part in the conspiracy was not proved and I got away scot-free. But I had lost an expensive machine, wasted several weeks' work and drawn attention to myself, and I feared that my major money-making gamble was at risk. My partner and I concluded that there was an informer at work and set about trying to find him. The problem was that once such a hunt started it was possible to see informers everywhere and we sought to avoid the hysteria of McCarthyism. One lesson I did learn was that I would never keep my diary in any one place for any length of time and thereafter it was hidden on a rotational basis in the cubicles of the few I could trust. At the same time I let it be known in the ears of my favourite informer that I was no longer writing one.

Round about this time I was sowing the seeds for what was potentially my greatest downfall, though I did not know it at the time. I was flush with the early success of the tape episode; I gloated that I was never out of tobacco while many of my former tormentors were constantly short of the stuff. I enjoyed smoking tailor-made cigarettes and the growing reputation I was having for my anti-authoritarian stance. Indeed, when I was fined for missing the tally a number of my early detractors suddenly became very friendly – it was as if I had won my spurs. What I could not see, of course, were the depths to which I, a former respected headmaster, was sinking. The cause of my going down was the system itself, which offered salvation only to those who were prepared to fight for their basic comforts. How much more difficult must it be, then, for those without my advantageous background and supportive family and large circle of friends?

I had become very friendly with a huge chap in the kitchen whose skills were many and various. He was doing a short sentence for motoring offences, had been a supremely highly trained soldier who seemed to have the pulse of the prison's underlife beating from his own heart. We trusted each other implicitly and decided to go into business. I claimed that I could arrange for a large quantity of tobacco to arrive at the prison if he would manage its collection and distribution. There were many ways of getting consignments of tobacco, alcohol, drugs and money into the place. One of the commonest was to arrange for a 'drop' to be made in a nearby quarry, from where the package would be collected after dark. I thought this method too chancy and crude. He decided that the best bet was to arrange for someone on the outside to be at a certain spot at a certain time; he, from inside the prison, would meet my supplier and there would be hand-to-hand exchange.

We discussed the theory countless times and decided that it would work if very few people were involved, if I had time to arrange a foolproof code with my outside contacts – he devised a simple substitution code for me – and if the plan did not operate to coincide with any of my visits. He had no visits by choice, so he could not implicate his family. I dared not tell my wife of this as she would have gone berserk with me; nonetheless I feared that if we were caught my visitors might quite innocently be brought into the picture. We planned and planned.

Both of us were interested in buying gold, which was often for sale in the prison. Men, short of money or tobacco, would sell rings or bracelets, even their gold-rimmed spectacles. Co-incidentally, there had come into the prison a man who claimed to be an erstwhile armed robber and current goldsmith. He was in my ward and because he was intelligent and articulate had gravitated towards me. He claimed to have passed A-level English Literature, a claim I doubted until, one night during a game of Scrabble, he quoted from Oscar Wilde's *De Profundis*. He had written a novel in prison, a copy of which he showed me. He was a keen bridge player, as was my huge friend, and the three of us quickly became trusting confidants.

One morning, my original partner came to me and asked if I was interested in buying a Rolex wristwatch. Its value was said to be about £900 but the seller wanted, I think, thirty ounces of tobacco. I agreed to the sale and instigated detailed enquiries. Because gold was involved, my partner Pete and I decided to involve Terry, our new-found and much trusted friend. Terry undertook the enquiries concerning the value and so on of the timepiece after Pete had received a detailed description. We even scoured the pages of *Exchange and Mart* to verify market prices.

The story was that the watch was at the women's prison nearby and would be brought in soon. Time went by and there was still no watch, and there was no way that I was going to part with tobacco or even arrange for its importation without seeing the goods. By this time Terry had offered to pay me £500 for the watch. Thus the picture was that the Rolex would be smuggled into Leyhill. I would part with thirty ounces of tobacco for it. Terry would pay me £500. So far so good. I stood to make a profit of over £450 from part of my consignment and the remaining thirty-four ounces of tobacco was already spoken for, according to Pete. The total deal was due to net me about £500. And there was a further delicious bonus. At no time would I see, let alone handle, either the tobacco, the watch or the money.

It was to work like this. I would arrange, by coded letter, for sixty-four ounces of tobacco to be brought to a prearranged spot by an outside contact. These would be handed direct to Pete. I would write a letter to arrive on a Thursday. At a visit the following Sunday I would arrange for final details of the place and time of the exchange to be passed on. I did not want to know these details until the Sunday. Thus I hoped to prevent any leaks at all. Pete would take the tobacco and pay the watch-seller – I did not know who he was and did not want to. Terry would receive the watch from this anonymous inmate and would send me £500 by an indirect route which I was to tell him at the last moment. Everything was going like clockwork but success depended upon total confidentiality. As far as I knew, Pete, Terry and I were the only ones in the know apart from the seller, and he knew only of Pete's involvement. My outside contact knew only me and would meet Pete briefly when the tobacco was handed over.

There was an added complication. We had decided to steal a large number of prison shirts for resale in London. The going price was about £25 per shirt. I had arranged to 'collect' twenty-five of these from a trusted laundry worker who would co-operate for a small payment. Pete was happy to pass the shirts out as the tobacco was handed in. The value of the total deal was now to be £1000 or thereabouts. I had no doubts about the trustworthiness of my three partners. Indeed, Pete was the only one to know of the shirts for I had to get his agreement to carry them over the wall to my contact. The laundry contact thought he was dealing just with me and Terry and knew nothing of the tobacco. Only Pete and I knew that the goods were to be personally handed over. The scheme was as foolproof as it could be.

It suddenly all went wrong.

# Breaking the Rules

First, the watch-supplier kept on stalling about the time at which he would deliver the watch. We suspected that we were being set up. At least, that was Terry's suspicion and he volunteered to make enquiries. I agreed that he could but told him not to involve me. I wanted to stay in the background, feeling that none would suspect me of improper conduct. I was, after all, a despised nonce and an ex-headmaster. I wrongly believed that these two facts would persuade the authorities and any nosey cons that I could not possibly be harbouring grudges and therefore be involved in illegal activity. The story came back that the watch belonged to a worker in the Administration Department at the women's prison and had been stolen from him. Alarm bells immediately rang. I could not believe that a humble pen-pusher would own a watch which had cost about £1500 or, if he or she did, that he or she would be stupid enough to bring it into prison.

We made further enquiries of the seller, who was eventually persuaded to say that the story was a fabrication and that he was only trying to get tobacco. It was pointed out to him that he had made a mistake and he was persuaded not to repeat his silly conduct. However, we still had the tobacco coming in and the shirts going out and decided not to cancel the remaining plans.

Three days before I was to receive final instructions from Pete about the hand-over I was informed by an inmate that a huge delivery of tobacco was to occur on a certain Monday. My heart, quite literally, started racing. I let the fellow talk on and gently probed him with questions. The result was that he told me in sufficient detail the operation of my own plan. He even knew things about aspects which I did not know and did not need to know. There had been an immense leak. I could not believe that Pete would inform against me and we both trusted Terry. The chap in the laundry knew only that I wanted shirts on a certain day and I knew him well enough to trust him completely. That left the disgruntled watch-seller.

I contacted Pete and told him what I had discovered. We decided to cancel the whole operation and lie low. I told the laundry worker that I no longer wanted the shirts but the big problem was to get a message to my outside contact. This would involve a phone call and it was not easy to set one up in the time available. (At this period there was no card-phone available to inmates.) I prepared a cryptic note to be read out over the phone.

Pete would arrange the call, through a channel that I knew not and did not want to know. Pete had promised to tell me how to use the phone once he was released. He was due out three months before me. The weakness of this was that now another con would be involved, but there was nothing for it but to take that risk. The final part of our cancellation programme was to send out some disinformation. Clearly the whole prison would know of the plan by now and that meant that the officers would as well. We laid a false scent with such success that for three days the security officers waited at a certain spot in the market gardens for our drop and got nothing but cold for their pains. I did not personally witness this but was told by inmates who worked in the gardens. The amount of contraband expected and the time of the drop coincided with my own disinformation.

The phone call was made and the whole operation cancelled. Several weeks of careful and accurate planning were wasted. The whole thing was a horrible anticlimax and, what was worse, there was a spotlight on me. Usually the drops were made in the nearby quarry or in the market garden. Our exchange was to occur at the opposite end of the prison among the officers' houses. We set about finding the leak.

Success came our way several weeks later and surprised us. The leak was Terry.

He was due on Home Leave for a week and had promised to deliver a number of messages to inmates' wives and friends. He left the prison armed with phone numbers which he said he would write on tissue paper and secrete before he went out. At the same time, he had promised, through his father-in-law, to arrange the purchase of a car for a fellow con who had given him his bank address as well as his home address and phone number.

To coincide with Terry's leave one inmate made a phone call home. If a prisoner did not receive visits he was entitled to a three-minute phone call instead. (This concession was removed when the card-phone was put in – another example of the meanness of the system.) The call home caused panic. Terry had contacted this man's family and asked for money for the car. He knew so much about the man on whose behalf he was calling that he nearly got away with it. Happily the man's mother was rather more canny and parted with nothing. But the man came to me in a panic. What the hell was Terry up to? After all, he was well liked and totally trusted. He seemed to be an old lag who would get into any amount of trouble just for the hell of it. He had lost remission for misbehaviour in prison; he was currently writing, with the authorities' permission, to a newspaper about his case. He was claiming to be innocent of certain charges. Or was he?

Pete and I decided to rifle through his belongings when he was on leave. We acquired the key to his locker and broke into it. Our search caused us real concern. The man was not in the least what he pretended. He was not married but was living with a girl. The photograph in his cube showing him in a Rolls-Royce turned out to be of the wedding of his sister. The mansion he owned in Oxfordshire turned out to be a small cottage owned by his parents. We did a great amount of 'digging' and tracked him down – I cannot say how – to a seedy flat behind Waterloo station. The gold shop he owned in the Ballspond Road, we discovered, did not exist. The web of lies stretched wider and wider. I wanted to look at his file.

If it seems fanciful to suggest that inmates can see others' files then all I can say is that it is possible. I knew of a man who knew of a man who would get the information I wanted. Again, for obvious reasons, I am not going to say how this happened, but the inside cover of Terry's file bore the words, 'Informer, use'. There it was in black and white. I spread the word.

Gradually it became apparent that Terry had left the prison having successfully conned dozens of men. He would have done me out of £500. He nearly got the same sum from the would-be car buyer. He left with the phone numbers and addresses of many other inmates. Some had given him money with which to buy contraband. The arrangement was to be that he would buy the stuff and drop it in the quarry on the day he went on Home Leave. I talked with the man who had agreed to collect the parcel, itself a risky operation. This chap, a young, crew-cut lad who was doing five years and who eventually absconded from Leyhill, went out to the dropping zone for three days in succession. After his third trip he came back with such a severe limp that I thought he had broken his ankle. He had fallen in the quarry and his leg swelled alarmingly. There was, of course, no parcel, and all the while we had been giving Terry the benefit of the doubt. At least, we had until his file entry had been seen.

A reception committee awaited him. He was such a plausible

conman that we thought he would try to talk his way out of trouble. He was going to receive rough justice. And in Leyhill that usually took the form of a battering with a PP9 battery contained in a sock. I was glad I was not him.

The prison buzzed with excitement and more and more people came to me with tales of his deception. I enjoyed being the clearing-house for information but strongly regretted the publicity I was getting. Some of the more experienced cons reckoned he would report back to the prison and ask to be shipped out to Bristol to be put on Rule 43. Plans were made at Leyhill to deal with him in Reception but it was reckoned that he would be closely guarded and that the best that could be done would be to pour scalding coffee on him. I have never seen such feral behaviour and it stemmed as much from the fact that cons were protecting the interests of their friends as from the fact that they, personally, had been conned. There was, after all, a certain honour among thieves.

Terry arrived back at the prison and duly demanded – it was his absolute right to do so – to be put on Rule 43 in Bristol. This was granted him, of course, and he went away unpunished by us. I learned later that a track was kept of his movements until his release, in May I think, and he was met from the prison and duly dealt with. Officers afterwards told us that he had done the same thing in other prisons and that he was known to be a conman. That he was an informer, too, was much appreciated by the authorities. I now knew why I had lost the tape-recorder and why much else about me was known. From the plausible Terry I had kept few secrets.

It also became clear to me why several inmates with whom I had been accustomed daily to walk around the playing fields had been warned by officers to stay away from me because I was 'bad news'. Pete warned me to keep a low profile because I was a 'marked man'. This was all very alarming. One particularly close friend who had known nothing of my tobacco plans suddenly started playing badminton in the afternoons instead of joining me in a walk. Even Pete, with whom I worked daily in the kitchen, was asked by Mr Ryan why he spent so much time talking to me. I was, indeed, being watched. I ceased all activity.

All the above happened after Monday 17 February. On that day I was in real trouble, as I shall now explain: I have written the events out of sequence to indicate just how great are the pressures to find 'constructive activity' in prison, particularly if one feels an added sense of grievance against the authorities. I regard my real downfall to be the events just described and not what I am about to relate. What I have related caused me to conform totally thereafter. What I am about to describe should have so taught me, but it did not. Resentment, as shall be seen, is a powerful motivator.

Terry went on Home Leave twice. The first occasion was a weekend leave from which he returned on Monday 17 February. He went out on St Valentine's Day – a day during which, incidentally, I acquired an officer's cap badge. My diary records:

> Terry back after a distressing weekend. Pete and Brian called by tonight. Terry talked with us and showed us photos of his wife – semi-naked. He claims a man is 'having it off' with his wife and wants someone to deal with the poor chap. A deal is struck up: £2000 worth of 'damage' is to be inflicted. Am I hearing right?

But before Terry had returned on the Monday, I had received a visit.

I had felt before the visit that I would be strip-searched that day and had arranged that no tobacco would be brought for me. I had received a couple of 'gipsy's warnings' and vowed to come out of the visit 'clean'. During the course of the visit one of my friends had run out of cigarettes and he left the visiting room to buy more. At that time I did not know that he could have bought them on site. He returned with cigarettes and tobacco for me. His gesture was kind, unsolicited and foolish. One of the officers on duty was my ward screw and I reckoned that I would probably get by with the ounce. Furthermore, I had been assured that I would receive only the usual frisk. (Again, I cannot say how this assurance was given.) So, despite my forebodings, I took the ounce.

At the end of the visit two of us were told to stay behind. It was obvious that we were to be strip-searched. The other man happened to have £10 on him but managed to get to a lavatory to lose it. I was searched first. I had already confessed to the tobacco, and the search was done in a discreet way. I disliked intensely having to bend down but I was not touched and the two officers were tactful in the extreme. 'Run along, young

Bettsworth,' they said. I resented the appellation but even more resented my own blind folly which had persuaded me against all my instincts to smuggle tobacco on that day. My diary entry of Tuesday 18 February takes up the story.

A terrible day. Nicked for one ounce of tobacco. I received the charge sheets from an officer who asked me if I was looking to be shipped out. I was hauled before the Deputy Governor again and given the most appalling verbal lashing. I pleaded guilty and merely said that the offence was unpremeditated. Of the many things he said I remember him asking me if I would prefer to be in Exeter on the rule. This was clearly a threat. I wanted to say 'Yes, I bloody well would' but 'Sir' clearly wanted me to say what a lovely place this is. 'I should have thought someone in your position would have been walking on eggs.'

Did I know my visitors were committing a criminal offence? He is sick and tired of the rumours he is hearing about me including 'smuggling out your writing and other documents and many other things we hear but for which we cannot put you on report'. He told me that if my name was raised again he would ship me out. So that's it, I thought. They know I'm up to things but can't bloody well catch me so are playing their hand. Very silly of them for I learned a great deal by listening and saying absolutely nothing. There is a huge leak somewhere.

My punishment is generally regarded as draconian. I have lost ten days' remission and two months of privileged visits. There is no doubt that someone here wants to do me.

This evening my cube was 'spun' – prison slang for thoroughly searched – by security on the pretext they were looking for a missing kitchen knife. My shallow jam pot was searched. The hems of my curtains and the spines of books!! They are obviously looking for a minute knife. Only one other kitchen worker was searched – Pete. Nothing, of course, was found, though the search was incompetent to an appalling degree. For example, I was not searched and my large tea caddy, full of tea, had its lid removed but the contents were not emptied out. It is clear that they were looking for drugs; the bottom on my tea caddy could have concealed several hundred pounds' worth. This annoys me for the one thing I don't deal in is drugs. Pete is so mad that he is thinking of resigning from the kitchen. He's already been warned to stay away from me. A real stir has been caused by this incident. But why me?

It must emanate from the reputation I've quite unjustly got. I know I'm unpopular with the screws because of my, for want of a better word, 'breeding'. I'll sleep on it but having been punished today for rumours – the word used by the Deputy Governor and threatened with a ship-out, I intend to lodge a formal complaint.

Another con, due to be released today, beat up a nonce last night and put him in hospital. His punishment was a loss of seven days' remission and a ship-out to Bristol. Causing Actual Bodily Harm is regarded in this prison as less serious than smuggling one ounce of tobacco.

The loss of visits causes me a problem. I must cancel all operations. Expensive on tobacco but the heat is on. . . .

At last I now know the true nature of open prisons. There is no dignity, openness, privacy or fairness. Screws at the highest level have acted against me on the unsupported (and in fact untrue, in the main) allegations of informers. This prison, like this country, is becoming more and more totalitarian. The general public would be appalled – even the bring-back-the-cat brigade – at how prisoners are treated here, particularly when theoretically we are being prepared for the outside world. The horror is that it is the enemy within which triumphs – fellow cons.

There is every logical and factual argument against my being suspected of anything apart from the ounce of tobacco – yet four independent and reliable people have told me I'm targeted for a ship-out.

Attitudes towards me have changed utterly in the kitchen and for the better. But it appears no knife was missing so I've been lied to by the authorities.

How can I tell Jen of the punishment?

The last question bothered me and the letter I received from her when I told her of the loss of visits was far worse than any punishment the authorities could impose. It was some time before I told her about the loss of remission. By now, though, we both calculated that I would lose parole anyway. But that story comes later.

The punishment and verbal wigging I received had the

opposite effect from that intended. I resented the severity of the punishment and even more resented the tongue-lash. I was spoken to in a manner far more insulting than I would have dreamed of using in addressing the naughtiest pupil in my school. Had the Deputy Governor not tried to intimidate me, had he spoken rationally and with a measure of respect in his voice, then matters would have been different. There had been no occasion in my lifetime of teaching when I had insulted or spoken to a pupil with anything but respect. I even refused to draw my red marking pen through appalling pieces of work; I preferred to accept the work as insulting but to show the erring pupil that I will not insult his efforts in return by putting a red line through it. Therefore, I expected him to respect me in return. But here was I, an adult and an intelligent one, being addressed as if I were a dog turd. One can draw but a lone conclusion. On both sides the gloves of co-operation had been removed; the bare knuckles of mutual loathing were bared.

I suspect that if I had not been fined for missing a tally and if I had not been so harshly dealt with for the tobacco I would have become a model prisoner. But a system so unreasonable – one which punished a tobacco smuggler more severely than a mugger – deserved to be abused and scorned. Punishment in Leyhill was certainly not 'impulsive to good'. It was only after the Terry incident and after I had been granted parole that I promised Jen I would behave.

I write at length about all this to give an insight into some of the undercurrent activities in prison and, more important, to suggest ways in which the system encourages bad behaviour. I, until now, had been a law-abiding supporter of the police and the authorities. My conviction had not really turned me into an anarchist and antisocial person. It was the experience of the prison system which did that. How much more likely therefore would recidivists, or even those whose respect for law and order had been slight before they went to prison, turn even more crooked both in prison and outside?

# 14

## SMUGGLERS, GRASSES, PREFECTS

*Good neighbours I have had, and I have met with
bad; and in trust I have found treason*

Elizabeth I, Speech to Parliament, 1586

In the previous chapter I have indicated how it was possible to circumvent the rules and I have tried to suggest some of the reasons why it was felt necessary to do so. In this chapter I will write more generally about the various attempts by other prisoners to smuggle contraband in and out of prison.

I have explained that the most simple method was to bring tobacco or whatever in during a visit. The risks were minimal, a strip-search being the only thing to be feared. Indeed, strip-searches regularly caught out would-be smugglers. In fact, very few inmates did not smuggle stuff in on visits. But it was those convicted of drug offences who were most at risk.

The only advantage these people had was that they needed one of only two commodities – drugs or cash. Significant quantities of both could be concealed anally and it was the case that trips to the lavatory during visits were not infrequent. I was glad I did not smoke cannabis: I had experienced enough difficulty using my alimentary system in its ordained way as a one-way street; the idea of introducing a contraflow system did not appeal. The usual strip-search would not reveal anything that had been pushed far into the rectum and as a probing search could be done only in the presence of a doctor the smugglers had few fears. It was also possible to put money and drugs into the mouth while leaving the visits room.

The problem came when one tried to conceal consignments of cash or cannabis. Some men constructed beautiful cigarette tins in which there were totally invisible secret compartments. Others hid the drugs or cash around the establishment or risked keeping the commodities on their person. It was not merely the officers against whom one had to be on guard, but also other prisoners. Drugs and cash meant power. And only a minute quantity of cannabis resin could be bought in a '£5 deal'. I knew little of values but was told that there was a threefold profit on cannabis compared with that which prevailed outside. No wonder some of the big dealers made hundreds of pounds.

Problems occur, though, when the authorities have a clamp-down, as they did unexpectedly on Friday 30 May. I went for my usual afternoon run but my diary then records:

Just as I finished my laps today I went to get back into the ward for my bath to be told that I could not. The prison was overrun by sniffer dogs and thorough searches were being made. Only the kitchen staff were not at work. I was very worried about the fate of my journal and got permission to go into the ward to put on sweater and trousers. The screw who followed me in was 'Roy Rogers' and so it was an easy matter to put the diary – which does not often remain long in my cube – down the front of my pants. It is 7.30 p.m. as I write and I still haven't had my bath. The dogs are now in the workshop and laundry. I know of two places were dope is hidden; both places have been thoroughly searched and nothing discovered. One place was literally at dog-nose height. The owner is much relieved. I suppose the exercise is as much propagandist as anything but it doesn't say much for the dogs. One theory explains their inefficiency by suggesting that they are being asked to do too much work at once. But what a waste of several hours – hanging around and, as a concession, being allowed to watch an old Randolph Scott film on television.

Several very worried cons came from work to find the dogs all over the place. I know of one bright kitchen lad who risked entering his ward to rescue the supplies of a friend. The rescuer spent several tense minutes with a mouthful of cannabis before deciding that he would not be strip-searched and so was able to transfer the drug to his pockets. And the dogs stayed. My diary on Saturday 31 May records:

Dogs are still here but nothing has been found except a post office rubber stamp! One screw has put his foot through the loft of the computer block! If I were doing the search I'd handcuff every con on the playing field and do a strip-search. There would be tons of dope left behind on the field. It is amazing how many cons have developed speech impediments. Or is it that they've mouthfuls of dope!!

Eventually the exercise was called off and the prison settled down. It was not unusual for wards suddenly to be searched or individuals to have their cubes spun. The mass search of the prison was rare. Generally, thorough searches were conducted as a result of a tip-off. But con incompetence contributed to our being caught very often.

I have said that it was common to use the market gardens or the local quarry as a drop-off point. After all, in an open prison it is not hard to go beyond the campus and the gardens were huge. However, those who tried to bring in consignments that way ran two risks. First, they could not always be certain that they could collect the parcel safely or, once having collected it, guarantee the silence of their fellows. Generally parcels were collected after dark and brought straight into the ward between tallies. It was impossible to bring in bottles of whisky, for example, and be certain that you had not been seen. The second danger was that whenever the authorities discovered a dropping place they marked it on a map. The place, usually a 'good' one, was hence dangerous to reuse. Further, if the authorities learned of a drop they would observe the spot and the package and catch whoever collected it.

Sometimes night patrols came across nocturnal perambulators and caught them that way. I remember two people leaving a ward after the 9 p.m. tally to pick up a consignment. The night patrol spotted them and gave chase. The two convicts separated. One ran out of the prison with the parcel and continued running. The other worked his way behind the patrol and followed it back into the main prison; he eventually regained his ward safely but without contraband. This loss of booty created a number of supply problems in subsequent weeks.

Perhaps the stupidest drop was that carried out by a man who came back from his pre-release Home Leave. He had been in prison for at least a couple of years and had been granted parole. On his return he went straight to his cubicle, changed into his working clothes and walked, in daylight, to the quarry to pick up the parcel he had dropped there minutes before. He was caught. Worse, he lost his remission and spent another ten months in prison. It is hard to sympathise with such incompetent actions, but I suppose the officers were happy to learn what 'serendipity' meant thanks to this man.

I suppose an even more bizarre case concerned a one-armed man serving a long sentence for drug smuggling. I had a liking for him. He used to leave his meal tray in the same place in the dining room each day and I enjoyed serving him his food, which he nimbly carried on the tray with his good arm. When I cleaned the dining-room tables I always wiped his tray and left it where I had found it. In an odd way his tray became a symbol for me, but I do not really know of what. Anyway, he too returned from Home Leave with contraband. He had filled his false arm with drugs, phone cards and tobacco! Various reports came back to us about quantities but our total reaction was one of incredulity. How could anyone have been so obviously unsubtle – unless he were trying a double-take. Sadly this man too was shipped out but it was not for two or three days that his tray was removed from the dining room.

Telephone cards were, not surprisingly, difficult to smuggle in. They could not be swallowed or inserted into the anus but it was possible to bring them in on visits by inserting them either into one's clothing or into one's shoes. One man went to the length of hollowing out the heels of his shoes as receptacles for cards and drugs and relying on his visitor to bring not only the contraband but also a quick-drying glue with which, in the lavatory during the visit, he would reseal the heel to prevent detection even during a thorough body-search.

The connivance of the non-inmate population added to our ways of bringing in contraband. Rumours abounded about one or two 'bent' officers but I have no personal knowledge of this. It was true, though, that one of the civilian employees was sacked for supplying alcohol to prisoners, but this is a far from rare occurrence in many prisons. Certainly, a variety of alcoholic drinks was available if you were prepared to pay. I could sell a bottle of scotch for £15, though in times of plenty the going rate was about £10.

But it was not only the case that contraband would be smuggled into prison. Sometimes it was produced with the ingredients already to hand. At other times our objective was to get stuff out of the prison.

There was a time when I was asked to supply raw potatoes to a friend. By this time I reckoned through various contacts that I could supply tobacco and alcohol and could get stuff out of the prison for people. I failed utterly to acquire the potatoes, even though I worked in the kitchen and had good contacts in the market garden. The reason for this was that the authorities conducted regular searches on the gardeners to prevent them from bringing potatoes out. Naturally, the need for potatoes was for the illicit brewing of Leyhill 'poteen'. Others succeeded in finding the raw materials and a pretty lethal brew was distilled.

The easiest thing to get out of the prison was oneself. If an inmate was prepared to risk being absent at a special tally then there was much opportunity to go over the (low) wall to make phone calls or collect parcels. Some men even went to the trouble of making assignations with their wives and hopped off for an hour's love-making. I was told that in past times wives would sometimes enter the prison easily disguised as an inmate to spend a night of love-making in her husband's room. It would not have been difficult. The lady need only wear jeans, a prison duffle-coat – easily got to her – and a hat to hide her hair. She could remain under the bed at tally times and leave the prison after dark with little difficulty. I have no personal knowledge of its happening in my time but would hope it did. As I have said before, there is nothing unnatural in a man wanting to make love to his wife, and prison, whatever else it tries to do, cannot deny basic or even sublime instincts.

All the above may seem disgraceful, even childish. But I think such illicit activity serves a number of functions, as I have explained. Once a man or woman is in prison 'society' ceases to care. That fact alone raises questions about society's motives and suggests that retribution is its sole aim. Furthermore this constant battle against regulations gave prisoners a *raison d'être*; it was often better to fight the system and take the consequences of failure than to do nothing. It was part of the survival kit each prisoner needs to alleviate boredom and to maintain an identity. Passive co-operation had no effect on the authorities. All cons were treated, at best, with indifference – usually, though, veiled hostility was the norm. I blame none for this. Cons will misbehave and it is the job of officers to control them. The system has gone on for so long and so many different types are thrown together randomly that nothing but a fundamental reappraisal will change the *status quo*. And one cannot easily see how a clean sheet can be produced so that a new start can be made. I was, though, surprised by the number of men who thought that by sycophancy and generally oleaginous behaviour they would gain favours from the authorities.

I have shown how we could have our misdeeds discovered accidentally and have referred, *en passant*, to informers. These latter types were as much despised as sex offenders. There was a built-in system for their use at Leyhill. It was known as 'putting a note in the box'. Any inmate who wanted to inform safely and anonymously on another had merely to write the name and offence of their victim on a piece of paper and post the item in the post box.

My name, I learned, was much used in this way – or, more accurately, was much abused. It always staggered me that the unsupported statements of cowardly grasses were acted upon, but they surely were. One officer told me shortly before my release that, though the officers hated grasses, they were happy to use them. Lifers who had spent years in long-term, high-security prisons told me that informing went on even in those places. This was a fact which mystified me greatly and still does. One can understand – just – that a short-termer, new to the system and desperately keen to get out, might be naive enough to think that by being a nark he would earn the gratitude of the authorities; one cannot understand how men who *know* they are to live together for years – even decades – can inform on each other. Perhaps it is to do with an innate sense of co-operation with authority which many have. I suspect some wartime collaborators might justify their action that way. Indeed, some have. I suppose, too, that the act of informing is little different from the eagerness with which we are prepared to tell strangers our complete life histories at the drop of a hat, whether the context be in a casual acquaintanceship struck up on a long train journey or during an interview with the tax man.

Be that as it may, the informers at Leyhill were as ubiquitous as the Royal Artillery is reputed to be. They cause many problems but did nothing for themselves. There was a man in my ward who openly threatened to tell the authorities if another inmate illegally played his radio without earphones. Yet this man was also a loathed nonce – he was serving years for incest with his daughter *and* his son. He had already received two knock-backs and he received a third shortly after I left. His informing was helping him not one whit.

Occasionally officers would try to build up their own system of informers as if they were members of television's fictional Sweeney or were themselves a sort of Dirty Harry. One man, whom I have already mentioned, was nicknamed Roy Rogers. He was new to Leyhill and spent his first few days practising what I imagine he had been taught at training school. He entered one's cube, asked about one's offence, family, photographs, and so on. I, in common with most others, regarded these visits as obtrusive and impertinent. I was not in prison to indulge in social chit-chat with the officers and I certainly was not going to involve my family, however vicariously, with any officer.

Roy Rogers, though, was persistent. One day he entered every ward and asked each ward cleaner to keep him informed of any misbehaviour. In return he would grant favours in the form of phone-calls or whatever. I know this to be true because I overheard the conversation between him and my ward's cleaner one afternoon; I had finished my run and bath and was sitting quietly in my cubicle sewing a koala bear. Roy Rogers had forgotten that kitchen staff were in the wards during the afternoons, as well as cleaners. Fortunately none took this man seriously and he became an object of ridicule and hatred. The verdict of us all was that he was trying to make a name for himself. He may have persuaded some to work for him but I do not know if he did or not.

So the risks abounded. The rewards were modest but successful tobacco smuggling, for example, removed a source of stress. Successful anything gave us a reason for being. However, penalties for being caught could be heavy.

I have already described my own punishments and have suggested that on both occasions I was hard done by. And it was the case in prison that disparity in sentencing was as extreme as it is in the courts. At Leyhill it seemed that the Deputy Governor was harsher than the Governor. Not all understood that. In Leyhill, on the scale of punishments, I never learned of the Deputy Governor giving an inmate the lightest punishment, a reprimand.

# Marking Time

Of course, for most of us the ultimate sanction was a delay in the date of release. Misbehaviour in prison could extend the length of our stay considerably – though the latest release date was one that occurred whatever happened. Thus a man doing eighteen months, like me, could hope for parole after six months or release after twelve – his EDR (Earliest Date of Release) – or after eighteen months. The last was an extreme situation. Equally, the man serving nine years could hope to be released after three, six or nine years respectively. Those who suffered most, as I have reported elsewhere, were the lifers. In the most extreme cases, of course, action could be taken in an outside court and an inmate could receive additional and concurrent prison sentences.

However, within the prison a number of internal sanctions applied. And all the penalties could be suspended at the whim of the Governor or his Deputy. I have mentioned fines being imposed and these were often extremely effective. A fine of £2 could wipe out a man's weekly pay, such that he relied on others for his needs. Or he got into debt or risked smuggling. In other words the punishment guaranteed that he would be in further trouble – unless, for example, the man could give up smoking in a trice or was happy not to write home more than once during that week. Certainly no cognizance was taken of a man's financial state before imposing the fine. Thus the system was self-defeating and caused resentment.

Loss of privileged visits was levied on those who had transgressed during the visit. As I have said before, this particular sanction was, in my case, a relief. Visits caused increased tension and their loss was often a good thing. However, to lose days was of a different order.

The maximum loss a Governor could impose was twenty-eight days and for such an additional sentence to be imposed the offence had to be very severe. I cared little that I had lost ten days at the time, though I was reluctant for several weeks to let Jen know and by the time my Parole Eligibility Date had come and gone I did rather regret my misconduct. What was more significant to me was that a mere Deputy Governor could, in effect, sentence a man to additional imprisonment for offences which in the outside world would not rate a charge or conviction – let alone a custodial sentence. This area is another in which I believe enormous resentment is engendered. I cite my own case – smuggling one ounce of tobacco not even for gain but for personal use. I received ten days' loss of remission and loss of two months' worth of visits. On the same day a man who had committed an offence which carries many years' imprisonment on the outside – Actual Bodily Harm – lost seven days. I come again to the point about the nature of the penal experience. Does one go to prison as a punishment or to be punished?

And all the above sanctions can be accompanied by a ship-out. To many this was the harshest penalty. What happens is that, unexpectedly, two officers come to one's place of work armed with handcuffs. They handcuff the inmate who is due to be shipped-out and march him straight to Reception and a waiting taxi. Before the man has time to think, he is in Bristol Prison in a cell. His belongings, or what remains of them, follow later. There were times when I longed for the privacy of my cell in Exeter Prison, but this was not a longing I felt for a protracted length of time, so it must be said that the threat of a ship-out to a bang-up was generally heeded.

Taken all in all, I am convinced that the sanctions imposed on prisoners did not work. Many would say, 'What are they going to do to me? Put me in prison?', when they were on report. The attempts by the administration to control us by increasing our financial hardship, for example, merely ensured that we *had* to recommit the offence because of the further hardship caused. If we had not been unreasonably short of tobacco in the first place we would not have smuggled. We were unreasonably short of tobacco because we could not earn enough to buy a 'reasonable' amount of the stuff. An imposed fine made us even poorer and less capable of satisfying our 'reasonable' tobacco needs. I define 'reasonable' as the permitted amount we were allowed to have which, as I have already explained, was far more than we could afford to buy.

In short, the psychology of dealing with errant prisoners was ill informed and counter-productive. If we had been a homogeneous unit with a common aim who accepted corporate discipline the system might have worked. If we had been children it might have been successful. But we were a large number of individuals who had already received the harshest sanction society could impose on us. To be treated like public schoolboys was absurd. And even when I accept that as convicted wrongdoers we could expect few favours I still assert that the whole thinking behind our treatment was barbaric and held the seeds of its own destruction within it. Riots will continue in prison until society rethinks, radically, its custodial policies.

Yet Leyhill even had a prefectorial body. There was a collection of inmates known as 'Top Table'. These men, elected ward by ward, formed the prison equivalent of a school's council. The object of the body was to represent the rights of prisoners to the authorities. Each ward had a representative whose function was to be, as it were, the constituency MP. Thus any point which needed to be made to the authorities was brought up at a meeting of the Top Table with the Governor and other members of staff. Regular minutes of meetings were posted. I think it is true to say that under 'Matters Arising' I saw trivia, like the privilege of watching a late film over a Bank Holiday period – which was granted, of course. As was the agreement of the authorities to underwrite twopence-halfpenny for a dart's competition or some such cause. Nothing of real substance was ever conceded.

I remember on one occasion that a member of Top Table managed to get the agreement of the group that there should be a non-smoking area in the dining room. No vote among inmates had been taken over this absurd decision but the kitchen officer came to Trevor, my workmate, and me, because the dining room was our responsibility, to invite us to determine the non-smoking zone. I pointed to an individual tile and designated that the non-smoking zone. There never was such an area while I remained at Leyhill. I much resented the intrusion into Leyhill of the small-mindedness which features in the world outside. The single-issue fanatic had no place in our prison. Besides which I could not come to terms with the notion of a quasi-oligarchy of prisoners. Yet there were elections to decide who should hold offices within the organisation. I never voted and tried to persuade others that the whole exercise was a confidence trick. How could prisoners run a prison? They could not and should not.

I was unpopular with one kitchen officer for referring to this august body as the 'school prefects' when one of its members had complained of the lack of hot water with which to wash his dirty dishes. It was my job to supply this. On one occasion the pipes had frozen so that none was forthcoming. A 'prefect' decided that he was within his rights to complain about another inmate just because he, the prefect, was on Top Table. Ugh!

Yet, I suppose, to visiting magistrates and others the fact that our enlightened Governor allowed a group of inmates to 'help to run the prison' would seem to be the epitome of liberal-mindedness. We would be regarded as lucky prisoners being cared for and reformed by an enlightened regime. What utter nonsense. The prison was run by the Chief Officer who was no lover of his fellow men. When the bitterly cold weather came in January he made it an offence for an inmate to wear a towel round his neck as a scarf. When the hot sun shone in May he reduced the sunbathing area to a tiny corner of the playing field and prescribed the exact sunbathing dress. Both decisions were ridiculous and were designed to increase the strains on the men. Over neither could the Top Table interfere any more than it could influence rates of pay, release dates, Home Leave or tobacco supplies. I think, though, that it might have been influential in dissuading the Governor from banning the monthly delivery of toiletries at visits.

What was more disturbing to me was that many took the group seriously – none as much as they themselves did of course. I could not understand how prisoners could so delude themselves into thinking the prison was some sort of club over which all members had control. For the same reason, as I have mentioned before, I resented the use of the word 'camp' as a euphemism for prison. 'Camp' and 'Top Table' are words which may cause the unwary to forget what their exact status was and lull them into a sort of fool's paradise from which they could at any moment be awakened by the reality of prison discipline and shortages. To this extent the device was extremely subtle. In an unguarded moment one might act forgetfully and treat the place like a holiday camp only suddenly to be brought low by its reality. That bringing low was part and parcel of the general undermining of individual morale.

Men's great hope lay in the daily knowledge that release for all, including theoretically for the lifers, was some time a certainty. But even this most delicious of thoughts was fraught with terrible dangers and much agony, as I shall record in the next chapter.

# 15

# PAROLE

*. . . the opening of the prison to them that are bound*

Isaiah, 61:1

The daily conversation of every prisoner concerns his date of release. This should come as no surprise to anyone, particularly when one considers the operation of the system as I have described it in preceding chapters. But above even the examples of stress which I have articulated there is an added ingredient which is hard to define. It is impossible to put into words not only the depth but also the nature of the feeling which is loosely described as 'being away from home'.

To be sure the lack of tobacco has an effect. So, too, does the need to live a celibate life. Absence from one's children is a daily agony. But the sum total of the desperate desire all inmates have to be 'out' is greater than the sum of the parts I can articulate. Indeed, this feeling of hysteria often becomes worse in a man who knows for certain when he is to be released; he gets what has been well defined as 'gate-fever'. It is perhaps true to say that lifers and other very-long-termers have learned to control their feelings rather more than short-termers, but nevertheless the excitement of a 'date' is still very strong for them.

Like everything else in the judicial system of this country, the system of granting parole seems to be an arbitrary lottery. As I have explained, most prisoners receive three dates when they first enter prison. The first is their Parole Eligibility Date (PED), the second their Earliest Date of Release (EDR) and the last, the LDR, gives the latest date at which they can legally be detained. In my case, the slip of paper containing this information recorded 14.6.86, 12.12.86 and 12.6.87 respectively. I wrote in my diary on Tuesday 17 December 1985 that the 'last date is a horror'.

I was convicted on Friday 13 December and the 'dates' were six, twelve and eighteen months hence, respectively. The discrepancy of days was because a parole date which falls on a

Saturday or Sunday is not exercised until the Monday following. An EDR or an LDR which falls on a weekend is exercised on the Friday immediately preceding it.

I was first conscious of parole in the cells under the courtroom. While my mind still reeled from the verdict and my head rang with the words 'eighteen months' imprisonment' I vaguely calculated that I could be out of prison in time for Christmas 1986, a year hence. It was my QC who told me that I would be considered for parole after six months and from that moment I was mentally adjusted to the fact that I could be out in time for my middle son's birthday on 21 June. In fact, I think for the first few weeks I assumed I would receive parole.

This confident assumption was based on a number of premises. First, I would do nothing to irritate the authorities and hence reduce my chances of an early release. Second, I was soon told that nonces had a good chance of a favourable parole decision. This was untrue, though it was commonly held at Leyhill that nonces do not get the dreaded knock-back. (This graphic compound word referred to every unfavourable decision a prisoner received. If he asked for an emergency telephone call and was refused, he had been knocked back. If his parole application was turned down he received the ultimate knock-back.) Further, I was sanguine about getting parole when I was told of some of the criteria. These included a suitable home to go to and a supportive wife and family. I had the first adequately and the second in superabundance. The chances of securing a job were taken into account but not in too rigid a way. The chances of reoffending were considered.

Thus I went to Leyhill determined to enjoy the same reputation for co-operation that I had had at Exeter. Alas, the experience at Leyhill did not allow me to be humble and co-operative, as I have described above. Be that as it may, from my first interview with the lady probation officer I set my heart on a June release but my brain on a December one. And the process started early.

The mechanism for parole was simple. A home probation report was sent to the local review committee together with a prison report and the inmate's own representation. Each man was interviewed by one or more members of the committee, and a recommendation made. If the application – yes, one had to state that one wanted to be released – was successful, all well and good.

If it failed it was possible to appeal; the chances of a successful appeal were about nil.

On Thursday 23 January 1986 I made the following diary entry:

> Found my parole application form on my bed when I returned from work. Will compose my thoughts tonight and write out a draft tomorrow. Must remember to use *black* Biro. I've already used a blue one on one form so have probably knackered the bureaucratic machine as a result.

Naturally, once I received the form there was much discussion about parole. All the time men were applying for it or being released or being 'KB'd'. The word 'parole' was the most common one in prison. Indeed, there came a time when our ward banned its use and I, whimsically, used it in Scrabble during the period of the ban and was nearly lynched. My discussions caused me great concern. One man told me that if anyone were to protest his innocence then he would get an automatic knock-back. He cited the case of a man at Leyhill serving five years for robbery who had consistently maintained his innocence and who had consistently been KB'd. When my wife and I discussed the process I told her to retain a neutral stance when the probation officer visited her; I asked Jen not to state very strong feelings about the situation in case I was given an unfavourable review.

For my part I spent a very disturbed day and night worrying about the Local Review Committee interview. On the one hand the world believes in my guilt because I am in prison. The effect of my sentence has been felt. I have lost my job and my integrity. Thus far have I 'served' my time and done my punishment. On the other hand I have been in trouble in prison and if I were to imply that the real cause of my bolshie-ness was the system I can hardly be judged to have been co-operative. My friends want me out as much as my family does. Oh dear, what shall I do? Thus did these and many other thoughts revolve.

I woke up on Friday 24 January and wrote in my diary:

> Governor's inspection tomorrow so I think I'll spring-clean my cube before writing my parole submission. I've been told that my misbehaviour will not count against me. This strikes me as odd. I'll write something neutral. . . . Written the following:

I am naturally keen to be reunited with my family and wish to be considered for parole. I hope the following considerations will help my request to be favourably considered.

On my release I will be returning to my home and family. As the lady probation officer knows, my home life is happy and stable. I love and am loved by my wife and family. I intend to raise capital in order to start a small business which is one of the reasons I am attending the Small Business Course run at Leyhill. The fact of my conviction precludes my being able to teach again and therefore it follows – if not strictly logically – that my offence cannot be repeated. I enjoy the support of a large number of people in Cornwall despite everything and I know that with their encouragement and with the guidance of the Probation Service I shall be able to recreate my life anew.

My wife is still employed at the school and may continue to work there *sine die* – the choice is hers. Her salary and my business income will ensure a regular income.

I can envisage no situation wherein I can breach any parole order.

Bullshit really.

The last comment I made indicates not that I had been mendacious but that I was sceptical about the value of my or any other application. After all, I was bound to say I would behave – and anyway I could not see how such a predictable promise of good faith had much value; no one would say they planned to misbehave once outside. Furthermore, it was not really necessary for me to write about my wife and home; the local probation service would make their own enquiries anyway. I was, moreover, unlikely to plead with the authorities to keep me here.

I sent in the application and waited. My relatively short sentence qualified me for release under Section 33 of a particular Act. Men serving sentences of, I believe, two years or more underwent a slightly different procedure in that their application went to the Home Office; mine was dealt with at local level by the local review committee. The constitution of this body was unknown to me. I believe local magistrates and other worthies sit on it. The man who interviewed me was, I think, an academic. He was certainly a delightfully charming man, as I shall describe later.

At the next visit I told Jen that I had had a good interview with a quite charming man. She was relieved and we both settled to the sensible view that we should expect a December release date but that an earlier one would be a bonus. My subsequent misconduct in prison had many inmate friends telling me that I would receive a knock-back. I, too, inclined to that view. At a further visit I told Jen to expect bad news. Her immediate reaction was to say to me that she was going to tell me the very same. I had, after all, twice fallen foul of the authorities, had been fined and had lost visits and ten days' remission. I tried to forget about the whole matter and let it take its course.

On Monday 24 March I noted in my diary:

My LRC is on Thursday at 11 a.m. with a Mr Holtom. I just hope that it is short and sweet though I may have dished my chances of parole. At least I feel the wheels are rolling onwards and if I get a KB I am passing time. I've now spent 101 nights in prison including tonight. Fourteen-plus weeks – it sounds better that way. It could be a thousand and one Leyhill nights. Even with my ten days' punishment I am more than halfway through my sentence if I get parole.

The preoccupation with numbers was everywhere. 'Only another fourteen weeks, five days and three hours to go – but I am not counting' exemplifies many a comment.

The night before my interview I recorded that I was 'nervous about LRC'. I went on:

What shall I say at the interview. They won't be impressed by my smuggling and loss of remission. Interestingly, too, Lyn reckons there's a chap here doing five years for robbery who has had three knock-backs for protesting his innocence. It's a mystery to everyone – including the staff – how the system works. Mentally I am more or less attuned to December. Ah well . . .

Thursday 27 March came and with it the prospect of a visit as well as the LRC. It was also a day which demonstrated something of what I have been saying about the nature of the prison experience, so I shall quote my diary extract for the day in full. I refer in the extract to my friend Pete, who had been granted parole and been released the previous day. Before he had been released he had promised his *Sun* calendar to another man in my ward, Russ, but he had forgotten to hand it over, so Russ asked me to retrieve it. Mr Ryan, of course, was the senior kitchen officer.

Was awake half the night deciding on tactics for the interview. Finally made up my mind and to hell with it.

Pete had promised a *Sun* calendar to Russ which Russ asked me to collect from the kitchen store room as Pete had forgotten to give it to him before he left. Accordingly I collected it and took it into the dining room while Trev and I were doing our morning work. Ryan came to work at about 10 a.m., saw the calendar on a chair and asked why it was there. I explained that Pete's wife had brought it for him and that Pete had promised it to someone else. Whereupon Ryan claimed it, saying that Pete had swapped it with Knight, the other kitchen officer, for another calendar! Unbelievable! Not only is trafficking between cons and staff strictly verboten but I never thought I would see the day when a senior officer's primary concern on coming into his department was the fate of a nude calendar. Oh dear, Princess Anne, if only you knew.

Fifteen minutes to LRC. I have not changed into my 'smart' clothing as one does for a Governor's call-up because I am told it is not necessary.

LRC seemed to go extremely well. Mr Holtom turned out to be a most civilised bearded chap who was tact personified. I felt totally relaxed in his presence. We talked generally and I was eventually asked how my wife and family had reacted to 'the allegations and conviction'. I replied that everyone had recovered from the shock and was adjusting magnificently to the horror of the situation. I said some rather strong things about the system generally. If I have dished my chances then the die is cast. J'attendrai le jour et la nuit . . . but not toujours.

Visit almost entirely good. The first time I've seen Jen and Tim for six weeks. There are potential flashpoints always – the tension and artificiality of the scene make this inevitable. Tim got a bit tearful at one point but Jay seemed well. . . .

Another couple of evening laps and a long chat with Trev,

while a keen game of Monopoly is played in the ward. A full day but my conscience is clear.

The above extract is typical of my diary, I suppose. The tension of visiting I have mentioned at length. The absurdity of the calendar incident – after all no one in the kitchen cared about its disposal and arguably 'men without women' might more enjoy the pneumatic bliss of Samantha Fox than a married officer – illustrates what I have said about the unnecessary stresses put upon inmates. Even more telling is that my extract records courtesy and tact from a member of the system who does not directly run prisons. So it is an outsider who, for a few brief minutes, gives me a feeling of being human again. I suspect that if the authorities followed that line more often there would be less trouble in prisons. At least it could be argued that open prisons which are supposed to cater for the least dangerous and disturbed men might like to give that alternative ethos a chance.

There was now nothing more I could do towards my parole. Presumably Mr Holtom knew of the lost days and so on but he did not mention them. As time passed I became resigned to the December date. One man, the jewel thief inevitably nicknamed 'Raffles', assured me I would get parole. I had known him as the librarian at Exeter Prison; he had recently been sent to Leyhill and now worked in the kitchen. He was a well-spoken, ex-public schoolboy in his late fifties or early sixties, who was serving his third sentence. He had already endured sentences of eight and five years and this last stretch, also for five years, was about a year old. He was wise about the ways of prison and its parole systems and had told me in conversation that I would certainly get parole. So certain was he that he bet me an ounce of tobacco that I would get it. Further than that he forbade me to mention the word 'parole' on pain of owing him even more tobacco.

He told me that while he was at Ford Open Prison on his last sentence he had helped an officer to work out parole statistics. He had also come to know a lady prison visitor who was chairman of the parole board for that area. She had told him that conduct in prison features not at all in the final decision. According to this excellent lady, local review committees were instructed that prison takes people in different ways and that conduct in prison was no guide to conduct outside. This was a relief to me, not only from the point of view of parole but because of the alarmingly anarchistic tendencies I was showing towards all authority in prison. I had sometimes wondered if my new-found rebelliousness would persist once I was released and if I would become a criminal! Further, Raffles indicated that home circumstances, likelihood of reoffending and so on were more important.

I argued with him that a number of people doing their first sentence of eighteen months had received knock-backs, but he countered by saying there was probably more to their case than they were letting on. I shall refer to some of these cases shortly.

In the event, he was proved right. On the morning of Thursday 24 April I received a call-up from the Principal Officer of my wing, Mr Owen. It was the day on which a well-known actress received a mere three months' imprisonment for drug offences relating to Category A drugs. Friends of mine serving up to three years for similar offences involving cannabis were less than pleased. My diary entry is low key:

> Got my parole today. I was called up by Owen, the Principal Officer, and told, 'The Secretary of State in his wisdom has decided to release you on parole on Monday 23rd June.' I said nothing but picked up my parole form, folded it, put it in my pocket and exited. There was no way I was going to register any emotion or ask for a phone call to let Jen know. I wanted no one to know, though they all know about the call-up. I've told all but Brian and Trevor that the reason for the call-up was to do with my teaching record.
>
> I've written to Jay and told Mum and Dad about it. I'll tell Jen at the visit on Saturday. . . .
>
> Feel *totally* calm about getting parole. I was to have gone out on 16th so I lose a week instead of ten days because of the weekend.

I wanted no one to know about my parole because I felt it was none of their business. Sadly, however, prison movement orders and leaky administration meant that many knew within forty-eight hours that I was due to be released. I also did not want to brag about my good news for there were many who would be wound up by it. One man, Shaun, in particular was due to be released before me and still had not heard. He was in my ward and I did not want to distress him, for he was very immature and liable to explode. In the event I was right, for as soon as the grapevine informed him of my good news he rushed straight in and gave me a severe telling-off for not letting him know. I explained that the news was personal and that, anyway, I did not want him to be upset. My diary entry on Friday 26 April takes up the story:

> Trev feeling rather low and Shaun very gouty. . . . He bet me the contents of his locker against that of mine that I had not really had my answer. He is a non-smoker so has rather a lot of 'goodies'. I told him the bet was silly because he would lose it but, in front of witnesses, he persisted and lost. He has, not untypically, refused to pay up. One judges people when they are under pressure; he's not the sort of man to go into battle with.

So the very thing I hoped to avoid by my silence happened anyway and Shaun was upset. Happily, though, he did receive a favourable answer and was released a few days before me. I mention him to demonstrate just how much emotion is engendered by the parole system. And I ignore the tremendous pressures some men feel a few weeks before their release. One Welshman wanted sleeping draughts on his last few nights inside because he could not cope with the excitement of release. For him the days dragged unbearably and he tortured himself the more by single-mindedly thinking of nothing but love-making with his wife. The old lags were, expectedly, as calm as a mill-pond.

I, too, was lucky. I did not find the remaining weeks a drag. Time went by as quickly as it had always done and I found that my task of having to complete a dozen koala bears in my last few weeks helped the passage of time wonderfully.

For many, though, the parole answer was unfavourable and I could see no system or logic in the nature of the answers. One man who claimed to be doing eighteen months for a motoring offence received a total KB. Another doing time for a similar offence and who had already broken a suspended sentence was paroled. Possibly the first man had skeletons well hidden in his cupboard. The, to us, illogic of the system was manifested daily.

And daily the urge to receive a 'date' pressed *forte et dure* on us all. It seemed that certain categories of prisoner, and here I exclude lifers, about whom I have written in another chapter, were doomed to an automatic KB. These included violent offenders and drug offenders. But they included, too, at least one old man of seventy who, through circumstances beyond his control, had lost his post-release accommodation and was languishing in prison. How I loathed seeing white-haired old men shuffling round the place, muttering to themselves. Surely, I vainly thought, society would not wish this to occur, but of course society neither knew nor cared.

Violent offenders had, understandably, to be 'made safe'. I could understand the caution with which they were given a date and offer no solutions to their predicament. But drug offenders seem to me to be getting a raw deal. I do not condone the use of drugs and accept that heroin and its associated chemicals are a menace. I ignore the fact that there is no evidence which suggests that cannabis is addictive and likely to lead to heroin addiction. I think I side with a former Cabinet Minister who has suggested that nicotine is far more harmful than cannabis. However, when it comes to deciding a man's date of release it strikes me as appalling that hope, the only blessing a prisoner has, should either be dangled Tantalus-fashion in front of him or removed totally.

The parole system can give three answers. Yes, you will be released. No, you will serve your full time. We don't know; we'll think about you again in a few months or years. The last answer was the cruellest and the commonest for drug offenders. I state again that the penal system would ease much of its load if it tried more mercifully to separate the crime from the criminal. I would go further in the case of drug offenders – particularly first offenders – and say that the hysteria being engendered about drug abuse by the Government is counter-productive. Superficially one can think of the attraction of forbidden fruits or the dangers of protesting too much. Over-exposure to the mayhem in Northern Ireland has blunted our susceptibilities to its horrors. Saturation bombing about AIDS will eventually cause us to become similarly careless. There must be some lessons to be learned from the Prohibition Era in America. But no, politicians believe that there is political mileage to be made out of the 'drug problem', that a firm law-and-order policy will please voters. And so it will. However, the success of such a policy ought to be measured in clearly defined terms. Law and order should be successful in solving crime, but it can only reckon to be truly successful if the offender is deterred from reoffending. That is, the punishment should not only prevent evil but should induce good in the individual. Prison does not do this.

Even more disturbing to me is the shocking disparity between sentences, particularly in drug-related crimes. Recent publicity would indicate that if a user of heroin or trafficker in cocaine or smoker of marijuana is a member of the aristocracy, rich, or a show-business or sporting personality then a token fine will be imposed. If he is an unemployed black – or white for that matter – he can expect to receive imprisonment. I exclude from this category the so-called Mr Bigs who receive decades in prison. Mind you, disparity of sentencing is rife anyway and it becomes something all inmates study closely.

At random I can cite the case of a police car which killed two old ladies while answering an emergency telephone call. The police were exonerated. A man in prison with me killed a drunk and received two years inside. According to this man's depositions he passed a breath test, reported the accident and was entirely guiltless of reckless or dangerous driving. A police sergeant receives seven years for kicking an elderly drunk to death in a cell. A young girl receives four years for stabbing the stepfather who was assaulting her. Both people were charged with the offence of manslaughter. In the case of my own charge, sentences have ranged from two years to probation. An MP is fined £250 for being many times over the legal limit of alcohol when he drove; a nonentity is given six months' jail for having twice the legal amount of alcohol in his bloodstream. A famous snooker player is fined £250 for assault causing Actual Bodily Harm. A labourer is sent to prison for twenty-seven months for an identical and first offence. The fact that the snooker player has been in trouble before is ignored. Each case I have cited is fully documented and I could cite a thousand more.

But I am concerned here to examine the workings of the parole system as it affects individuals and in the light of the supposed objectives of the punishment. I have already suggested that generally speaking a man in prison cannot easily reoffend. To this extent, then, prison has deterred him – if only temporarily. Has, though, the punishment deterred anyone else? For deterrence is supposed to be one object of our penalties. Obviously, unless our man were the first transgressor of the particular law he broke, the penalty has already failed to act as a deterrent. After all, he risked committing the crime! Even if he were the first offender and a few months after his conviction for, say, four years, people were still thanking their lucky stars that they were not the perpetrators of the deed – a highly fanciful notion in itself – can it really be imagined that one, two and three years later *anybody* is deterred by our man languishing in prison? Will anyone except his family and close friends remember him?

The idea is insane. What function, therefore, is served by keeping him in prison for years on end? It might be argued that his small section of friends and loved ones would be deterred for they would not wish to languish in a cell for three years. That argument presupposes that all his friends, or even some of them, are inclined to his misconduct. Equally absurd.

Let us further assume – and I will suggest later how this assumption is tenable – that our drug offender has been a model prisoner, that he accepted his notional four years and reconciled himself to spending at least sixteen months in prison. Let us further suggest that he has been so put off prison that he will never smuggle again. What purpose, then, given everything I have said above, is served by making him remain in prison for another sixteen months, apart from the fact that he is a convicted drug smuggler? Our hypothetical man has paid the price, reformed and will never repeat the offence. If he were a robber or tax evader or sex offender he would get parole more readily. He may serve as long in prison as the policeman who stamped an old man to death. If the policeman were to receive parole he would be released within twenty-eight months. Our smuggler, without parole, would serve thirty-two months.

If there were any evidence to suggest that the smuggler is likely to reoffend by being granted early parole, but that he would not so do if he is made to serve another sixteen months, then one could understand the system. Sadly there seems to be no correlation between prison sentence and reoffending. We are left with the conclusion that our imaginary smuggler is doomed to lose parole because he is a drug smuggler. No inroads have been made into the problem of drug trafficking by stiff penalties – not even in Malaysia, which has been hanging offenders for several years. How, on the scale of human activity, can one decide that drug smugglers are somehow 'different' from other men and that they need harsher treatment? What is the point of a parole system if some sections of the prison population are automatically – not in theory of course – precluded from it? Might it not be the case that the drug smuggler, desperate and resentful, will feel that the only way he can survive when he is eventually released is by committing further crime?

How much more disturbing would the picture seem if one pointed out that identical crimes receive very different treatment. What sense would be made of a system which indicted two people on exactly the same charges, found them guilty and sentenced one criminal to twice the period of imprisonment as the other and, to add to the inequality, granted the shorter-serving inmate parole and denied it to the other? In our example let us assume the one prisoner received four years and the other two. The two-year prisoner, *for the identical offence*, serves ten and a half months; the other serves thirty-two months. Would not this seem monstrous – particularly if the person receiving the shorter sentence had lost some remission for bad behaviour and the person serving the longer term had been a model prisoner.

The above may seem very fanciful. I have been quoting a real story. Now I shall 'humanise' it by introducing the players properly.

In late January there came into the ward a short man whose prison nickname became 'Short Person' but whom I will call Pedro. To tell his tale I shall use diary extracts and invite the reader to follow Pedro's story while remembering the points I have made above about parole, about the nature of imprisonment and so on. When I first knew him Pedro had already served about thirteen months. I write exactly twelve months after I first met him; he is still in prison and likely to serve another seven months.

### Wednesday 29 January

Pedro had heard others discussing me and my case. He thinks my conviction was bizarre and flatters me by saying how tough and wiry I am. I enjoyed the talk for it allowed me to boast about my school and educational philosophy. I read him, at his request, extracts from pupils' letters. . . . He said they must do my ego good. I agreed but also said they had the potential to tear me apart. He then told me about himself.

He and his common-law wife got four and two years

respectively for bringing cocaine back into the country from Amsterdam. They had some debts and thought they could wipe them off this way. His wife was a courier and he was a successful disc jockey (though he does not like the term) for local radio. He hosted a highly popular programme of nostalgic music – Glenn Miller, Tommy Dorsey, Frank Sinatra. He moved to a station nearer London and had a prime-time breakfast spot and was doing well. He had been short-listed for a job with the BBC just before the balloon went up. He had arranged that about £8000 worth of cocaine would be sold by a contact of his. The contact's house was raided by the police and a letter from Pedro found therein. The police raided Pedro's house and found the drugs. So the £3000 he had borrowed from the bank to buy the drugs has turned into a £12,000 debt and several years in jug.

At his trial – he and his wife were to plead guilty – not only did the solicitor not turn up but Pedro found a new and uninstructed barrister was to represent him. Before the trial, because of his co-operation with the police and former clean record, he was told that he would get a maximum sentence of two and a half years and his wife would receive a suspended sentence. Thus, the poor boy, whose foot was on the ladder of success – fan mail, celebrity appearances, etc. – has lost everything.

He is a small man . . . moustached and with a perfect 'radio voice'. He wants me to grow a beard!

At the time of the above entry Pedro's girlfriend had been released with what is known as a 'late date'. Instead of receiving parole a third of the way into her two-year sentence she served an additional ten weeks, partly because she lost time for mis-behaviour in prison. Pedro, therefore, was optimistic about his chances of a reasonably favourable decision. He defined this as a 'six months late date', i.e. he accepted the fact that his crime was regarded as appalling and thought that the authorities might make him serve twenty-two months rather than sixteen – the shorter period being his parole eligibility time. Note, too, that he accepted the initial disparity in sentence.

I now take random entries from my diary starting with one on 4 April 1986:

Pedro the disc jockey out at the dentist in Bristol today; he eagerly awaits news of his release and expects a six months late date. His parole date is in April so he hopes to be out in October at the latest. His girlfriend got parole so he's optimistic.

A week later I wrote that there had been several KBs on that day, Monday 14 April. Of Pedro I say:

Pedro went to see the Assistant Governor about his date. MacAllister (the AG) will ring the Home Office and let Pedro know tomorrow. This parole game sure is a wind-up – fortunately I've got several weeks to go before the fever hits me. Indeed perhaps two visits and Trinity Sunday will pass before I hear.

Pedro, it will be noticed, has passed his parole date without the authorities contacting him. Some men go months beyond their PED and hear nothing. The system would be improved if they were told immediately that they are not going to get parole first time round. After all, that decision must be made before the PED. On 13 May I noted that Pedro and I had a long chat about his Home Leave. He had found after sixteen months that 'nothing has changed'. I wrote, 'I hope he gets a late date.'

On 19 May:

Pedro went to see the Governor today about his parole. He and I had a long chat yesterday and I said he must go to the top. No decisions are allowed to be given over the phone and the Governor can't expedite decisions but at least he can ring the Home Office.

The following day I record: 'Pedro has been told to wait another fortnight for his answer – with no guarantee that he will get it then. . . .'

By this time, of course, Pedro was a month past his parole date and did not even know when he would receive an answer – even less whether or not he was to serve another month or another sixteen. By this time I knew I was to be released. My continued presence made it harder and harder for Pedro, who from time to time exhibited irrational and tense behaviour. It was the not knowing which caused the strain. And let it not be forgotten that this mental torture was inflicted also on his common-law wife and on his widowed mother.

*This* is the reality of being in prison. If society wants this form of suffering then it has it in full measure.

The following day – one during which Pedro was visited by his girlfriend – I recorded that he was happy after his visit, 'during which he planned his immediate post-release marriage and a fortnight's honeymoon thereafter'. It would seem a marvellous achievement that two young people should survive the joint ordeal of imprisonment and still be sufficiently in love and optimistic to be planning to wed. Surely one could advance the argument that neither would dream of being separated again and thus would not reoffend. I *know* that Pedro would not touch drug smuggling for a million pounds.

Shortly after this Pedro returned to the Assistant Governor only to be told that his parole answer had been sent to his previous prison – an establishment which he had left six months before. Even though the answer was known it could not be relayed by telephone and Pedro had to wait for it to be readdressed. When the Home Office cannot find the right prison, one wonders if it communicates the correct decisions.

The decision arrived on Wednesday 11 June:

No mail but a *black day*. Pedro got a total knock-back and on four years that is devastating. About £10,000 of cocaine – unfortunately the importation of – a 'guilty' plea – a first offence. His girlfriend, convicted on exactly the same charges, gets half the sentence and parole. She was done for smuggling booze in prison and was released only ten weeks after her PED. She visits him today.

The poor boy is, in prison terminology, 'gutted'. I've promised to help him with his Home Office petitions and to explore every avenue with and for him. . . .

I shall start on Pedro's petition tonight. We must take an original line. But the Home Office is still a mystery. One guy imports cannabis in a gang and gets three years and a six weeks late date. Shaun robs a post office and buys cocaine with the proceeds and gets first-time parole on an eighteen-month sentence. Pedro's 'wife' gets out with half the punishment. I've told him to get married now; at least his girlfriend would qualify for financial assistance. But the Home Office policy seems hell bent on destroying the lives of two young people who have paid their debt and see their future hopes recede. He could go back into crime as a result of this.

Mercifully his visit wasn't too bad. His girl is a resilient lass by all accounts. I've nicknamed her 'Josephine' but Napoleon is less than a conqueror at the moment, poor chap. We're planning appeals, etc.

Suffice to say that I spent many hours composing letters to people on Pedro's behalf. He is still in prison – a man with a loving 'wife' and a distressed mother.

To those not involved – the great majority, that is – Pedro's story will have little impact because they do not know him. To those of us who knew him in prison as a witty, intelligent human being, the thought of his languishing away for another year and a half seems monstrous. He and thousands like him are being treated inhumanely. The risk is that he and his family and friends will become inhuman. And Pedro was not alone at Leyhill.

I spent a great deal of my time trying to compose appeals for inmates. The exercise had no effect whatever. Pedro, like the others, would receive an automatic review after six months. One often wondered why the appeal procedure existed. Even the officers told us that it was a waste of time to exercise one's right of appeal. One went so far as to say that he had never known an appeal affect a Home Office decision. It was all part of the process of humiliation.

In Pedro's case his probation officer had supported him and cited the case of Pedro's wife and how well she had coped with probation. The wing officer at Pedro's previous prison had told him that he, the officer, would support his parole application. Was Pedro doomed because he was a drug offender? It would seem so. But what of his girlfriend?

The drug theory was well tested in Leyhill for there were two other offenders who used me regularly and fruitlessly as their creative amanuensis.

Joe was serving eight years for a drug offence and when I knew him he had served three. His crime was so pathetic that I could weep for him. He was a sailor who had been asked to point out a particular container on board his ship when it sailed from

# Parole

Bermuda to Liverpool. He would be paid £3000 for so doing. He was led to believe that the container contained a suitcase of drugs. In the event it appeared that there was a huge amount of drugs on the ship and that Joe had become the unwitting member of a large gang upon whom the eyes of the Excise men had long been resting. Joe's co-defendants received sentences ranging from nine to fourteen years. In Walton Prison Joe was banged up with one of the co-defendants who, when Joe asked him where the £3000 for him was, told him to forget it if he wanted his wife and family to remain unharmed.

So silly Joe received eight years' imprisonment and no money. At no time did I hear him complain about his initial sentence but he, like Pedro, said to me one day that he reckoned that after three years inside he had done enough. On 27 April I noted in my diary that I had written a letter to his probation officer for him, pointing out that he felt he should again be considered for release. Joe went on Home Leave and saw this probation officer, who agreed with and supported Joe's application. Joe's wife after three years' separation from him wanted him home. A year later he is still inside – patient, co-operative but mystified by the system of parole which passes him by.

Dino, a cunning likeable rogue from Pakistan who always addressed me as 'Master', was a demanding 'client'. He had been convicted of dealing in heroin and had received just under three years. Like Pedro and Joe, he was also denied parole. By the time he came to ask me to write letters for him he was at loggerheads with his probation officer, who came to the prison to tell him that he, the probation officer, was not recommending him for parole. I was asked to write a 'snorter' to the man and did so. Unfortunately, as a postscript to my reasoned but firm letter, Dino added the words 'Are you a racist?' The reply was swift and conciliatory but the stumbling block was Dino's home circumstances.

He had a wife and a mistress. And all the while he consorted with the latter the authorities, not unreasonably, regarded his home circumstances as less than stable. Oddly, though, his long-suffering wife knew of the existence of her rival – a lady for whom Dino said all his passion was now spent – and was still desperately keen to have her husband back. Matters became so taut that Dino even asked me to speak to his wife on the pay-phone to advise her of what to write to the Probation Service in support of her husband's plea for parole. I refused to do this but I wrote down the exact words which I thought would help him so that he could relay them to his wife. All to no avail.

Dino even went to the prison authorities for help. When asked by the principal officer of his wing about his mistress, Dino told me he had replied that he 'loved' his wife and the mistress was merely the lady he used to 'fuck'. His problem was undoubtedly greater because his English was not good and the prison experience was adding only to his store of expletives and scatalogical expressions.

Indeed, it came as a surprise to me to learn that another Asian in the kitchen, whose command of English seemed excellent, had scant comprehension of our language. He asked me to teach him better English, which I tried to do; I soon realised that many of the misunderstandings which punctuated our dealings with this man were the result of poor English and not of bloody-mindedness.

There was, obviously, nothing racist about the decision to keep Dino in prison. He was not an uncooperative inmate and his wife wanted him home. True, he was rather idle and crafty, and he had an appetite that made Gargantua seem positively anorexic. No. Like Pedro and Joe, Dino was victim of the 'hard line' the authorities were taking on drugs. Sadly and ineffectually the only ones benefiting from the hardness were those directly concerned who had learned their lesson.

The myth that all sex offenders got automatic parole was easy to explode. A number did but many did not. I helped a convicted homosexual and a man bizarrely convicted of the attempted buggery of a girl put in applications to gain their freedom. My help was in vain. The first man, whom I have mentioned before, had received eight years for homosexual acts with males under the age of twenty-one. On appeal his sentence had been reduced to six years. He was not a paedophile but had fallen victim of our absurd laws on the age of consent.

He had spent years in the Regular Army and was, to that extent, institutionalised. He was friendly, kind, unobtrusive and lonely. He openly admitted to his sexual leanings and was sometimes ribbed, sometimes respected, for that fact. I first wrote a pre-parole application for this man based upon information he had initially supplied.

He had some money and occasionally I would compose letters

to his bank manager for him. His sole interest in life was soccer and being released into a hostel. I composed letters for his hostel application; he received promises of jobs once he was outside; he accepted 'treatment' for his homosexuality – though I am not sure how I could be 'treated' for my heterosexual orientation; he was no threat to children or to himself. He was knocked back.

The other man was a tragic case. He had been accused, on the say-so of a disgruntled business colleague, of attempting to bugger a young girl. The girl denied the assault and the parents made no complaint. (I know this for I have seen all the documents and got to know the man and his family well.) The alleged victim was a family friend – and still is – whom my co-inmate used to taxi from place to place on a regular basis. The man was not tried as such but in a special judicial hearing he agreed, under duress, that his hand may have touched the girl's bottom while he was tickling her knee. There was no forensic evidence to suggest that anal penetration by finger, let alone by penis, had occurred. The man convicted himself in his confusion by agreeing that maybe he had touched the girl's bottom. He received three years. I believe him to be totally innocent of the charge.

But that does not matter. What is important is that the victim's family support his release. His wife wants him home. His neighbours miss his presence. In prison he was popular, hard-working and well regarded. So much so that the majority of inmates thought he was in prison for an entirely different offence. Thus his 'secret' has been preserved by – in his case – a totally sympathetic regime. Even the Reception cons who tend to know everything have kept silent. Such is the depth of sympathy for this man.

He was due to be released on parole just before Christmas in 1986. But he had an enemy in an unexpected quarter. His female probation officer was an interfering do-gooder. She desired to make a case out of him and was constantly visiting his wife and demanding that the facts of his case be talked through *ad nauseam*. The wretched woman insisted on a strange social worker being introduced to the home. And all the while the wife and family wanted to be left in peace to pick up the threads of their lives again. The probation officer would not let go.

I became involved when one day the man received a letter from his wife which reduced him to tears. She was at her wits' end because of the prurience and negative interference of the probation officer. It was at this time that the man told me his full story. I promised to say nothing, though there had been occasional rumours about him. Whenever his name was mentioned in the future I denied that he was anything except a thief. I advised him to go to the prison probation office and enlist their help. At the same time I said he could sack and replace his probation officer and certainly could get rid of the social worker. We composed a stiff letter to that effect, thinking it not unreasonable that if the so-called helpful agencies were causing acute distress they must be replaced.

For a short while after receipt of that letter matters improved. The man's wife was left to live her life and the probation officer came to the prison to restore relationships. I would have staked a large amount of money that my co-inmate would be spending Christmas at home. By now he would be fully integrated into the community, at one with his family and gainfully employed.

His wife rang me to say that he had received a total, one-year knock-back. She put the blame fairly and squarely on a vindictive, interfering female probation officer. As I write, this man is still in prison and I grieve for him and his family. If his probation officer had had the sensitivity and skills of my own – whom I could not admire more – he would, today, be a free man, saving the state about £300 per week.

The parole system is as much a lottery as Premium Bond prize draws. With its unpredictability and unfairness, it is a source of indescribable anguish. It is the sole source of hope for thousands of convicted men and women – most of whom accept the justice of their punishment but long for, and often fail to receive, the mercy of a 'good' answer.

The callousness within the system is best demonstrated by a small entry in my diary on 29 April 1986. In it I note that Dave, a man serving four years for robbery and accidental arson, seeks parole information:

Dave is now twelve weeks after his date and still has no answer. He went to MacAllister today and was told that if he heard nothing by September to come back!! September!! This is appalling and some moron from the Home Office said on the radio today that a three-year sentence should mean three years and that additional time should be added for bad behaviour in prison. This statement underlines what is essentially wrong with the system; no one who decides, rules, legislates or releases, knows what it is like to be in prison.

The only thing it's taught me is how to steal, to be underhand and to trust no one. Oh, and I've also learned how to commit a number of crimes – and that it is absurd to say that all those in prison are failed criminals. Many have got away with countless crimes though they are paying the penalty for some others. Others – and they seem not to be few in number – are in prison because they were grassed up. . . . If a tithe of the crimes planned in here are effected then Leyhill will sorely stretch police resources in the future.

And it is to be remembered that Leyhill is an open prison in which all men expect – or are led to believe – that their chances of a favourable parole decision are high. Dave had already served three months after his PED and was now being told to wait another five. He was being told this not by a member of the Parole Board but by an administrator in his prison whose function was not to speak, *ex tempore*, for the Home Office. Happily, though, and unexpectedly, Dave was released into a hostel on the same day as me. This fact alone, when set beside the heartless advice of the Assistant Governor, tells its own story.

Would to God that the Home Office spokesman I referred to in the diary extract knew what he was implying by his remark. If the system of punishment worked I would applaud and share his view. That the majority of criminals accept their punishment and honestly expect parole should encourage the system to show compassion. After all, it is not the convict who invented the parole system. But its abuse by those who run it is a significant cause of the discontent in prison and a major cause of reoffending outside.

It is, finally, interesting to record that old lags, who were brought up before parole existed, loathe it. They blame it for increasing the length of sentences at conviction stage and for effectively resentencing the criminal at parole stage. Thus a man who might have received a three-year sentence twenty years ago and have served two, now received six years because the judge knows he will have some chance of being out after two. In practice, the longer the sentence, the more serious, rightly, is the crime adjudged to be; therefore, the chance of the prisoner getting parole is reduced. In essence, then, the parole system is doing precisely the opposite of what it was intended to do. And in so operating it is causing unspeakable mental torture to prisoner and family alike. And, of course, relatively short sentences do not qualify for parole. That fact, too, gives pause for serious thought.

# 16

## LIFE OUTSIDE

*The sober comfort, all the peace which springs*
*From the large aggregate of little things;*
*On these small cares of daughter, wife, or friend,*
*The almost sacred joys of home depend.*

Hannah More, 'Sensibility'

I wrote the following letter to my wife on the morning of Saturday 14 December 1985. I had been in prison fourteen hours:

Dear Jen, Jamie, Tim and Jay,
    There is only one thing that you must all understand and that is that I am *perfectly* all right. It's now about noon and though I am still confused by all the things I have to get sorted out here I am in no grim way distressed. The staff I've met so far have been most helpful and my fellow holidaymakers are excellent. You need have no fear of [*sic*] my personal safety. I am at no risk whatsoever. We arrived last night quite late; one of my fellows knows Tony Wood and Podge. It is a small world! Now to facts. As far as I can work out you are entitled to visit me any time you like and thereafter at twenty-eight-day intervals. All of you may come. I'm allowed my pipe and I could have brought my tobacco in. Please send the pipe and a radio (not VHF) and batteries. Send enough cash for me to be able to buy a daily *Times*. Toiletries, tobacco cannot be bought from private cash. £5 at the moment will suffice. I am allowed to send two letters a week and I may be allowed more. I may be able to receive stamps and notepaper and envelopes. But the rules still confuse me. All I will say is that recent publicity has made me well known and elicited many comments – one from an officer, who, surprisingly, had a great deal to say about the case.
    You are probably more distressed than I am at the moment. When you get organised, darling, tell Trevor or Jon Cooper or Andrew B to sort out my tax, pension, your two-term contract,

the personal effects in school and our loan. John H will need to sort out J's fees. Keep him at school as long as possible. When you move out sell most of my books – keep the antiquarian ones but raise as much cash as you can. John G and Ron must be galvanised to sort out the mini-market and net store respectively. Cash from the school will help, I hope.

I am confident that you will be well looked after by our many friends. The more 'good' publicity we get the better. I would love to receive many letters from everyone, but you must explain that I will not reply to them for the reasons explained above.

It is likely that I shall be transferred but only at a time when I can go to another prison anonymously. This is likely to be after Christmas but, of course, you will be informed. I will be eligible for parole in six months but it does not follow that I shall get it. It does, though, seem likely that I shall be home in May or June, but we'll see.

Jay must, if he so wishes, go on his Ben Nevis trip. We must decide whether or not Tim comes to Sennen permanently. How is he? Actually I cannot begin to express my love for you all in case I become drowned in sentiment. Send some photos – in giving you my wallet I forgot I had none. Is Jamie going to look for work in PZ now or what?

I take it the shock waves have passed through all the families and friends. Neil was going to ring this week from Canada. He may offer you help financially – if he does accept the help. You mustn't be Yorkshire stubborn, angel. I have ruined everything we've worked for and I find it hard to believe that your sacrifices since May should lead to a wrongful conviction. A common feeling here is that I was convicted by public opinion. Ah well, it is a new experience and I will try and make use of it. I am not worrying about whether you will all survive materially – our friends will guarantee that. That you will survive as a family is equally certain. You are such a wonderful family to have that you will all care for each other – and boys, you could not have a more competent and loving mother.

Please thank – inadequate word – the superlative support in court everyone gave and ask people to write. I just feel I have let everyone down and destroyed the school and the education of so many children. That our enemies and evil have triumphed is hard to accept but we must all make a new start. Try not to let my absence give too depressing a Christmas. Imagine I am back in the USA or something and will return in the summer. I love you all so very much and hope to see you in the next few days or so. I will be thinking and praying for you but ask you not to worry. Don't forget Tim needs *Samurai Blades. Fondest* love to you,

Yours restrictedly,
Mike/Dad

(Pass on the above address to everyone please.)

My letter was accompanied by useful information from the authorities about visits and so on.

This first letter, written on 14 December, was posted, second class, on Monday the 16th. It thus arrived after the visit Jen, Jay and Tim paid on the 16th. They spoke little of how life had changed for them but it was significant that already Jamie, my eldest son, felt unwilling to see me in prison. He did, though, visit Leyhill several times. It was only much, much later and from friends that I learned how Jen had spent the days immediately after my conviction.

Once the verdict was declared and I had been taken to the cells, Jen, in tears, was supported by our equally tearful friends. The group of them loitered at the back of the court room avoiding the press. The press had badgered Jen for a press conference if I was available at the end of the case. In the event she did not have to go through that ordeal.

Eventually Jen came to see me in the cells with Jamie, as I have already described. Penny, a staunch and dear friend, with the help of the senior prison officer in court, arranged to take her car to the rear of the building where the prison bus was waiting. Jen was slipped out of the back door and invited to wait in the prison bus until Penny's car was accessible. Just as Jen was mounting it the car arrived and she and Penny drove off to a prearranged meet in a garage forecourt, where they were to meet with my secretary Lora and the wife of a colleague. The three of them drove to Lora's home, where Jen and I had been staying with Tim during the trial.

Jamie, meanwhile, went home with another friend whose mother, Lois, had come for the last day of the trial, bringing with her her daughter, Helen, and one of my pupils.

Later that evening Penny and her husband returned to the court to collect my car.

While this was going on Lora's husband, Alan, had been deputed to collect Tim from school and bring him back to the house. Alan had been informed of the verdict before he collected Tim but could not bring himself to tell him. Jen remembers walking into Alan's house and seeing the look on Tim's face. It registered comprehension, having read the expression on Jen's own tear-stained face. Tim asked, 'Is Dad with you?' Jen said I was not and they both collapsed into tears while Lora and Alan tactfully made tea.

My middle son, Jason, was travelling home from boarding school and would not arrive until the following morning. Lois and Jamie met his train and told him the grave news. He was taken to Lois's house where he and Jamie were due to stay. Jay rang his mother later in the day but was speechless. He could say nothing but merely wept down the phone. It was only at the end of the day that he could face Jen with some measure of control.

Saturday was spent constantly on the telephone. Calls of support poured in and Jen made many outgoing ones. One, to Exeter Prison, amused Lora. Jen was put through to what she describes as 'a nice, Yorkshire warder' who chatted about their mutual county of birth and gave her information about how and when to visit and so on. Jen asked if he could relay a message to me. He agreed to and did. As I have said, I shall never forget his quiet, Yorkshire voice saying 'She's all right. She sends her love. She's coming to see you on Monday.' And even now I feel profound gratitude to this anonymous prison officer who was the first contact between my wife and me after I had started my sentence.

Another close friend volunteered to drive Jen to Exeter. Jamie, fearing that the visit would take place in a cell, did not come. Jen, Tim and Jay arrived early at the prison. Lois had packed them a picnic and they chewed their lunch while waiting in a public car park. Then they walked to the prison, where Jen remembers going through a gate to the main doors. There was a queue ahead which built up behind as they waited. A few at a time were let through a Judas gate, after which they gave their names to an officer and were ushered into a waiting room. Jen remembers holding the baby of another visitor while its mother folded the pram. Previously in the street the lady had changed its nappy. Eventually they were called from the waiting room, went across a courtyard and through doors into a screened-off part of the visitors' hall.

My letter had not arrived, so Jen had no notion of what she could or could not bring in to me. She asked for a list and was initially given that which pertained to remand prisoners. Her name was eventually called and the visit occurred.

Jen remembers wanting to leave the prison as quickly as possible after the visit. She thought the Christmas decorations in the hall were pathetic – in the proper sense of that word – and she loathed seeing an officer, perched in a high chair like a tennis umpire, and his three peripatetic colleagues supervising the visit.

So Jen went home to Lora's where she spent the next sad week. She took the family up north for Christmas and I lost track of them for three weeks because of my transfer and the tardiness of Christmas mail. In the New Year she returned to her hundred-hour-a-week job at my school, where she remained a loved, vital colleague, until she resigned a few weeks before my release so that she could welcome me home.

Jamie went to London until my release and Jay and Tim returned to school. None now wishes to articulate his feelings at the time. Suffice to say that they all suffered, and in ways which have not yet, perhaps, manifested themselves. But two years after the verdict Tim – now a teenager – is still unable to attend school and is undergoing weekly psychiatric treatment. A suicide threat was taken seriously by the specialist treating him and we daily watch in the hope that happiness will eventually return to him. At the moment his life is destroyed.

I received 327 letters or cards during the six months or so I spent in prison. During that period I wrote 133 letters. Rationing necessarily meant I could not reply to all the letters I received; equally, even if I could have written an unlimited number of replies, I could not have afforded to. It was absolutely the case that letters were my sole joy in prison. Each day I eagerly consulted the letter board for my number. I think I am right in saying that there were only six days on which I was not written to. Some days I received as many as ten letters, but generally a couple of missives arrived per day. One of my early detractors at Leyhill changed his tune towards me once he had learned how a veritable confetti of correspondence was showered upon me daily and that many of the letters came from pupils.

A dozen pretty, intelligent teenage girls wrote regularly to me. Their penalty for this loyalty was to receive a koala bear each. And they suffered from my imprisonment. They wrote of the school discotheque Tim and Jay had told me about on their first visit, and how it had been an occasion for tears and deep upset. Another ex-pupil ran a private disco after this one. In other ways, too, the pupils were affected and wanted to help. I was told of a pupil-intention to approach the Prime Minister – a wonderful gesture but one which Jen and I discouraged, not least because it would fail to have effect. But also we did not want to involve the school in further adversity. In like manner we dampened down the enthu-siastic group of parents and friends who wanted to approach the television programme *Rough Justice* on my behalf. Nonetheless it was good for me to learn that those 'on the home front' were fighting on and the moving *ex ore innocentium* remarks of my pupils were profoundly sustaining.

The very first letter I received in prison was from my secretary Lora, with whom I had not worked for very long. Fate was to decree that this should be a permanent state of affairs. She wrote the following wonderful letter on Saturday 14 December while she and her husband were 'nursing' Jen and Tim:

I know you will be eager to hear, above all else, that Jen and Tim are being absolutely wonderful. Tim took it so well, and is bearing up bravely and knows it is going to be 'liveable with'. The telephone has been hot with calls of support and sym-pathy, and our undercover operation to duck the press with Jen succeeded, so we felt we'd managed to cock a very small snook at the whole lot of them! Jen and Tim will stay here for as long as it seems helpful to have so many friends so nearby. You'd all have hated Greece at this time of the year anyway!

Already a feeling is emerging (I'm sorry, that must have offended, starting a paragraph with 'already') from the talks we've had on the phone with Jim and Julian that the ranks must close to do battle for the school against any adversities that may be imminent and to perpetuate what you started. I don't know how you'll be feeling about that – somewhat more callous about the place, perhaps – but it is their intention to insist, with

# Life Outside

Andrew's help, on being present at a governors' meeting next Wednesday, so that at least they can't pull off anything absurd with Common room's knowledge. We shall see, but it's bracing to see that everyone's spirit hasn't been utterly eroded.

Jen has enclosed this fiver so that at least you can get your hands on *The Times* and a Biro! I hope sincerely that you'll find something in the life you're going to have to put up with for the next few months that will be sustaining in one way or another. I imagine that you might meet some rather interesting people along the way to lighten the ordeal a little!

We're thinking of you all the time. Please know that the family will get all the support they need from the vast 'network' of people down here – I'm sure you do know it. We expect to see Jamie and Jay later this afternoon when they come back from a run to Sennen to pick up the mail. Tim is looking forward to launching himself at Jay for a good bellow but is being doggedly selective about his moments of such release, and is currently cheerfully playing a mediaeval jousting game with Alan! One can cope with most things if challenged and your brood look as if they are rising nobly to this occasion – I'm sure you imagined they'd never do anything else.

I shall continue to fire a steady barrage of letters your way and hope that those who have to read them first don't get so fed up with me that they can't bear to open anything addressed in my handwriting! I will try to be more brief if necessary! Alan says *nil carborundum illegitans*!

with much love
Lora

It would be hard to imagine how Lora's letter could have been improved. The family was secure and loved. My school would survive if my colleagues had anything to do with it. The letter reduced me to tears – but more of relief and happiness than of regret and misery. And, true to her word, the wonderful Lora wrote regularly and even managed a visit with Alan and Jamie.

Christmas approached and with it came many letters and cards from friends all over the country. With these I 'decorated' my cell and sent replies to various 'clearing houses' of strategically placed friends who would radiate my messages. I wanted so much for everyone to enjoy their Christmas in the knowledge that mine was not unbearable.

Just before Christmas I received two messages from the outside world which moved me deeply. One was the large Christmas card signed by the majority of pupils and staff at my school. The other was the letter from the girl involved in my case who had unwillingly and confusedly been compelled to testify against me. Her testimony had been rejected and the absurd charge based on it dropped. I recorded the following in my diary on Sunday 22 December:

Just before going to church received a wonderful letter from a girl in relation to whom charges against me were dropped. She writes, 'I am writing to apologise to you. It is very difficult to write down what I want to say but I do hope you understand what I mean. The school is carrying on as best as possible but I think I speak for everyone when I say it will never have the happy, friendly, family-like atmosphere it had when you were headmaster. . . . I cannot think of much else to say except that I do mean I am really sorry. . . .' What a generous remark. She has seen Jamie and Jay . . . and tells me about her plans. I look forward eagerly to replying to her. I think the judge unsettled her in court.

So there was one very worried girl on the outside. The hysteria which the police investigation caused forced her into adolescent fantastical conclusions of which she rid herself during the trial. Now the poor girl thought she had sent me to prison. I replied telling her she was blameless and that I was delighted to hear from her. She wrote again on 23 January to say, among other things, that my Leyhill address was posted on the school noticeboard because many wished to write to me. Again I was touched and grateful that the youngsters – creatures with notoriously short memories – were still thinking of me. I did not reply this time as I had no available spare letters and was, by now, having to adopt a rationing system.

I had six letters a week to distribute. Five were already spoken for – Jen, Jay, Jamie and my parents were all at different addresses and I tried to write Tim a private one each week too. It meant that my dozen weekly correspondents had often to accept that their letters would remain unanswered. I tried, too, to respond at least once to all those from pupils. This time the girl would receive no reply.

Her story does not end here for she wrote a third letter to Leyhill, which I answered. This event caused great anguish and anger to Jen, who already had enough to cope with. I noted down the mail I received every day. On Thursday 3 April I recorded that I had received a letter – 'a charmer' I described it – from a girl 'who was involved in my case'. I further recorded that it was the third unsolicited letter she had written and that I had replied to it 'with great pleasure'. By this time there was no real censorship at Leyhill – despite which Jen constantly told me she never felt confident enough to write intimate letters in case they were read by others. It did not matter to me, by now, because I was practised in the art of letter-writing and in writing fairly neutral but, I hoped, diverting missives.

On Friday 4 April I wrote:

A very unpleasant episode today. Out of the blue I received a call-up from the Governor. I went to get changed, having asked Ryan what it was all about; he didn't know but didn't think I was in trouble. Conscience doth make cowards of us all and mine was working overtime. I knew that they had failed to pin a number of little pranks on me but wondered if at last I'd been found out. I had done nothing nasty since Jen's bollocking except send out the odd unofficial letter. I'd sent one out yesterday whose contents would be better unknown! I feared it had been intercepted but my 'postman' said it had got to the post. The arrangement was that 'stiffs' [illegal letters] should not be put in post boxes near the prison. Mine was due to be posted in Cheltenham or South Wales! I worked out in my head an 'explanation' for its contents if, indeed, it had been discovered.

A number of inmates awaited the Governor's pleasure. Each was called in by his surname and number by the Chief Officer. I was called in last with the gentle words 'Will you come in please.' No surname, no number. I stood before the Governor in the presence of the Chief – Governors are always ac-companied by the presence of an officer. On his desk was an unopened letter! My heart leaped – literally. But it was not my 'stiff' – it was my reply to the girl who'd written yesterday. I was shocked. Questions and answers started.

'Why are you writing to a girl involved with your case?'

'Because she's written to me.'

'Does your wife know you're writing to her?'

'Of course she does.'

'Do you write to the principal girl in your case?'

'Certainly not.'

'Do the girl's parents know you write?'

'I assume so. I always ask the girl to give them my regards. I assume she shows them the letters. In fact, I've only written her two, though she has sent me three.'

'What does she say in her letters?'

'Just general news about what she's doing.'

'What have you written to her?'

'Open the letter and read it.'

'I don't like opening letters. I never did like censorship.'

'I'd rather you read the letter. Please open it.'

'I'd prefer you to tell me.'

'Please open the letter. It's merely a response to her unsolicited and kind letter.'

'I'd like to see her letter. Bring it to me this afternoon at 1.45 p.m.'

'I thought censorship had been abolished.'

'I'm allowed to open any letter. Bring it to me this afternoon.'

In other words there was still censorship!

I left the office seething with rage. First, he had insulted me by implying I was conducting a sort of clandestine postal affair with a girl who had figured in my case (and who lived to regret her misleading testimony – and which she withdrew in court and which was suggested to her by the police). Next he insults my wife and the girl's parents. But how, if censorship is over, do they spot my letter and know who the girl is? I've written to about a dozen girls since I've been in prison and this is the second letter she has received. The one from Exeter and my reply went through the censor with no trouble.

I returned at 1.45 p.m. and sat in the waiting room. After a while the Governor came out and said, 'Oh there you are.' I said I'd been waiting for a summons from the Chief Officer and didn't know the drill. This time he was on his own. He read the first page of the girl's letter, having first invited me to sit, and remarked, 'Oh, it's only chitchat.' That's the nearest he got to being plastered over his own wall. What did the dirty-minded little man expect? I was curt to the point of rudeness. He noticed her letter ended 'All my love' and remarked that he expected that it did not mean anything. But he also asked how I'd ended mine. I said I couldn't remember but that all he had to do was open it and we'd both know.

Eventually he started talking of Winchester. I stood up – conscious that this was not a social occasion and that I was still, in his mind, a guilty sex-offender. He remarked that he had seen my parole report and we spent some time talking about my case and about Winchester generally. We discussed his schooling and the changes there had been in the city over the past decade or so. It was a bizarre experience given our respective positions. His parting shot as I ended the interview was that he would have a word with the censors and 'see what could be done' about my letter. He showed surprise that so many pupils still wrote to me and wondered if I had written to my MP. Presumably, he surmised, my school had now closed. Thanks be to God it hasn't.

The whole affair has left a nasty taste. I understand – at least in part – his concern and responsibility. Shades of things to come, I suppose. But several people have, to my mind, been besmirched – mostly my own wife.

Even Ryan showed some concern when I went back to the kitchen. 'Everything all right, Mike?' he asked. As a courtesy I told Ryan all about it. Despite what I've said about him I did feel he was genuinely concerned – not gratuitously curious. Apparently Brian and Trevor were very worried. They know of some of my exploits and are both rather close to me and expect me to be shipped out at any moment. Brian had asked Ryan why I was with the Governor; Ryan amusingly told him that my promotion to Assistant Governor had come through!

The whole episode meant that the girl could no longer write to me – a fact that might well add to her already developed sense of guilt. I told Jen of the incident and she was extremely angry. She resolved to write a snorter to the Governor and demand to see him. I told her that she was well within her rights and that I looked forward to her letter. When she is mad, as I told many cons, she is the only thing on earth that frightens me. She would turn the Governor into rissoles. A week later she wrote to say that she was in the middle of composing her 'Exocet'.

I was glad she was fighting but resented that further *Angst* and stress were being placed on her – and over something so trivial. Two innocent outsiders were being made to suffer more by the operation of the system. Shortly after all this I was given parole and that cheerful fact caused Jen to abandon her attack on the Governor.

And all the while I was worried about the welfare of my family. Jen in an early letter had quoted from a favourite love sonnet of mine – I have quoted the lines already – but the fact that she so wrote indicates the effect on her of my being in prison. In 'normal' circumstances her reticence would have made such a gesture unthinkable. Generally her letters revealed that she was working desperately hard at her cardinal job in the school as well as coping with all the financial matters affecting my demise. She looked after the boys wonderfully and hid most of her worries from me. But there was one letter which she wrote which revealed that she was under enormous stress. Unwittingly, I was the cause of burdening her even further. She had always disapproved of my antisocial stance in prison and had tried to dissuade me from misbehaving. For this reason she knew virtually nothing of my smuggling and other activities. Indeed, I dared not tell her of the ten days' loss of remission until she had learned of and assimilated the news of the loss of visits. Even that news I sent via my secretary.

One day, after Jen knew of my punishment, I received the following letter:

By the way I am livid with you – you will not listen when I had begun to think maybe you would for the first time in nineteen years.

There are many things we need to discuss alone and I feel that one visit ought to be just me. There are many adjustments that need to be made and for once I am not going to do the adjustments and giving way for the sake of peace and quiet.

Those I need desperately, and need to lay things on the line otherwise I can see problems. You are altering and I suppose it is inevitable because of where you are and whom you meet, but it won't do and you must make no decisions without me being fully aware of all details. Do not hit the ceiling – this worm has turned. Use your intelligence. I have nearly killed myself for three and a half years and I will not commit myself again blindly.

Inside may be hard but it is extremely disagreeable on the outside in my position – which is nil.

Before you write again – think long and hard. I do not want a slanging match but sense. Hard work again I expect and do not mind, but founding a school, even though you had to learn a lot of business, does not make you magnate of the year. For once my pessimism must be taken into account. Yorkshire 'nous' counts for a lot and must be taken into consideration. You cannot write a concerto before you have learned your scales.

You must realise how different things will be when you get home. There will be no cash left and debts to pay off. After all, by then I shall have no job here. . . . I worked for you and I have continued here for you so that this place will continue – after all you founded it and that cannot be taken away from you. But I often feel like the spectre at the feast and there is no incentive now. . . .

Sorry about all this but things crystallise over the months. Put it down to tiredness if you like, but it is what I believe. Admittedly my brain is very woolly but at least you are not here to side-track me and make me lose my train of thought.

The above letter shattered me. Initially I thought Jen wanted to leave me until I realised that she was under inordinate strain – as much strain as me – and she had lost her 'status' in the school because of my conviction. That night, I remember, there was one person whose murder I could have effected – and it was not Jen.

My diary entry of 1 March records that 'I have had a heavy, heavy heart all day. I am too busy to weep.'

I replied on 3 March:

My Darling Jen,

I cannot tell you how relieved I was to see Lora, Alan and Jamie yesterday. Your last letter I took entirely the wrong way and spent a sleepless night! In fact, I could not read it all at the first attempt because I was so stunned. As Lora said we are both under pressure in different ways, don't have each other to turn to and become introspective. You have lost much of your original identity and I have lost all of mine. . . .

. . . as I said in my last letter there is no risk of my being in further trouble in here. After all if Jono had not bought the tobacco I could not have smuggled it in. You refuse to bring it to me, ergo, I cannot get into trouble. . . .

For an insane twenty-four hours I thought you were hinting that the peaceful life without me was beginning to suit you. I was desperately frantic.

All your points have been taken on board. But obviously you know I will have, well, it could be eighteen months' pent-up energy to release. . . .

I love you so much and can't wait to see you at the end of the month or so. Don't worry too much; things will improve.

Fondest fondest love,<br>Mike

Jen's reply to this letter further revealed the nature of her painful experience and the thoughts which occupied her.

Darling,

Just taken Tim to karate after which a friend will pick him up, give him lunch and then they are going to roller skate at St Austell for Karen's birthday treat. . . .

As for us – I'm sorry. I don't mean to put all the blame on you, but my brain doesn't function and it is hard to appear normal and not let people see how hurt one is by all that goes on here – or doesn't as the case may be. My head is woolly and every trivial thing sets me off. Every day I dread the post even though I know eventually the bills will be paid. . . . It goes on and on like a treadmill. If I could just switch off for four weeks with no decisions to be made I could recover my equilibrium but that is not possible.

I do need you and love you, but for years I have played second fiddle to one hanger-on after another. So I suppose I retreated and I was exasperated when you had been out and by what I had to listen to when you returned. That cannot happen again. . . . we shall find it hard enough to pick up the pieces and outsiders around are no help.

Even now I feel I am not expressing things properly, but always there is the feeling that others will read this and the antibiotics I am on are making me rather dopey – I just want to crash out instead of cooking Sunday supper for all the boarders. You will come bouncing out full of a desire to get on and I shall just want to have peace and time to ourselves so both of us will have to be very careful.

But it takes very little to make me fly off the handle and that terrifies me because words spoken in anger can never be properly retrieved and you have always tied me in knots verbally and always had the last word. Please don't misunderstand – I do want you back – even if life is quieter now!! Look what we did over the last three and a half years but equally we must have time to spend together – as you rightly say, in a few years we shall be on our own and I would rather our future was together not apart. But we shall have to walk before we run – and I always walk and you always run. If all this sounds as if I'm putting the onus on you again please believe me it isn't meant to. . . . I want you back. Hang on to those four words whatever.

<u>All my love</u>

Jen

She had never underlined before; all was well!

In a way, of course, Jen was much luckier than many convicts' wives. She had been to a good school and was literate and articulate. Both of us could communicate with reasonable accuracy by letter; even so, the strains of our respective environments and positions caused there to be occasional hiatuses in our correspondence. How much worse, then, for the many who were unaccustomed to the written and read word – and for them there were none to intercede.

At the time Jen's first letter came and I was concerned, generally, about the family's welfare, a remarkable letter came from Tim. He had suffered much and presumably will bear the scars for ever. He is a deep thinker for an eleven-year-old – as he was then – and had rationalised my predicament and that of the whole family.

Dear Dad

This is a short note to continue my last letter to you. I keep on composing a letter in my mind. This is it. One day, before your trial, you said, 'This is all a test from God.' I thought of this and I think that, well, the school just made you and Mum tired. So God thought, 'I will get him out of this. I will make him a £1,000,000air [sic]. So I will send him to prison for a year to show his sons never to go there and he will meet a very successful man (Terry) and also have a gaurd [sic] and friend in prison (Pete). When he gets out of prison his last days will be very comfortable.'

Good hey.

also, you know those notes you made in Court, may I have them. Where are they and I will be going on a birthday date – Karen's birthday with Julie and Karen, roller skating, then eat, then listen to music. Prep has ended so I must go.

Lots of love,<br>Tim

How does one cope with a letter like that? I wept copiously and showed it to all my friends in prison.

Tim wrote regularly and developmentally, as it were. Many of his letters were accompanied by allegorical drawings of my progress. With no prompting he invented his own Bunyanesque Hill of Difficulty and as the weeks and months went by I was portrayed nearer and nearer the summit. He added other figures to the drawings – Pete, particularly, became a hero of his for I told him that Pete was 'protecting' me. Until his downfall, Terry, too, occupied a place in Tim's imagination. For on visits I had described Terry as a friend: at the time it seemed important to reassure Tim that I was surrounded by friends and helpers. These people became part of Tim's mythology. It was as if, by himself, he had invented his own *Piers Plowman* rolled into Bunyan's allegorical landscapes with a touch of John Donne's 'Satire on Religion'. I was at once impressed and concerned. The whole affair had caused Tim to develop a very old head on very young shoulders.

But the commonest effect on friends and family alike was one of shock. One friend wrote:

My Dear Mike,
I am so sad for you. I really believed that British Justice would stand by you in your 'hour of need'. I never dreamed that an innocent person could be treated so badly.

There are many of your friends and colleagues who are shocked and numbed by what has happened to you.

May the Good Lord show us all a way to channel our positive thoughts into a pool of productive energy to help you in your dilemma.

My friend, you, with the power that you have been blessed with, if you had a mind to put pen to paper, could you not tell the world of your injustice and with such eloquence.

You are always in my thoughts and my family's.

God bless you.

Roger

PS. Penny sends her love and has reminded me that I am supposed to be life's jester and suggests I ask you, now that you have time to yourself, do you think you could make 'it' clap now?

Perhaps I should sign myself, JW 1891.

NULLI CESSURA FIDES

'Roger would have killed you if he thought you were guilty,' his wife, Penny, told me. I say this to show the depth of feeling there was about my case and also to reveal how yet another law-abiding citizen had had his faith in our legal system shaken. The Latin quotation at the end of his letter was my school's motto – Good Faith That Will Yield to Nothing.

The 'it' refers to an occasion when during the performance of *Macbeth* – the school play I had produced that year – I had criticised Roger and the audience for sitting silent during the performance. I told Roger that I had seen more life in a stale dog turd. Several days later a suspicious parcel arrived at the school for me. Roger had sent me an artificial turd to which he had inscribed the challenge 'Try making that clap.' He was reminding me of the good old days and doing what he was so good at – cheering me up.

His son, a pupil of mine, resented not being asked to testify at my trial on my behalf, and he also wrote. He movingly signed his letter, 'Your friend for ever'. His sister, who went to another school, also wrote. Penny did not, so I wrote and asked if she were literate. A few days later a postcard arrived for me which had on it all the letters of the alphabet and was signed 'Mother'. For a minute or two I thought it was some elaborate code. But it was from Penny, who, with the rest of her family, was keeping up the constant flow of cheer for me.

A rather surprising effect of my conviction was felt by my accountant, who had told me before my trial that he now had to conduct himself differently in the office. He was making the point that almost any remark or gesture, if taken out of context, could be misconstrued. The same applied to all my teaching colleagues. They would never be able to teach in the same and successful way. Tactile contact was now 'out'. And I defy any successful teacher to do his or her job without there being occasional, and proper, physical contact. But for the senior partner in an accountancy firm to feel threatened by the application of the law relating to my case . . .

As the months passed none let up their stream of letters. One friend, an agnostic, and I conducted a postal debate about free will and predestination. Her daughters kept me informed of what was happening to my school. Swedish parents were prevented from ringing the Governor to demand my release! Their middle son, a twelve-year-old, dropped convention and in writing to me started his letter, 'Dear Mike'. The same family arranged to give Tim a free holiday in Sweden during the summer. Generosity and concern came my and Jen's way constantly.

But the scars will remain and, though they have never deserted me or doubted me, it is the case that my friends' lives were as radically affected as my own. Like me they tried to maintain a brave face and never tired of keeping in touch.

Some, though, attempted to write to me, but failed to complete their letters. I learned this afterwards. They just did not know what to say. It was, to them, worse than writing to bereaved relatives.

But I was not dead, and the day of release approached.

# 17

# RELEASE

*Half to forget the wandering and the pain,*
*Half to remember days that have gone by,*
*And dream and dream that I am home again!*

James Elroy Flecker, 'The Dying Patriot'

Most 'dreams of home' that I had in prison were unclear and harmful reveries. The thought of being 'on the out' was a luxury which few prisoners gave themselves; the thought was too corrosive. It was far better to shut off memories of what had been and too speculative to imagine what might be in the future.

Naturally, as the time of release approached, we allowed our minds to wander into the paradise of home and hearth. I found that the parole date – news of which I received two months before my release – had not unsettled me too much. Its real effect was to cause me to plan for the loss of celibacy and I felt increasingly excited about the prospect of sleeping with Jen and of close contact. It was rather strange – planning to sleep again with the person to whom I had been married for twenty years and with whom I had created three sons. A mixture of second honeymoon with a dash of 'forbidden fruit' added to the nervousness of a 'first night'. I found the cocktail of responses to the prospect unnerving and exhilarating, with a faint hint of the absurd. Before that, though, other responses were to the fore.

First, I banked on nothing. A few hours after I had received my date a man who worked in administration and who was privy to 'movement orders' informed one of my ward companions that I was to be released. This second man – to me a suspected informer – came conspiratorially to my cube to tell me that he had just heard that I had got parole on 29 June and that he thought I would like to know. I affected a nonchalant pose, told him I already knew and that he had got the date wrong.

He was clearly put out that his scoop was, after all, second-hand and in injured tones told me that he had thought he was doing me a favour. I reckoned him to be the chap who had done me the favour of a loss of remission so did not hail him as a long-lost brother. His news, though, worried me. I was annoyed that news of my parole was general information but more than that I was worried lest the date I had been given was wrong and that I would, in fact, spend an additional six days in prison. I returned to the parole document and read:

> The Secretary of State has decided to release you on licence subject to the conditions which will be explained to you. Provided circumstances do not change you will be released on 23rd June 1986 or as soon after that date as arrangements for your release have been completed to the satisfaction of the Governor and of the probation officer under whose supervision you will be.

I studied the document again. The licence conditions were all right but my date of birth had been wrongly entered. Oh dear, I thought, if they can get that wrong, perhaps they've got the date wrong too; my informant says that movement orders state that I'm to be released on 29 June. I sought inmates' advice and was told that the licence itself is never wrong – what of my birth date? – and that I should not worry. I was concerned for I had learned that nothing in the transitory life of imprisonment is certain.

Even if the date on the licence was correct it was merely a *terminus a quo*; it was not a *terminus ad quem*. Such is the conditioned response of prisoners. I could have double-checked with the authorities but decided against this; I did not want to put ideas into their heads. Besides, between news of my date and the date itself, many things could happen which would prevent my release. I wanted to make assurance as sure as I could by imitating, as far as was possible, the actions of a potted plant. I had at least two months to survive. It was a case of head down and struggle on.

Two days after I received my date I had a visit. Jen was delighted by the news of parole, as was Tim, who was there. I was encouraged to behave like a saint. At the end of the visit I was strip-searched again. I thought, 'This is almost harassment but I won't complain. It's as if "they" want me to err. I must be very careful.'

# Release

Fantasy images of being with Jen became commoner. Visions of seeing all my friends and celebrating grew in strength. The dream of drinking decent claret drew nigh. A hundred images seethed in my imagination and a kaleidoscope of 'felt thoughts' tumbled crazily in my head. Each of these prospects pleased, but the vileness of my fellow man became apparent.

For the last few weeks in prison – with the rare exceptions of my few friends – I despised and abhorred my fellow inmates. It was as if I had suddenly realised that what I had come to accept as the norm was a distortion of the human condition. It was not amusing to listen to tales of criminal derring-do. Frank confessions about Home Leave sex were neither erotic nor entertaining. There was no real satisfaction to be gained by thwarting the authorities in simple ways as a means of survival. I was not like the majority of my fellow convicts. I was not better than they. I was different.

Even now I find it hard to define exactly my response. I remember feeling guilty that I had come to loathe so much of the prison experience at the very end. Guilty because what I was loathing were its products and not its administrators. At the same time my sympathies and intellectual response were on the side of the convict. I suppose I came to realise that in part – difficult to quantify – the men with whom I laughed and wept and suffered were so much the victims of themselves. Rarely did their decent selves come to the fore. They, like me, were degraded by the system and thus reacted as expected.

My intolerance was reflected in my diary extracts: Saturday 3 May: 'Gambler Tony is burping his way to freedom. He is disgusting and deliberately breaks wind from any orifice whenever he sees me – safe in the knowledge that I loathe it.' He had been doing it for five months and until now I had not remarked upon its foulness. Monday 5 May: 'Raffles, Dave, Pedro and I am getting heartily sick of the arseholes in this place. How have I tolerated them for so long?' Wednesday 7 May: 'Gambler Tony's walkabout day. How glad I shall be when the smelly, selfish bastard has gone.'

Again, I recorded dozens of releases before I had received any parole date and had always written that I wished the men well. As my return to the real world approached I grew in intolerance. I even grew obviously intolerant with the officers. On Tuesday 12 May I wrote:

Allowed myself to get extremely wound up by Knight today. He came back on duty after a week off and gave everybody hell. Eventually he came into the dining room and told Trev and me that the place was a disgrace. I told him (a) that it was not and (b) there'd been no complaints for five months and we work just as hard as we did and (c) that his superior, Mr Ryan, was satisfied. Knight replied that the place was a disgrace, told us to scrub the walls, window ledges, etc. He said finally to me, 'You ought to be ashamed of yourself, a man of your calibre.' He pronounced the last word as Tony Hancock used to – 'cal-eye-ber'. This is revenge for a row he and I had a couple of weeks ago when he refused initially to give us new mop heads, saying there was only one spare. I pointed out that spares were what they said – there to be used in cases of need. I ended up saying I didn't give a toss about his floor if that was his attitude. This exchange was witnessed by cons who were amused by Knight's discomfiture; he gave me the mop head.

Anyway this afternoon we saw Ryan who complimented us on the state of the place but fairly pointed out the odd corner needed more attention. The toad Knight knows I am not going to do anything to get a KB.

Normally I would have taken the criticism but now I was gradually and in a mental way emerging from the trammels of my totalitarian state. It was interesting to note that not only was the physical circumstance of prison totalitarian but my mind had accepted the subservience too. My mind was now regeared to the free world in every sense of that adjective.

Two days later I was referring to the new draft of prisoners as 'real riff-raff'. The entry for Friday 16 May demonstrates a little how my mind was working:

Phone broken again – people are still revarnishing used cards. The bloody thing was only fixed yesterday. It'll soon be permanently withdrawn. As someone said at breakfast, 'You always get arseholes' – Hear Hear.

Horrid dream that Jen denied me sex until 'tomorrow'. I remember nearly strangling her. I hope I'm not being prophetic. How the mind works – I suppose it'll come up with some surprises when I'm out. One can't go through a seven-month pre-trial experience, a one-week trial and six and a half months in prison without after-effects, I reckon. We'll see.

A social worker has just been admitted. Involved with little boys and girls but no more details yet.

On to koala number three.

Friction in the kitchen because of the easy number Trev and I have – excellent, for the place is full of arseholes and I do like to see them riled.

A few days later I write, 'The days are becoming identical: work, run, sew, crossword, darts, bed,' and 'Time is slowing down and I'm feeling tense. Aware of outside problems, perhaps?' My anger and frustration boiled over on Saturday 24 May:

One of the newer intake in the kitchen is gossiping rather maliciously about nonces. He is making life particularly hard for the young lad who works on the coppers. I hear, too, he has taken my name in vain. I visited this chap today and threatened 'to kick shit out of him'. Sadly, I meant it but was warned off by Pedro who rightly says with a few weeks to go I'd be silly to get shipped out. I've frightened this bloke, who denies the charge; I told him the only reason I was not plastering him all over the wall was because he would rush and tell the screw. He said he wouldn't but as soon as I'd finished with him he went to Knight! Knight told him that he doesn't blame me; he also told the original victim that it is better that 'Mike deals with it than you do'.

And so the entries which reveal my preoccupation with release continue. I write of 'gate fever' being on me and of planning my post-release Jersey trip with Jen. In June I rowed with the tea-maker because he made weak tea. He told me that 'the lads liked it that way'. I told him I didn't give a bugger how the lads liked it. He made it stronger. I commented in the diary, 'It's time I left. Jen is right; this place has changed me.'

On the day when I would have been released I received a super Fathers' Day card from Tim. Surprisingly I was not resenting the extra week's imprisonment. There was too much to do.

On 17 June the authorities screened the video of Olivier's *Richard III*, which passed that evening splendidly. It was the last play I had produced at my school, so a few pangs were felt. By then, though, I had been told that I could send my letters and toys out early and had taken them all to the respective dispatch points. Jen was due to visit on Sunday 22 June, stay the night in a nearby hotel and pick me up at 7 a.m. on Monday 23 June. But the best laid plans. . . .

On Wednesday 18 June I recorded the following in my diary:

Shocking letter from Jen. She's badly injured her leg so cannot drive and hence cannot visit on Sunday to take the stuff out. Dear Penny has offered to drive her up on Monday morning to collect me. I am beside myself with frustration and rage. What a thing to come out of prison with. The most important moment of my life in many ways will be shared; it will not be private and polite conversation will have to be made for hours in a car. I want to talk and think about making love but what with the probation visit and plans for the rest of the day I can see myself being celibate even longer – perhaps until Jen's leg heals. I am so disturbed – angry and more angry with myself for being so angry and ungrateful. Oh God what a bloody mess. . . . Eventually recovered from the shock of Jen's letter after a walk round the field with Pedro and the writing of a cathartic snorter, which, of course, I did not send.

The last few days were recorded thus:

*Thursday 19 June*

Woke early to a glorious sun but felt very tired. Still don't know if I'm working on Saturday or Sunday. I hope not as I want to sleep and sunbathe. We'll see.

More mail – very gratifying at this stage. Just pushed my last stores' trolley and got a box to pack my few possessions in. The beginning of the end. Sent Jen a conciliatory and sympathetic letter; now I'll write to Jay and Tim.

Tomorrow is to be my last 'official' day, as it were. Its function is that the soon-to-be-released man walks about the prison putting into reverse the reception process. A formulated sheet of paper is carried round and signed by the respective departments.

The process begins with the hospital and ends with the Chaplain. All property and clothing is handed in, as are the library books. Why we have to go to the Education Department and the Chaplain is anybody's guess. The visit to the Governor informs us of our financial state and gives a pep-talk.

My own case is rather different in that my 'walkabout' is three days before my actual release. No releases occur at weekends so I have to kill a long Saturday and Sunday, having experienced the excitement of the walkabout on the Friday. Normally it is the morning following the walkabout that a man or woman is released.

I had planned to work over the last weekend and give Trev my pay. In the event, I decided not to as I'd hoped to sunbathe and generally assemble my thoughts before the Monday morning. I was, too, reading the lesson in Chapel on the Sunday and preferred, for once, to do that unhurriedly; usually Trev and I have rushed to church in our whites and rushed back to work at the end of the service.

Several days before release one was expected to collect the necessary forms and plan for departure. I had already arranged for the toys and letters to go out at the visit. But, as I have explained, there was a good chance that Jen could not make it because of her injured leg. My plan, therefore, of leaving prison as I had arrived, with just the clothes I stood up in, was now thwarted. Even my prized possession, the padded Christmas card, had been due to go out before me.

I record what actually happened below:

*Friday 20 June*

Today is walkabout day. It is cold, wet and windy. Slept well.

Hospital at 7.45 a.m. 'Any problems?' 'No'. 'Okay.' I was weighed – about 66 kg – whatever they are – but I seem to be wasting away.

Forwent breakfast but had a cuppa with Trevor and Raffles.

I've given away my 'good' chair and dispatched my belongings. 9 a.m. went to Reception to confirm everything could go out on the visit. (Jen now thinks she can get here. Thank God.) I was asked where my teapot and strainer were. I have to bring them to reception at 4 p.m. – 'So many get left lying around that the Chief says they must be handed in. The Chief hates you to pass them on. There's a box, which when it is full we throw away.' Thus spoke the Reception Officer. I've arranged to bring my stuff at 6.30 a.m. on Monday morning so that I can use it over the weekend.

Consternation, too, over the whereabouts of my nail-file. I've arranged that everything can go out on the visit. Checked my own clothing but skipped the clothing board – I don't want any hand-outs. It was a real pleasure to see my own stuff again.

The Education Orderly has signed me off and arranged to take my soft toys down to the visiting room. I've now nearly packed for the Clothing Exchange Store. Trev has to work with Dino in the dining room – that's just what he didn't want.

Letters from Eli – she can't visit and has sent the Visiting Order to Jen – and from Prue. Lovely at this stage.

Returned my books to the library, been to canteen and bought tobacco and letters to give to Trev and others. Now Governor and lunch.

Read the papers before seeing the Governor. Soccer and other GBH yobs get *weeks* in jail. Learned from a chat that one of the men in the Harry Roberts policeman murder case is in here. This man has done twenty-three years. Dino informed me his co-defendants got eleven years.

The Deputy Governor saw me. I gave no parting handshake though I'm told it is customary. I declined a travel warrant and learned that ten days had been added on to my EDR as well as having served an extra ten days. I shall be on parole until 23rd December. I have £18 in private cash, one week's dole money, £3.50 expenses and 88p in earnings. 'Well, good luck and I hope we don't see you again.' Tight-lipped and fuming I left the presence of the person.

Still no sun and a fierce wind heading straight into my run, which, the last one I shall do, was very hard. Reception in half an hour, then Chaplain, which I'll skip, and walkabout is done. I was wished good fortune by the CES people – how different from my reception five and a half months ago.

I'm still very hungry, I wonder why? Dave was to have trimmed my hair but hasn't yet. Mike has gone out on appeal.

Dave and I were cold-bathed unexpectedly – though the Leprechaun did give a hint by asking, unexpectedly, if he could speak with me at the end of the ward. His custom is to charge unannounced into my cube. So my remaining clothes are now soaked.

Jim found some fresh field mushrooms and kindly invited me to share them. Trev is up again. Raffles regaled me with stories of cat burglars of yore and described his post-war escape vehicle – a motor bike with special tyres. . . .

Poor Chris attended the funeral of his brother today – victim, I think, of a road accident. He was granted one day's parole – but I don't think he knew the brother well so his grief is somewhat bearable.

Dear Inch is mopping up the water caused by our ducking; he's good like that. I am wet and chilly and just hope Jim's mushrooms were not poisonous. Roll on tomorrow and tomorrow and tomorrow. . . .

I don't get the 'Next Out' sign; Dave has it – well, he's waited long enough.

The sign was a cartoon of a cricket ball hitting stumps and removing the bails. It was pinned outside the cube of the next inmate to be released. I think my release date was the only one of our ward which coincided with the release of another man in the same ward. I was sorry not to have it pinned outside my cube, but Dave had waited two years for his release.

### Saturday 21 June

Cold, cloudy. Rose at 10 a.m. I'm not working this weekend. Wrote to Jay for today is his birthday and but for my smuggling I would have been out to celebrate it. He has received a present from me, though – by arrangement with Jamie.

Received a typed letter from Emma! What a wonderful last letter to get in jail. She's been off school with a broken 'choler' (*sic*) bone. So that's why she was bad-tempered sometimes!

Headache, bored, very tired. Watched the cricket but I no longer feel I 'belong' here. Three in an adjacent cube are having their 'fix' but very quietly. It is tea-time and I have the film to endure – despite the headache. Maybe brought on by the lie-in or by wearing my glasses all afternoon. I don't know.

I'd thought of replying to Em but decided against. I'll give my spare letters to people in here. Tomorrow should whizz by as long as I get to sleep tonight. I couldn't have stood much more of this – tho' if I'd not got parole there'd have been no trouble. Done my last laundry – mainly as a result of last night's

ducking. I shall pass my bucket on to someone else; Lyn gave it
to me. . . .

Another early tally because of the soccer. Trev came up after
supper. His wife has yet to make progress on a business idea.
I'm getting increasingly frustrated by him and by this place
generally. He must, so to say, give me up. I'm enormously fond
of him but want him to survive when I'm gone.

Today has brought home to me the futility of this place.
Thank God I worked every weekend. But the order of events
when I get out? There's so much to do but much of it does not
bring me in money immediately. . . .

This will be the last entry smuggled out unless I have
anything tomorrow morning before the visit.

It is finished and I am thinking 'white' – a cryptic reference
which need not be explained.


*Sunday 22 June*

*The Last Day* got off to a bad start. Inch failed to wake me so I
was late for church and I was reading the lesson. Came back
after the service and verbally lashed him. His response: 'I'm
allowed to lie in.' 'Not when you promised to wake me you're
not.' I then called this dear friend a 'little, fucking bugger'.
Prison has done much for me.

The gipsy of the ward asked me for milk. I said, untruthfully,
I had none. He then complained to two newcomers how tight I
was. I went spare. I'd kept this ward in food for nearly six
months and . . . what the hell? I am happy to say I am so angry
that I shall get through this day with ease.

How I *long* for Jen. . . .

That was the last entry I wrote in prison.

The visit came and passed wonderfully. The only slight hiccup
was that the Education orderly had forgotten to arrange for my
remaining soft toys to be liberated so I would have to bring them
out with me. It was glorious to be able to say to Jen and Jamie, 'Au
revoir. See you in the morning.'

I do not remember clearly how I spent Sunday evening. There
were many valedictions to make and I made sure I promised to

write to no one. I took out a number of messages (which I did deliver) but I felt in limbo.

Few fellow ward members wanted to have much to do with me. I knew why. I had felt the same. I now no longer 'belonged'. I had got the vital date and would soon be making love, having a drink and rebuilding my life. The others did not need to be reminded of that nor did they need to be unsettled by any loose talk on my part.

Old lags like Raffles came up for a final cup of coffee and apologised for intruding. He and another Jerseyman, a lifer, had given me advice about the island to which Jen and I were going to repair for a few days on the Tuesday after I was out. The lifer's family still lived there and I promised to visit them. His story was bizarre in the extreme; it seemed that he had fallen between the two stools of Jersey and English law and that a conspiracy of sorts was keeping him in prison without a date. Apparently he had fallen foul of the ruling 'junta' and would be an embarrassment to release. I felt for him but could do little to help save visit his elderly parents, which Jen and I did when we arrived in Jersey.

The 9 p.m. tally came and went and I continued reading Iris Murdoch's *The Sea, The Sea*. I went to bed having arranged that the night staff would wake me at 5.30 a.m. I think I went to sleep quite quickly. I was certainly awake before they came round. I headed for the bathroom only to find its light on and the door shut. I imagined Dave was having his final prison bath. I sat on my bed frustrated for a quarter of an hour. Time was passing and I had things to do. I returned to the bathroom to get him out and found that it had been unoccupied all the while!

I bathed and shaved leisurely, made a cup of tea and took one to Pedro and Inch, both of whom had asked me to wake them. I gave the remains of my tea, milk and sugar to Pedro – I had distributed the bulk of my stuff the day before. Another man, Louis, rose and came to bid me farewell. I collected my bedding and cutlery and reported 'off' at the Unit Room. It was about 6.30 a.m. and I was on the way with Dave.

At Reception we were ordered to put our bedding, cutlery and other impedimenta into a huge basket. Nothing was checked. We stripped naked and threw our prison clothing into the same basket. Naked we proceeded to the changing room where, bliss oh bliss, we were given our own clothes, which had been laundered. I could still tie a tie and to wipe my nose on a real handkerchief after months of using paper was a joy.

We were given our parole licence and money and waited for the main tally to be cleared before marching to the gatehouse. The lifers who worked out all day were with us. One or two, including the egregious Jock, were also present. I stood apart and felt totally isolated. These men had done more years in prison than I had months and resented my departure. I felt their indifference acutely.

Dave had asked me if I was going his way so that I could give him a lift to the station. I said that I was not, not least because Jen did not want to start the new life with a fellow con. The order to go to the gatehouse was given. I felt very calm.

There in the car park was the car. Inside were Jen and Jamie. I went quickly towards them, only to be called back by the officer. 'You can't go yet. Tally's not cleared.' I indicated to Jen to wait and went to the gatehouse. There I was given my remaining toys to carry out. I dared not even carry them to the car in case I was called back and delayed again. I stand motionless, hardly daring to breathe. Nervously I roll a cigarette. Dimly I am aware of a tapping sound. I turn towards the gatehouse window; an officer is tapping it with a bunch of keys. He gives me the thumbs-up sign. We may go. Go. Go. I walk to the car and climb in. The gate is lifted. Jen drives out. I look neither to right nor to left.

Jamie hands me my pipe and tobacco. Within minutes we are on the motorway and I am puffing contentedly. It is as if I have never been in prison. We stop for breakfast on the motorway. I am overwhelmed by the taste of real butter and by the brightness of everyone's clothing.

I am going home.

# 18

# WHY IMPRISON?

*The liberty of the individual must be thus far limited;*
*he must not make himself a nuisance to other people.*

John Stuart Mill, *On Liberty*

John Stuart Mill's words quoted in the epigraph to this chapter
hold the key to the dilemma of the authorities when they come to
consider the fate of wrongdoers. Most crimes cause nuisance to
others; the perpetrators of these crimes must have their activities
limited. The question is, how? I have sought to show in the course
of this book that prison solves few problems. Generally, though, I
have tried merely to identify areas of difficulty; their solution is far
more complex. Further, my own prison experience is very limited,
not only by its duration but also by the nature of my fellow
inmates. That I was in an open prison suggests that the majority of
my fellow clients (to use the term I found in the *Prison Officers'
Journal*) were not dangerous or violent. In the main this was true
and even the eighty-plus murderers could legitimately *now* be
regarded as of the same, relatively harmless status as myself.

In this and the following chapters I will suggest ways in which
the prison system could be changed to cause fewer tensions. In
the course of my arguments I will assume that the men and
women of whom I speak are non-violent, have no history of
mental illness and are not recidivists. I acknowledge, therefore,
that I have no 'solution' for the violent psychopath nor for the
habitual offender. I have suggestions only for the rest. I recognise,
too, that all men are different and that the function of 'authority' is
tremendously complex.

My final premise is that the prison objective is not only
to contain but also to reform. This last assumption is very
contentious.

That 'society' – an indefinable concept, but whose predomi-
nant characteristic is one of unthinking hypocrisy – seeks to react
to evil-doing has to be conceded. That it reacts to those who are

'caught' while at the same time accepting the existence of the eleventh commandment has never seemed to bother it. That in the nature of crime and punishment it can be utterly feral on the one hand ('Hang the Moors Murderers'; 'I'd birch soccer hooligans') and totally sentimental on the other ('Public demands release of tug-of-war love baby's mother', when the mother has been convicted of theft and drug offences) never seems to give it pause for thought.

The reason for the inconsistency is, of course, that society does not care to acknowledge the existence of its 'dirty washing' and that its response is unthinking and topical. It is not affected so it does not care. Nonetheless, there is general agreement that a structure of 'law and order' has to be erected within which a system, however flawed, must operate. Our 'system' has often been called the world's best. I can only say I would hate to be under the control of the world's worst.

That we no longer execute felons is one of the finest points in our judicial system. It always seems odd to me that those eminent politicians – often of the Tory persuasion – who profess a deep religious conviction can reconcile their faith in God with their vote for the restoration of capital punishment. Conversely, socialists who profess agnosticism or worse (!) would almost rather die than vote to kill their fellows. It seems that both parties have lost the significance of the Crucifixion. Be that as it may, I believe that it is a secure and sympathetic state that does not execute its citizens.

By the same token, however, it must, on behalf of its constituent members, register disapproval of antisocial acts. The problem comes in the quantifying of these acts, for essentially they are all of a kind but of widely differing degrees. Let me illustrate by a few examples – all of which are potentially imprisonable offences.

A man fails to pay a fine. He is imprisoned and so 'pays' his penalty, but the person to whom the fine is owed does not receive any money from him. Who is satisfied? Many men in Leyhill with me received an extra week or fortnight's imprisonment for failing to pay a fine. The extra 'time' did not unduly inconvenience them; their creditors can have received scant satisfaction from the custodial sentence.

A woman shoots her unfaithful husband. She receives 'life'

imprisonment which can range from seven to fifty years, say. What is the object of the punishment? Society has not been outraged. The woman has. No one has suffered except her unfaithful husband and the woman herself, who has been betrayed. Adultery, in Christ's day, was a 'stoneable' offence, as it is in modern Teheran. But Christ also forgave the adulterer. Should not the wife have forgiven her husband? Should not we forgive the wife? But who the hell are 'we' anyway? The problem is acute. It is unlikely that the situation would repeat itself in this particular case, and one imagines that the shock from which the murderer is now suffering would be a life-long punishment, anyway. Yet in our scale of values we feel we must imprison the woman; a fine, or community service, or probation are regarded as insufficient. We must deter others. But then was not hanging meant to be a deterrent? There is evidence to suggest that many types of murder fell in number immediately after the abolition of capital punishment. Where does that leave us? (Perhaps, though, the situation has changed. Crimes against the person often now seem to be treated less severely than crimes against property.)

A financier, through insider dealing, makes a fortune. He is fined heavily and imprisoned. He is doubly punished. The recent spate of adverse publicity about illicit share-dealing elicited the immediate response from a Home Office Minister that the maximum prison sentence would be increased from two to seven years. If we ignore the typically British skill of bolting the stable door after the errant nag has galloped off, we are left wondering why the Minister, or anyone else, thinks that 'more is better'. The Minister is not responding in anything except a political way. He cares little for the effect of his Bill save that it will show the country that he is being tough on crime. Unfortunately he fails to see that prevention is the only real answer and that increasing sentences is no cure.

An absurd example of this hard line was witnessed recently in the United States. The West German Government agreed to extradite a suspected terrorist to the States only if the US authorities promised that the man, if found guilty, would not be executed. A report in *The Times* a few days later stated that the American authorities were searching for a severer punishment than life imprisonment!

A man rapes and murders a young child. He receives the same

sentence as our hypothetical murderess above. He may, though, be given a minimum period which he must serve. I invite the reader to list the differences, as it seems to him or her, between the two cases.

Three people plan to rob a bank. The robbery does not take place but their plan is discovered. They receive years in prison. Three others regularly send in fraudulent Inland Revenue returns and are eventually found out. They protest misunderstanding and accidental errors, repay the tax and are 'free'. Which of the two trios is more culpable?

A woman chains herself to the perimeter of a US Air Force base and ends up in prison either because she is a regular protester or because she has failed to pay a fine. She is guilty of trespass or causing an affray or damage to the property or whatever. She is treated in the same way as the child murderer.

A pop singer is addicted to heroin and is caught with some in his possession. He is imprisoned – well, even that is unlikely; pop singers and sports stars tend to get off – but his craving is still there and ironically so is the availability of his vital drug. A woman is caught in possession of cannabis with intent to supply it to her friends. She has been caught in possession before; she goes to prison. In prison she still has cannabis and her friends find a new supplier. When she is released she is likely to repeat the offence. What has been served by her imprisonment? I ignore any discussion about whether or not cannabis is harmful; it is against the law and so punishment must, sadly, follow detection of the offence, as night follows day. But why imprisonment?

The question is harder to answer when, on the same day that the girl is imprisoned for her drug offence – and a 'harmless' drug too, according to certain experts – an MP is charged with driving with many times the legal limit of alcohol in his blood and is fined £250. Alcohol is a known poison with many harmful side-effects; drunk driving is a serious offence. Cars are deadly weapons. The combination of a deadly weapon and a drunk in charge of it ought to raise the hackles of the flabbiest liberal. Why was the MP not subjected to the full majesty of the custodial law? (That is a rhetorical question, by the way.)

All the cases I cite are imprisonable. All the convicted persons receive the same treatment within the same regime. Admittedly their length of sentence is different and the nature of their institution changes. But one cannot help asking the question 'What does the custodial treatment seek to achieve?' It cannot deter, or people who have been to prison once would not go again. The nuclear protester, a latter-day martyr, is happy to go time and time again, as the history of Miss Pat Arrowsmith testifies.

Our murderess is highly unlikely to repeat her experience whether she goes to prison or not. The habitual cannabis-user will still use the stuff. Indeed, I know that many people develop a liking for it only because they have been to prison.

The MP would have been shocked by the prison experience and maybe learned a lesson. And here is the only justification for prison that I can think of: it does, like corporal punishment in schools, deter a minority. I do not mean in the 'short, sharp shock' way with which Lord Whitelaw failed to solve the problem of juvenile crime. I mean in the sudden assault upon one's sensibilities by the totally alien environment of the totalitarian prison. Funnily enough, though, many of the parents who oppose corporal punishment seem, if they are correctly reported in the press, to condone imprisonment and even judicial execution. The implicit double standard operates again; a caning might well have deterred a future criminal.

The only common factor which binds the above examples together is that the perpetrators were liable to, or did receive, imprisonment as a punishment. Imprisonment is the harshest reaction our society can impose on its members. It is a symbol of extreme disapprobation and must be seen to be so. So far, so good. Society must reassure itself about its own standing, for failure to do so would cause a lack of confidence in its constituent members. On that basis, the punishment cannot be faulted.

That it seeks to deter the criminal is, as I have demonstrated earlier, at best a highly questionable justification and at worst risible. Criminals either do not expect to be caught or, if they are 'professionals', calculate the risks if they are caught. One man told me that he had got 'one more stretch' in him before he retired. He had planned not to go to prison after he was forty. But remember, we are discussing minor offenders and not hardened criminals or those with mental illness.

Justification for imprisonment on the scale practised in this country – more widely than in any country in Europe, including Turkey – would be easier if it were the avowed intention of the authorities to attempt to reform the wrongdoer. I would argue that reforming zeal comes rather late by the time the man or woman is in prison, particularly if he or she is a regular, petty criminal. Further than this I would state that the one-time perpetrator of what is regarded as a serious crime – drug smuggling, say – may well have committed the crime out of naivety, believing that the offence was trivial, and in his own eyes he may not see himself as a suitable case for treatment.

Far-fetched? I think not, as the case of Pedro suggests. He was shocked at the enormity of being caught and, like many an incest prisoner, was still trying to discover what had made him do it in the first place. He was reformed even before the judge passed sentence. What he needed was not an exemplary punishment but help as soon as the offence was discovered. Certainly the incidence of drug smuggling was not reduced when he got his four-year sentence. And here is another acute problem. I say what I have said about Pedro because I know him and like him. Of thousands of others I might well say that they should serve a term of imprisonment. How can the state apparatus begin to view forty thousand cases in that personal light? It cannot, so it plays safe. These comments about reform are, in any case, misplaced. There are few attempts made in prison to reform or rehabilitate the offender.

We are not getting very far in attempting to justify custodial treatment. Let us concede, finally, that withdrawing a person from circulation prevents that person from reoffending. We are left with, at best, four reasons which would support imprisonment as an acceptable part of the judicial process. Society can feel secure and properly upright. The inmate cannot reoffend while he is in prison. The inmate may be deterred, as may others who witness his demise. The inmate may be reformed.

The first two reasons seem irrefutable. The second pair are absurdly missing the mark. Criminals continue to commit crime, or rather the crimes for which they were convicted continue to be committed by themselves or by other first-time offenders. First-time offenders have not yet had the opportunity to be reformed for they are not yet, for the purpose of my argument, in prison.

I have attempted merely to suggest some of the complexities of the situation. At this stage I am not interested in looking at the alternatives to prison. I accept – and so do the majority of criminals to whom I have spoken – that wrongdoing merits a punitive response. I accept, too, that society's attempts to 'humanise' its judicial punishments are genuine. We no longer execute felons. We attempt to reduce, through the parole system or alternatives to custody, the suffering of the wrongdoer. (Though the Draconian cries for longer and harsher regimes which gush from the bellies of some hard-line politicians make us wonder sometimes.) What concerns me here is that the prison experience all too often has the reverse effect to that intended.

Remember, still, that I speak of the first-time offender or of the man who, like myself, was ruined by the punishment. In fact, many professional people who fall foul of the law are ruined by the publicity anyway. That a headmaster or a doctor or a lawyer loses the chance to ply his trade would seem the harshest penalty of all. His family suffers great economic hardship, an appalling stigma and the annihilation of a secure future. If society really wants more than that then I cannot see why public beheadings, amputations, castrations and floggings should not become the norm!

A number of people remarked to me that the prison experience had 'changed' me; more honest commentators used words like 'degraded'. The change, such as it was, had little to do with my resentment at being in jail; at Exeter, after all, I received maximum Brownie points for co-operation and humility. It was the daily humiliations and deprivations that bit deep, as I have described. The negative aspects of prison are many and lie largely below the surface of what a visiting magistrate or resident probation officer will see.

It is a truism that prisons are universities of crime. Even relatively harmless institutions like Leyhill are full of expert professors of thieving, readers in fraud and lecturers on smuggling. Conversations are mainly concerned with crime and its rewards. I learned how to cheat my electricity board and how to perpetrate what I regarded as a foolproof fraud – expert advice supplied by ex-policemen, bank managers and accountants. I know how to launder the proceeds of crime – at least in theory and through several countries. I am fairly certain that if I concentrated hard enough I could smuggle most things into the country with a slight chance of being caught. I know of many causes of detection; criminals told me how they were caught and patterns emerged. I made conversational contact with jewel fences, 'heavy mobs' who did the dirty work of others, and smugglers.

I was propositioned a number of times and my 'brain' was used to assist in the analysis of putative crimes. It was all heady stuff – particularly when one saw from the depositions of a few men that they had got away with large sums of money. One such was told by the prison authorities that he had no chance of parole precisely because his crime had been, financially, so successful. He was nonetheless paroled. In his case prison was clearly absurd. He would serve less than a year, he had avoided being liable for criminal bankruptcy proceedings and he would return to his private life with over a quarter of a million pounds. He also found every day in prison a 'joy': 'I need never work again.' How much more effective it would have been to fine him £250,000 so that restitution could have been made to those from whom he stole, the cost of keeping him in prison spared and, by leaving him with enough capital to earn his own living, avoiding any dole or other benefit costs. By this means he would have been very, very hard hit. Thereafter a supervision order of some sort could also have been imposed.

This man was discussing with others ways of investing his profits to make even larger gains; his discussions involved illegal as well as legal activity. Any gaps in his criminal education were amply filled by the prison experience.

A second negative aspect of prison life concerned drugs. I had never even seen cannabis until I went to prison. There, I smoked it twice but found I hated it so much that I would not wish to touch it again. I resisted, too, the opportunity to trade in the stuff, though I could have done so and made good profits. Some men were learning much about the drugs world and *would* leave prison dependent upon them and likely to commit further crimes in order to satisfy their craving. Some of these men, like me, had never touched drugs before going to prison.

Even those who intended to keep to the straight and narrow in prison found, as I had done, that one could not afford to buy even the basic allowances of tobacco, tea, letters, and so on. In order to supplement their allowance they got into debt, offended in order to get out of debt, often got caught and fined, and so got even further into debt.

The strain on family life, and in particular on marriages, was acute in prison. One brave chap, on receipt of marching orders from his wife, applied to be banged up in Bristol Prison until he had recovered from the shock sufficiently to ensure that he was not tempted to abscond. For those who have never been married but who are heterosexual and have to spend a long time in prison the unnaturalness of being without women is harmful. It is harmful precisely because it is unnatural.

That prisons do not encourage men or women to reform, or at least to feel as if they are still human and belong to the human race, is the worst indictment of all. To be as low as society can place you and then be trodden on is no way for a humane society to treat its errant members. There is no need for men to be addressed by their surnames or by a number; it is even more insulting to a woman. The insult is in the prison sentence. The judgment has been made by then. Thereafter it should be the aim of the authorities to restructure personality, rebuild hope and cease to judge. In absolute terms there is none living who can cast the first stone. If one allows that mighty Parliament is entitled to hurl a great rock, then it should follow that no other should join in the volley.

All the above negative aspects and their attendant problems are exacerbated because the prisoner is essentially being held *incommunicado*. When a crisis looms it cannot easily be dealt with. I remember one man desperately needing the help of the Probation Officer. It so happened that on the day he needed it I had a pre-parole appointment with her. At my appointment I apologised for committing potential *lèse-majesté* but told her of my friend's acute problem. I suggested that she defer my appointment, which was merely a form-filling exercise to tidy the paperwork before I was released; she declined, saying that my appointment was equally urgent and that she would see my pal on Friday. This was on a Tuesday morning. In the event I sent my anxious co-inmate to the Deputy Chaplain, who allowed him to telephone out and solve his own problem.

Matters are made even worse by the quality of men who 'guard' prisoners. The educational qualifications are essentially nil. Physical requirements are minimal. Training is of a pathetically short duration and one training school was closed down while I was at Leyhill. Pay is too high and the practices against which the Government is fighting have resulted in a closed-shop mentality which will ensure that no significant reforms will occur while they are maintained. And, dammit, the officers are there to help the prisoners as well as to serve the community. If officers and prisoners were to get on, then strains for all would cease.

Charges of brutality, sometimes false, sometimes true, should cause no surprise to anyone who has experience of the system. In a way no one is to blame, except of course those who offend in the first place. But, having said that, it is worth repeating that there are alternatives to custody which would benefit all concerned. I was glad to record my own pleasant experience at the hands of the Exeter officers. I was treated like a human being with courtesy and tolerance. I was trusted. At Leyhill the reverse was true and, though there was no instance of physical intimidation of prisoners, the main attitude of the staff to the trusties – for that is what we all were – was not even friendly contempt. It was inimical disdain. The officers were socially and intellectually inferior to many of the inmates but in the main behaved with a swaggering superiority. I except one or two but the wisest and most skilled in dealing with us all was one of the civilian workers.

He was an interesting, never empty, fount of verbiage *and* wisdom. He was in charge of a gang of maintenance workers and treated his men with complete honesty, total trust and extreme paternalism. He would allow no man to insult another – particularly were nonces defended. He would assist any problem to the limit of his prescribed authority. He ran an armchair travel club. He referred to me as 'a gentleman', not as 'young Bettsworth'; he knew about me and was happy to concede my superior intellectual education in discussion. He deplored the present standard of prison officers, stating that they were poorly trained. The man of whom I speak, Peter Quick by name, had been in the prison service for forty years and spoke with accumulated knowledge. 'Their attitude's all wrong,' he often said. He did more pastoral work in an hour than did Welfare in a week – only because he was prepared to talk on equal terms with all-comers. True, he had no official role in men's welfare and that was, obviously, a large reason why he was so effective. Even so, I suspect that if a leaf had been taken out of his book by many of those in authority, life would have been easier for all. None dared take advantage of him either.

But even if one were to applaud the staff to the hilt – and I certainly could not do that – it was obvious that their morale was low. The conditions under which they worked made their lot less pleasant than it need have been. The prison – all prisons – are vastly overcrowded. The backlog of parole decisions, the increase in some crimes, the lengthening of other sentences, the air of hopelessness and dilapidation, all played their part in making the lot of prisoner and guard unnecessarily unpleasant. And if those in authority are sick at heart, then their underlings must suffer.

It is depressing to see the extent to which the Prison Officers' Association is resisting attempts to make changes from which all would benefit. But the real changes must go nearer the source of the trouble. These changes require a drastic, new approach to the problem of crime and punishment.

That there will always be criminals is certain. That some men and women must go to prison is sure – and some, perhaps, for the course of their natural lives. That there must continue to be punishment is equally certain. But it is the nature of that punishment that I wish to examine in the next chapter.

# 19

# REFORMS

*He will not always be chiding: neither keepeth he his anger for ever.*

Prayer Book

If we agree, then, that custodial punishment must remain in our system, and no one denies that obvious truth, then our attention must be directed towards improving its nature. I have argued in an earlier chapter that it is *the act* of going to prison that is the punishment; one is not going there *to be punished*. The distinction is often a hard one to draw, as I have explained.

Prison is prison is prison. The word carries an eternal stigma. Integrity is absolutely lost. The mark of the sinner is indelibly branded into the person's psyche. This is the same whether he is incarcerated in a suite at Claridges or in Makindye Prison under the control of Idi Amin. If this principle is accepted then I can proceed, hypothetically, to make life more bearable for prisoners and warders, reduce insider dealing of the custodial kind and diminish the cost to the state.

First and easiest. All men and women should be paid enough money to enable them to buy the prescribed amount of goods. A bonus is paid at Christmas, for example, which lifts the morale of all. If the regular money allowed the smoker to buy more than twice as much tobacco and the non-smoker even more chocolate, fruit or whatever, much smuggling, discontent, debt and fighting would be reduced. Fewer men would need to rely on the expense of the black market. That the black market would continue is equally certain, but its grip on the whole population would be lessened. Another ounce of tobacco per man would prevent the degrading scenes which precede the two days before pay-day when borrowing, begging, grovelling among ashtray debris and so on are rife.

The increased cost of the scheme would be more than offset by the reduction in prison time spent, for example, by those caught smuggling tobacco. Let us assume a modest £300 per man per week. My smuggling of, say, thirty ounces of tobacco for private consumption in the course of my sentence would have cost the authorities about £35. The extra days in prison for my actual smuggling of one ounce cost them ten times that amount and an unnecessary amount of paperwork. This 'remedy' may sound ineffably trite but all smokers know the irritation caused by running out of cigarettes at a time when the purchase of new supplies is impossible. In prison, that unpleasant state is potentially omnipresent.

To be able to buy enough letters in order to reply to most of those one receives is, again, a reasonable demand. Open prisons are more relaxed institutions than high-security prisons; censorship in them is virtually abolished, therefore no real increased workload would result from many more letters being sent and received. The reduction in frustration and anxiety which would follow this simple concession would be a positive advantage. So, too, would the availability of more than one telephone for over three hundred men and the more just allocation of telephone cards. If one machine is available, why should ten not be made so? Why, too, may men not buy many more telephone cards than one per month – and buy a larger-denomination card out of private cash? Those who want to use the machine(s) regularly may then do so; those who do not are not affected.

Lest the above suggestions seem appallingly 'soft' to our puritan-minded hard-liners, I would merely repeat that the prison sentence does not state 'and that the prisoner shall be kept short of tobacco and have only limited non-physical contact with his family and friends'. If the object is solitary confinement, it ought to be stated.

What about the physical contact? Visits are prescribed as one per twenty-eight days for thirty minutes. Privileged visits can increase the duration and frequency, as I have explained. But why one visit per month? Is it that more frequent visits would cause too much disruption to the authorities? I doubt it, because the huge host of remand prisoners are allowed a daily visit. Is it that the prisoners and their families only 'need' (define that if you can) to see each other for six and a half hours per year? I think not. Why, then, not a weekly visit for three hours, a daily visit for two hours, one visit every decade?

The visiting arrangements are such that those with a large

circle of friends either have to cut off all contact with them for the duration of their sentence or have to reduce the number of times they see their immediate families. Is this healthy? The breaking-off of social contacts with one's *innocent* friends, the better to allow one to rub shoulders with *guilty* acquaintances, hardly augurs well for a reformed future.

And what of the nature of the contact? Large groups of strangers trying to keep their close relationships alive and with hope have to do so in the equivalent of a rush-hour crowd. Any form of intimate physical contact – by which I mean a close embrace or a kiss – is not only frowned upon but is, for most inmates, too embarrassingly public. It is a hard price for anyone to pay – but for a fine-defaulter or someone who drove an uninsured car for the third time? 'And make the punishment fit the crime . . .'

My argument here would seem to be leading to the advocacy of conjugal visits. Is the idea – after all it is practised in some countries – so shocking? Brothels have long been made available to serving soldiers – one remembers the punning joke that *hors de combat* is a synonym for 'camp followers'. If unmarried as well as married soldiers, for example, have in the past been issued with contraceptives and had 'approved' brothels placed at their dis-posal, it would appear that somewhere along the line the need for sexual intercourse has been accepted. Why not, then, for men under as much strain as soldiers (if not more)?

Now, one can see that conjugal visits to prison would be difficult to arrange. It would be like visiting a brothel. But Home Leave is granted to certain categories of prisoner, as I have already mentioned; is it too absurd to allow all Category D prisoners the opportunity to go home regularly and at their own expense? The difficulties and inequalities would be enormous, but the old principle of 'dog-in-the-manger' has always struck me as absurd. It has the same effect as mass punishment. The truly guilty go free; the overwhelming number of innocents harbour a grudge. If some men had their load reduced, a beneficial result would accrue.

It is not, either, as if long-termers cannot meet members of the opposite sex. I knew one man in Leyhill – a prisoner of sixteen years' duration – who was conducting a very proper affair with a young lady he had met when he went out of the prison on an educational course. Sadly, the liaison ended precisely because she could see no future in it. The man had no 'date' but was constantly promised one; there was no opportunity for the love affair to blossom in the hothouse of privacy and intimacy. So it died. The effect on the man was catastrophic. I know because for weeks he pestered me for advice and help. I assisted him in the writing of love letters. I was recruited to help him to 'read' the metaphorical entrails in her 'last' letters. He was young, too, and had a strong desire for a durable relationship within wedlock. Even the one man who was married from prison was not allowed to consummate the marriage before returning.

At no time am I, for the purpose of this argument, forgetting that the offender is a wrongdoer. Nor am I, in the same context, saying that none should go to prison. If it appears that I protest too much I can only say that the experience *is* as I have described it. It is almost impossible for a person who has not been to prison to conceive of these pressures and it is not sufficient to say that the convict should have thought about it before he offended. Such a response does not cause the pressures to recede – much less disappear.

Can you, dear reader, conceive of running out of cigarettes for two days at the same time as your wife is away for one week and you are feeling as concupiscent as the proverbial goat, you are out of beer and the off-licence is closed, your children are *denied* you, your phone cut off and your television broken? If these things happened for a week and simultaneously you would feel a little under pressure.

Imagine, further, that despite all these deprivations, you are expected eventually to receive these gifts again as if nothing had happened and resume a normal life. Difficult, eh? And I have only scratched the surface; I cannot adequately define the emotional stress of the stigma of prison; the inner-core mental suffering of young children whose mother or father is taken away from them is incalculable. I know. I have seen it in my own and to me quite wonderful – not to say innocent – children.

That which I have sketched above approaches the reality of prison. If that is what society wants, so be it. The problems the system causes are acute and some can be mitigated. The current vogue is to increase sentences across the board in the vain belief that more will be deterred. I have explained the absurdity of that notion. The only real effect will be that more resentment and, worse, despair will result.

I concede, though, that prisons of every sort are full of recidivists. But is that a reason for making their lot worse? The *act* of going to prison is the punishment. There are enough pressures without adding to them. Indeed, a more realistic approach – a better word might be humane – to the custodial offender just might ignite a small spark of appreciation. Kindness – a word which properly means acting according to species – from the system might result in a reciprocal appreciation by the offender.

In many ways the system does have a heart. Parole, for example, suggests that the man or woman has a chance of being released sooner. That it exists suggests that society wishes this to be. But the workings of the system, as I have described, ensure that what is given is given grudgingly, stintingly, unequally and irrationally. Its effect has been to lengthen sentences, on the one hand, and to cause an outcry from the public when it is exercised, on the other.

The whole system is currently under investigation by a group chaired by Mark Carlisle. It may well come up with some harsher recommendations – not least because of the publicity released murderers receive if they reoffend.

The existence of suspended sentences has resulted in an increase in the prison population. The thinking behind this punishment presumably concedes that imprisonment is not the answer. The offender is given a kind of gipsy's warning, which he often ignores. His stupidity results in the activation of the suspended sentence. This happens in many, many cases. I cannot understand how, if it is inappropriate to send the offender to prison initially, it is appropriate to send him the second time round. Either the offence merits – however that is defined – imprisonment or it does not. The English compromise here works as well as it does in most areas of endeavour. Is it not truer to suggest that the existence of a sanction known as the 'suspended sentence' implies that there *ought* to be an alternative but that we do not know what it should be? In the eyes of the offender, clearly, the threat of prison is no deterrent. It is not unreasonable to assume that the fact of imprisonment will be equally ineffective – indeed more so, as the resentment, felt in the absurdities of the system which I have highlighted, will work negatively on our inmate.

## Reforms

All the above should be seen in the context of the other, non-custodial, effects of the prison sentence. For many, as I have shown, the prison sentence is only part of the punishment. The real punishment is the permanent loss of a job or the total disbarring from one's own profession. For a man whose sole skill in life is as a dentist or teacher or accountant, from which occupation he is banned, life seems somewhat harsh. And it is not always as if there is a choice between going to prison and losing everything or just losing everything. But there is sometimes this choice and the unfairness of the system is legendary and inevitable.

For statutory offences the system prescribes maximum sentences but not a minimum. This, on the face of it, seems to be reasonable. Only the court knows all the details of a particular offence and all the circumstances of the defendant. It has to weigh these factors with that of the 'public good' in terms of making an example and so on. But huge disparities still remain. In the case of my own offence sentences have included probation, conditional discharge and the maximum two years' imprisonment. Additionally, teachers who have committed unlawful sexual intercourse with (willing) pupils have sometimes been disbarred from the profession, sometimes not. One was recently retired on full pension. The same apparent inequalities exist in all offences.

That concern about these disparities is felt is manifest almost daily in the press. A random week's sampling of *The Times* produced the following headlines: 'Sentences Brought to Book' – an article about the research work of a criminologist who has produced 'the judge's unofficial bible', *Principles of Sentencing* and another work entitled *Current Sentencing Practice*. The article refers to the outcry caused by too lenient sentencing and to the view some hold that there should be a prosecution right of appeal against lenient sentences. I would argue that no prison sentence is lenient.

The academic who has produced the two 'encyclopaedias' on sentencing as a kind of judicial *vade mecum* is quoted as saying, 'There is a growing reluctance in Parliament to trust courts to work out their own criteria. Now legislators want to spell out what is simply common sense.' Ominously, the academic continues, 'It's a waste of time to worry about disparate sentences when – as a result of the widely criticised new parole for short-term offenders

– most of those sentenced to less than two years will only serve six months.'

I am sure that the first comment meets with the approval of those on the other side of the wall. But what about the convicted persons? It's the prisoner who does the worrying. His family and friends would be quite happy to 'waste' *their* time looking at the whole system. 'Only six months' is a lifetime to the man or woman in prison. This is what is wrong with the system. *No one who has been in it as a convict is ever consulted about it.* Neither hard-liner nor liberal *knows* what the prison experience is. True to form they will both 'imagine' (patronisingly) themselves into the system rather as they will 'understand' the workings of an infantile or disturbed mind and prescribe a 'treatment'. Yet, as I say, much current thinking is devoted to making sure that sentences are *severe* enough.

From the same week's *Times* as the article I have just mentioned there were the following headlines on different days: 'JP courts thwarting jail policy'. This piece cites a finding by the National Association for the Care and Resettlement of Offenders. Vast disparities between one magistrates' court and another are reported. The article states that Home Office research has found that one magistrates' court sent 7 per cent of burglars to prison, another sent 47 per cent. Fewer than 1 in 200 first-time offenders were sent to prison by one court, the figure was 1 in 10 in another.

These statistics may 'concern' the general public; they are a matter of life and death to the inmate. And the article reminds us that Britain has the highest prison population in Europe but also a greater number of alternatives to prison. More depressingly it is stated that we 'have made no inroads into the use of custody in the decade from 1974'. It is suggested that 'A National Crime Policy Committee, including judges and representatives of other parts of the criminal justice system, should be set up to plan crime policy.' The first priority of this body would be 'to reduce the use of prison'.

Fine, I say, but why not invite a few ex-prisoners to have their say. No harm would be done by a poacher-turned-gamekeeper policy. The views of such members could be ignored if they were too fanciful. Perhaps they could be co-opted members who would, at least, define the experience of imprisonment as it affects family as well as inmate. But, alas, this country would rather play safe than be radical.

Two other articles in the same week were headed 'Magistrates abusing power' and 'Young criminals are being locked up unnecessarily'. Both articles concern the treatment of juvenile offenders – potential adult criminals, of course. Not surprisingly, the articles report huge discrepancies in sentencing policy and one contains the comment that 'in spite of a revolution in the way juveniles are dealt with in England and Wales, the proportion of those sentenced for indictable offences and given immediate custody has remained virtually unchanged over the past seven years.' Concern is expressed that, because of the laxness of the policy of sentencing, principles of natural justice are 'being offended'. And one way to cause resentment in a young offender is to be seen to be unfair.

Three criteria are suggested in this same article which should be applied before a custodial sentence is imposed. At the moment only one is used. These are that the offender should have a history of failing to respond to non-custodial penalties; that a custodial penalty should have to be deemed necessary 'for the protection of the public' and for the added reason of 'protecting it from serious harm'. Further the sentencer should have to consider whether, if the offender were over twenty-one, 'the nature and gravity of the offence are such as to require a sentence of imprisonment'. I ignore the questions raised by 'nature and gravity'.

Interestingly, too, the article states that contrary to the belief that courts are being too soft on young offenders – an argument advanced by those who do not want the courts to be provided with stiffer conditions which must be satisfied before they impose a custodial sentence – the 'facts show the reverse to be true'. It is further stated that the rise in the number of juveniles being imprisoned over the last two decades has been faster than the rise in juvenile offences.

The article also reports that a scheme in Northampton which seeks to keep juveniles from the courts and offer them different treatment from custody has, between 1980 and 1985, reduced the number of prosecutions by 80 per cent, custodial sentences by 65 per cent and the overall juvenile crime rate by 3.2 per cent. So it can be done.

The last headlines from one week's reporting which I shall

refer to include, 'Prison officers prepare for dispute', 'Concern for the rights of prisoners on remand' and 'Carrot may be used with the stick to avoid jail troubles'. The first two headlines speak for themselves. The Prison Officers' Association will resist pressure for change, a resistance founded on a specious concern for the prisoners. The Home Secretary will therefore impose a new scheme of working practices. In the struggle that will follow, the prisoners will suffer. Education, recreation, visits, releases, transfers and mail will all fall victim.

The plight of remand prisoners is notorious. All are technically innocent but are treated with the same indignity as are convicted persons. Their situation is beyond the scope of this book. Suffice to say that cost-cutting by the present Government will have the effect of further reducing the rights of access to the courts that the remand prisoner has. In fact a third of remand prisoners eventually receive a non-custodial sentence and 4 per cent are acquitted.

It is the last headline which is most germane to some of my arguments. It concerns new measures to deal with disturbances in jails:

> Until now British jails have been unusual in relying on loss of privileges and remission, but that has failed to prevent disruption. The approach now being examined is to provide incentives to good behaviour; the carrot as well as the stick. . . . Making sure that there are no more unsentenced prisoners in custody than necessary is one of Mr Hurd's two main strategies for dealing with the prison population increase. The other is the building programme.

Remand prisoners do not concern me here. That one solution to the disturbances is to build more places where disturbances occur seems odd. The thinking behind this, too, is faulty. Jails are crowded. True. Let us build more jails and reduce crowding. True. Or is it? The prison I was in has been emptied of inmates, who are now in a brand-new adjacent one. No new places have been created – and indeed the inmates prefer the 'more relaxed' ethos of the old place. Second, it is the case that the current prison population has already exceeded the number originally predicted for the mid-1990s. There is no way that a building programme will catch up unless a radical change in custodial policy occurs.

This brings us to the headline above the article to which I am now referring: 'Carrot may be used with the stick to avoid jail troubles'.

Implicit in the headline is that the jail population will change little, if at all, in the foreseeable future. Therefore all the causes which make for an unruly prison population will remain – except that grown men, many of high intelligence and with a deep level of cynical worldliness, will now be offered incentives 'to be good boys'. It does not work like that. Such an incentive might make the cynical conform to get out of prison earlier but it will not affect the prison experience and its results. It will deepen the cynicism. I know of several men at Leyhill who attended church every Sunday in order to 'get a good parole answer'. I know of two who ceased to worship from the day they received their date. Besides, the parole system itself *is* an incentive but it offers nothing for drug offenders. Will they, too, be exempt from the 'carrot' because political expediency is rated more highly than humanity or compassion?

My experience as a headmaster tells me that 'carrots' cease to affect adolescent children who regard such bribery as childish and false. And just as the jail 'stick' proves to be a failure, so too will the putative 'carrot'. The measures proposed by the Home Secretary fail to examine the root cause of prison unrest – and the unrest is not confined to hardened and dangerous recidivists.

The simple truth is that too many people are in prison and for too long. Home Secretaries generally recoil from any policy of executive release. They do not like the idea – and judges even less so – of prescribing what is the 'right level of imprisonment'. Neither do they see merit in increasing the gap between length of sentence and the actual time served. I agree. That would be illogical given that it would deny all the premises upon which a custodial sentence was imposed and the length of that sentence. I say again, such thinking misses the main point. Too many people go to prison and for too long.

Having said that, it is timely to remember during the last prison crisis that Mr Hurd did accelerate the release of about 3000 short-term prisoners to alleviate the serious overcrowding; less than a year later the jails were bursting, some prisons were refusing to accept additional inmates and police cells were so overcrowded that six men had no difficulty in escaping from one police station. One of the escapees was described as 'dangerous'; two others had been charged with murder but were not so described – a point about murderers which I have covered elsewhere in this book.

But to continue. The criteria which are being suggested for juveniles could well be applied to adults. In my own case little was served by sending me to prison. I lost my job and my right to practise my profession. I had no history of failing to respond to alternatives to custody, I was given no chance to respond to those alternatives. *The accusation ruined me.* There was no need for a vengeful society – a puritan, insensate concept at its best – to imprison me and add to my and my family's suffering.

It did so to make an example of me, I suppose. But loss of livelihood and integrity is pretty exemplary. And what of the car offender and the shoplifter and the fine-defaulter? They pose no threat to society. Many who go to prison are first-time offenders who may well reoffend precisely because they have been so harshly dealt with.

There is, additionally, a strong case to be made for adopting the practice in some countries abroad of allowing a man to work from home during the week and return to prison at weekends. That way he remains in touch with his community, is gainfully employed, has the love and support of his family (who in turn have his), but is reminded that he has transgressed by his compulsory attendance in prison at the weekends. If he abuses this privilege then, assuming he merited imprisonment in the first place, he would have to attend permanently.

Much publicity surrounds the suggestion of keeping contact with a convicted person through an electronic 'tagging' system. Howls of outrage have come from unlikely as well as likely quarters. Prison-reform organisations have predictably described it as 'degrading' and 'inhuman'; even the Probation Service, which is one of the true beacons in the darkness of penology, is against it. It argues that it is able to supervise offenders better than an electronic device and that given the resources it would do just that. I suspect most prisoners would vote for it – a fact which, if used as an argument against 'tagging', I would accept!

The current thinking, as expressed in a *Times* article by Home Office Minister John Patten, is to be wholeheartedly welcomed. The Minister makes the point that there has been a 250 per cent rise in the number of remand cases in the last decade as well as an increase in the prison population of 9000. He says that the building programme will cater for an extra 22,000 places – that is depressing, of course. He states, too, that imprisonment is appropriate for crimes of violence, serious burglary and major fraud. Well, Lester Piggott found that out, but Geoffrey Collier did not, and one wonders if the eminent men arrested on allegations of financial impropriety in connection with the Guinness affair will, if found guilty, go to prison.

More tellingly Mr Patten, who suggests that a reconviction rate of around 70 per cent 'does not inspire much confidence', invites penal-reform groups to ask themselves whether 'it is more degrading for an offender to wear a monitoring device and to continue living with his family or to live for months, perhaps slopping out each morning and evening, possibly three to a cell designed for one'.

Furthermore Mr Patten reminds us that 'tagging' would be a means to an end – not an end in itself. He urges 'radical thinking' and the adoption of a policy which not only keeps people out of prison but causes offenders 'to face up to the damage and distress they have caused'; they can do this, he suggests, in community service which emphasises 'discipline and paying something back'.

This approach should be wholeheartedly embraced by all; sadly, I am not surprised by the reactions of NACRO (the National Association for the Care and Resettlement of Offenders), for example, who seem to fulfil no function but that of a rather cross maiden aunt. I am bound to say, too, that so unhelpful did I find them after my release that I wrote a bitter letter to their president. When I asked them, after eighteen months' frustration and disappointment, how I should find employment, I was told to go to the Job Centre and answer advertisements. I had not thought of that myself, of course.

There would be much less strain on all concerned if prisons operated more completely like hospitals – that is, if only the 'most urgent' cases were admitted immediately. Less serious illnesses would have to 'wait for a bed'. This would allow the sentenced person to return home after the sentence, put his affairs in order, adjust to the fact of his enforced absence and be ready to go to prison when he was called up. After all, many men and women who wait for months for their trial are not remanded in custody.

They appear for their trial; there is no reason to suppose they will disappear after they have been sentenced. Most have loved ones with whom they will wish to spend the maximum amount of time before going to prison.

Discretion will make a few mistakes, of course. But for the majority this system would reduce the strain on the prisoner who, anticipating as many do an acquittal, has no time after conviction to prepare for prison by putting personal affairs in order. And as I have explained, once you are in prison you are not allowed to conduct any 'business'. Were such time granted then I *know* untold misery would be avoided.

But, one suspects, such radical changes will be rejected out of hand as 'too risky' or 'too soft' or because 'we've never done it before'. Not least, one can see that such a flexible system would disturb the cosy practices of 'the Department' and the Prison Officers' Association. It would be too irregular, too untidy. If that is the response, then prison unrest will continue. The building of another thousand prisons will not remove the root cause of disruption – which, as I have said, is not concerned with slopping out or with living three to a cell.

If the country's public purse cannot afford to build new prisons then I would advocate the much discussed proposal for private prisons. They work successfully in parts of the United States. They would need to be licensed by and subject to the control of the Government of the day. They would, more successfully, operate with run-of-the-mill petty offenders and could, additionally, take the remand strain off the main system. That such a radical venture is opposed by the Prison Officers' Association comes as no surprise. No closed shop likes to be 'opened'. That some prison-reform societies oppose the move is more of a mystery to me. Cost-cutting has been achieved in America. A faster building programme has occurred. Private schools, nursing homes and hospitals exist; why not private prisons? After all, the other institutions are the public concern of all; the physical welfare of the aged or ill and the emotional, physical and spiritual development of the young are highly specialised and vital areas of concern to the body politic. So, too, are prison populations. Nothing in logic argues against the instituting of private prisons. Economically and for the good of employment figures they make sense, for the sort of inmate about whom I have been speaking,

although I suppose there is no reason why long-term and dangerous men could not be incarcerated in a private institution.

An added effect, one would hope, of the privatisation of prisons
is that at the same time they would be largely depoliticised. And
this neutrality of management can only be good. One will never
forget how education was ruined in this country by alternative
governments. The excellence of public schools – one of the few
remaining symbols of freedom in our *soi disant* democracy – is
constantly threatened by the left wing only as a conditioned
response of intellectual penis envy. The implementation of the
comprehensive ideal, like ideal Marxism, is marvellous in theory,
but has failed abominably in practice. So, likewise, has the 'prison
issue' become a political football. Tories are proud of their 'law
and order' stance. By this is generally meant that Tories are
'tougher' and hence more law-abiding. It is deemed a virtue to
advocate hanging or birching or longer prison sentences, the
theory being that revenge and lack of compassion is a virtue.
Left-wingers on the other hand are denounced as flabby liberals
whose aims are anarchy. I polarise the arguments to illustrate
the point that there is an in-between stage which even Shylock
learned.

The control of erring human beings is an a-political, a-
religious responsibility, the exercise of which should be carried
out upon two criteria. The first must ensure safety to the general
public and, by extension, to the offender. The second should
recognise the sinfulness in all humanity and accept that 'treatment' should be applied according to man's highest virtues. At
present the system assumes that all inmates are lying, thieving,
conniving, irredeemable pieces of flawed creation. To a greater or
lesser degree all but the saints are like that. And many saints have
given their fellows a hard time!

That there exist 'evil' people I imagine to be true. I do not think
I met any in prison. I did, however, meet many men who admitted
their guilt, accepted a degree of custodial punishment but felt
increasingly enraged and desperate that they were not to be
released on parole. They felt that they had 'done enough time'
and were ready to go home. A percentage of these men were
determined on a life of different crime when they were released
for they saw no other way forward.

For any progress to be made there needs to be a spiritual

revolution in this country. Social ills like unemployment, poverty, the profit motive taken to extremes, the idea of 'getting on', need to be replaced by a more realistic 'each according to his needs' ethos, a society in which we care for our fellows who rate us as well.

Crime would still occur, of course, but a profounder level of universal *caritas* might well receive a reciprocal response. It would, at any rate, be a more acceptable reaction to the 'problem' of law and order than the Pavlovian response of building more prisons, imposing longer sentences and reducing to a worthless state the dignity of each human being – a precious creation in the eyes not only of God but of the prisoner's family and friends.

# 20

# AFTERMATH

*I shall go softly all my years in the bitterness of my soul.*

Isaiah, 15

Our plans were to go to Jersey for a few days before returning home to live; I did not want there to be an immediate memory connection between my last visit to my house – the night before my trial opened – and my next – the day I returned from prison. Before the holiday, though, I had to report to my probation officer, sign on the dole and drop off the hire car Jen had used.

We dropped Jamie off with friends and went to the Probation Service, where I clocked in with a charming lady probation officer. She initially suggested we went and had lunch; we declined that suggestion as we were keen to be alone as soon as possible. Stupidly, as it turned out, we forwent our visit to the DHSS because I wanted privacy. I visited them on our return from Jersey only to be told that I had lost a week's benefit by not signing on the day I left prison.

This piece of bureaucracy struck me as heartless in *my* circumstances, though I see the sense of it generally. Yet the thought of queueing in that dreary place for hours and explaining all about myself seemed far less important than being alone with my wife.

We went home.

The house was chaotic, as Jen had recently resigned from her job in my school and moved out of our flat there. Bottles of red wine awaited me and we enjoyed each other's company in privacy for the first time in a year. (We had never been on our own during my pre-trial period.) Jen took the hire car back and I planned to follow her in our battered Ford. She went off. My car would not start. Rain began to fall as I waited for nearly two hours for the Rescue Service to start it. I rang Tim, who was by now with friends, and exploded in a storm of rage at the car, the weather, the Rescue Services. Not a good start. Here I was, sitting in a wreck of a car, in the pouring rain, outside the village shop a few

235

hours after being released from prison. I assumed, probably rightly, that the whole village was witnessing my return and my frustration. Jen, meanwhile, was ten miles away wondering what had happened to me.

Eventually the car was started and we went off to meet Tim, who was carried shoeless from our friends' house where a restrained reunion occurred. It was almost as if I had not been away.

Later that night we stayed with other friends before being fog-bound on our way to Jersey. We waited for the flight to be called and I remember feeling rather proud that I had money in my pocket and that I could order coffee at will. I bought a copy of *The Times*. The banner headline concerned the jailing for forty-five years of a terrorist. I flinched and said loudly to Jen that I thought the sentence Draconian. She told me to keep my voice down.

The Jersey holiday was a success. During it, as I have said, I visited the mother of a Leyhill lifer who took us on a tour of the island, a tour which included the prison; shown to us, I believe, because she wanted me to see where her son stayed on his visits to St Helier.

By the time we were back I was accustomed to normal life again. Apart from the weekly visits to the Probation Service all was relatively smooth as the summer wore on. My sons were at home and we converted my outbuilding into a study; I started writing and gardening, sure in the knowledge that a job would come along. I was keen to keep up some of my prison contacts and had promised to undertake a number of (legal) commissions for them. Jen was less happy about this. I knew and had lived with these men and was extremely fond of a number of them. Occasionally we would clash about this contact until I realised that I was the one who had changed.

I became obsessed with all news of prisons, the law and judicial process. I kept huge scrapbooks and commented on what I thought were excessive or inconsistent sentences. There were many such in my opinion.

By the time January came and I had transcribed my prison diaries I started to seek employment. I had been banned from my profession with the possibility of a review in the not too distant future. But I do not want to teach again, for I still feel badly let down by the profession I had served for nearly twenty-five years.

I put in for a wide range of jobs – each time opening my letter of application with the details of my conviction and sentence. Rejection after rejection followed the one interview I had for a joint job in York. We did not get that and during the lengthy interview process Jen decided she wanted to withdraw from it anyway, so nothing was lost.

After a year's total frustration, relieved only by my taming my huge cliffside garden, we began to grow desperate. My writing had brought in no money. My countless job applications were consigned to oblivion, yet I was not applying for well-paid posts. I remember offering my services as a rehabilitator of ex-convict drug offenders, for as time passed I was feeling more and more strongly that I should use my knowledge of prisons to help other offenders. However, the poacher-turned-gamekeeper mentality availed me nothing.

I wrote to the Apex Trust (a charitable organisation whose primary aim is to help ex-offenders to find jobs), who offered persistent, personal help and advice and, though they did not find me a job, they did all they could to help and would still be helping me now if I needed it. I feel deeply grateful to them and, were I a rich man who loved cats, I suspect the money I would have left to the Cats' Home would go to the Apex Trust.

In final despair I answered the advertisements of a number of headhunters, one of whom offered me free help and invaluable and – to him – time-consuming guidance. Weeks after meeting him and through using his method of approach I received an interview for a post in Essex. I did not get the job but was told at interview that the final result would not depend upon my conviction. I believed that then and I believe it now. Shortly afterwards I was offered a job by a friend and am happily employed.

The contact I have with one or two of my ex-inmate friends is now more marginal. Some seem to have jobs of one sort or another and they are pursuing a law-abiding path. Two have since been back in prison – two out of the five with whom I am in touch.

As I read through the manuscript of this book I am conscious that my anger and bitterness shine shamefully through much of it. I wrote as I felt then and have made no attempt now to dilute those contemporary thoughts. The book may well appear slanted and too much on the side of the criminal. At the time I was of their number and of the devil's party, possibly without knowing it. Now that I am back within society I am much more of society's party. My reactions to recent high-profile court cases have been more as they would have been before my conviction than while I was in prison.

I applaud the tough action against soccer hooligans and believe the Birmingham Six to have been bountifully treated by our judicial system. I think all insider dealers should be fined heavily and sent to prison *pour encourager les autres*. I am in two minds about Lester Piggott's sentence but admire his attitude to his condition. I deplore the constant press criticism of the police when they fail to catch a mass-murderer for a few weeks. Above all, I feel for prison officers who are held hostage by violent men in overcrowded Scottish prisons. When that happens the victims are the man's family as much as the man himself.

And it would be a mistake to imagine that no criminal feels compassion for his victims. The unwritten code of conduct among criminals is complex. A large number of burglars are totally without morals and will steal anything from anywhere. There is an equally large number who, for example, would never steal from a private house. Their reason is that they would not like anyone to steal from theirs.

The attitude of all criminals to sex offenders is equally understandable. They would not like their children to be molested or their wives to be raped. Oddly enough, though, while unlawful sexual intercourse with a fifteen-year-old girl is regarded as heinous, defrauding old ladies out of their life's savings comes low on the list of veniality.

And murder is regarded as the king of crime (except child murder, the perpetrators of which are looked on as the lowest of the low). Most lifers have an aura about them – or, perhaps more accurately, other prisoners accord them a special status which some enjoy. As I have recorded, Inch felt no guilt about the woman he killed – 'What's a fucking woman in a box?' he asked rhetorically about the prostitute he claimed to have killed; at another time he protested innocence of murder. Yet another lifer, Dougie, who had killed his wife and been in prison for fifteen years, told me that he asked himself every day of his life why he had done it. He was a popular man, simple-minded and retiring, who seemed to me to be utterly, utterly harmless. But I would not wish to be the person who authorised his release.

The lifer who shot his unfaithful wife was regarded as a criminal by none; even prison officers remarked that he was not a criminal.

The above general remarks do not apply to professional criminals. Most of the men I met in prison were either opportunist offenders – small-time burglars or one-off murderers, for example. A few, however, were fully professional and they looked down upon their part-time colleagues.

The man who told me that and reckoned he had 'one more stretch in him' before he 'retired' believed that 'Crime is a full-time profession.' Prison, to him, was an occupational hazard which he was prepared to accept. Having said that, it is right to record that his crimes were non-violent and 'clean'. That is to say, his victims were anonymous. The goods he stole in huge quantity after meticulous planning belonged to massive corporations. He airily allowed insurance companies to foot the bill of his wrongdoing, declaring that they could afford it. The companies from which he stole lost nothing; the general public was affected not a jot; the insurers were in the business to take such risks – that was his philosophy. But he played for high stakes and when he lost he was out of circulation for a long while. That he had been so several times before indicated to me that crime must, for him, pay and that the risk was well worth the candle. His depositions suggested he had made a good living from his work. Only a life sentence would keep him out of harm's way.

Interestingly, too, the professionals were not nonce-bashers, in the main. They despised all petty criminals as so much riff-raff and were unimpressed by lifers.

The second category of professional criminal was of a different order. They were professional men of violence or of murder who had served many years. They thought nothing of their crimes but were universally feared. One such had single-handedly subdued a drunken rugby team with a pick-axe handle when the players were making a nuisance in his club. He had no remorse for what he had done, believed nonces should be hanged and advised our ward to smash in the head of a man who had stolen from fellow cons. Julius Caesar would have agreed that 'such men are dangerous'.

Generally, it was the herd instinct which prevailed. Privately men were different and on a personal level deep suffering was felt. The man accused of attempting to bugger a child wept in front of me as he recounted the 'facts' of his bizarre case. Oddly enough, after his release he went back to live in his former community and was taken up again by the family he was accused of wronging. I think this suggests his case was doubtful to start with but it shows a great compassion, too, on the part of his 'victims'.

That society at large recognises that the victims have to be compensated is right. I am not sure, however, how a rape victim or the widow of a murder victim is compensated. I wish I could say that the perpetrators of the crimes were, on the whole, remorseful; they were not. Their apparent unconcern stemmed less from callousness than from a desire to suppress knowledge of their actions. They would excuse their appalling conduct on the grounds of mental illness or suggest they had received provocation.

I have sought, in the course of this book, to do two things. First, to record the facts of my own incarceration and to show how I felt at the time. This knowledge, personal and individualistic, is not designed to 'prove' anything. Second, using my experience as a basis for discussion, I have tried to enlighten the general reader about the prison experience and to stimulate some debate. I have posed many questions but advanced few answers. If I have demonstrated that the problem of crime and punishment is fiendishly complicated, I have in part succeeded.

I am now on nobody's side for I have learned that each case is unique and that my reaction to a newspaper report about an individual trial and sentence cannot be based upon all the facts. I try, now, not to judge. Should the folk-hero Lester Piggott have received three years' jail after repaying some of his owed tax and the police sergeant who stamped a drunk to death receive four? Should Boy George receive a non-custodial sentence for heroin offences and an unknown cannabis offender receive two years? Should Geoffrey Collier have received a suspended sentence for his insider dealing and Keith Best, initially, be sent to prison for a less lucrative crime? Should Mrs Lawson's driving offence be tried with indecent haste and in relative obscurity while that of an 'unknown' perpetrator of the same offence has to wait and be publicised? Should President Nixon have been impeached? Should Kurt Waldheim be President of Austria? Should George Bush stand for President with the Iran–Contra affair hanging over his head?

In our self-righteous smugness – and we all have it to a greater or lesser degree – we would do well to pause for thought. Which motorist has never broken a speed limit? Are there millions of businessmen who have never once evaded paying some tax? How many people do not own a television licence? How many adulterers are there in our society? How many under-fifteen-year-old girls are not virgins? How many homosexual acts between twenty-year-old males occur each year? How many parents have never slapped a child? How many 'respectable' people are there who have smoked cannabis? How many 'county' types have unlicensed shotguns? These are all common crimes. Some carry heavy penalties; the possible effects of others carry heavy penalties. Let he who is without sin cast the first stone.

Meanwhile, too, let us recognise that, though our system be flawed, it retains an essential humanity. The fact that one policeman may be corrupt or that one priest may be a paedophile does not mean our 'system' is rotten, any more than one wrongful conviction means that the law's effects should be diluted.

Those who believe that our society is lawless and out of control are wrong. Spectacular successes by Drug Squads are recorded almost weekly; soccer hooligans are being brought to book; fraudulent financial transactions are being successfully detected; DHSS fraud is declining massively; income-tax evasion is on the decrease; tougher laws to combat the possession of lethal weapons have been introduced; neighbourhood watch schemes have reduced local crime; television programmes have, with massive public support, helped to solve criminal mysteries.

The negative response of retribution as an end in itself is being ousted, it seems, by a greater compassion. That compassion is not 'soft' – it does not displace the need for punishment to follow crime – for it does include severer sentences for some crimes. However, the severer sentence (so often translated to mean a longer prison term) that is now being discussed concerns tougher community service and the possibility of the victims of crime being, wherever possible, compensated by the perpetrator.

The biggest revolution that could occur – as big as that which abolished flogging and hanging – is one which recognises that a custodial sentence is not the only response to aberrant behaviour. Dangerous men and women must be removed from society. Other wrongdoers should be made answerable to society in society. Cost-benefit would follow, prison officers would be able to exercise their profession in more congenial surroundings, prisons would cease to be academies of crime and the daily awareness that society is actively involved in the correction of its deviant members' actions would benefit all.

To society, generally – and I believe it still has a long way to go before it is as comprehending as it might be – I can do no more than ask that in judging and condemning our fellows we remember the words of the Prayer Book

He will not always be chiding: neither keepeth he his anger for ever.